SELECTED PAPERS

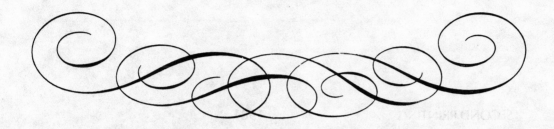

THE JOURNAL
of
IRREPRODUCIBLE
RESULTS

Edited by

George H. Scherr, Ph.D.

Published by
The Journal of Irreproducible Results, Inc.
Box 234, Chicago Heights, Illinois
60466, U.S.A.

SECOND PRINTING   1981

THIRD PRINTING   1983

ISBN:0-9605852-1-4
Lib. of Cong. Cat. No.:76-365410

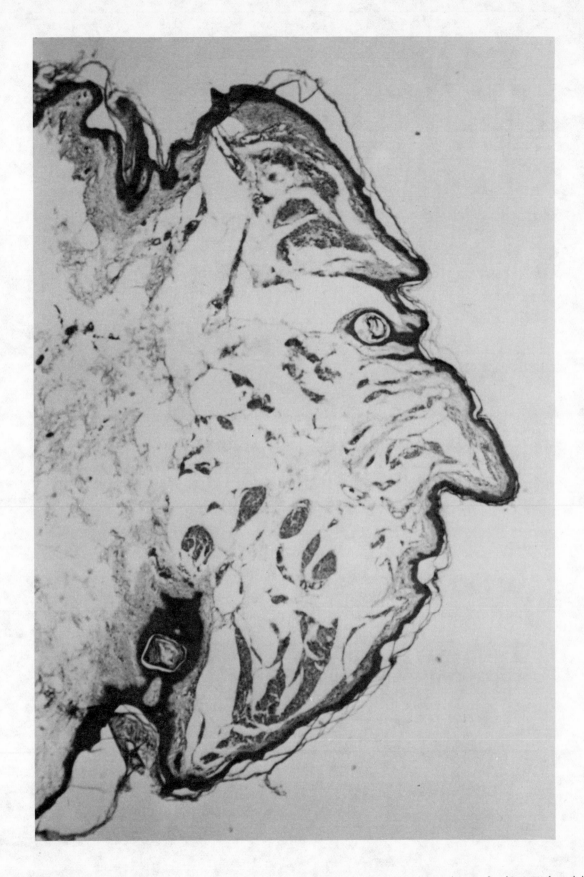

Submitted by: Walter H.C. Burgdorf, M.D. Dermatology
Oklahoma City, OK 73104

Shave excision of intradermal nevus, fixed in 3.7% formal dehyde stained
with hematoxylin and eosin photographed at 30x.

Selected Papers

* * *

THE JOURNAL
of
IRREPRODUCIBLE
RESULTS

A selection of superb and

irreproducible research from the illustrious

and irreproducible archives of the Society

for Basic Irreproducible Research

Preface

The innumerable bombastic, pompous, and verbose reports that were finding their way into the scientific literature prompted Dr. Alexander Kohn of the Ness Ziona Research Institute in Israel to collect a number of examples, and by adding a few contrived papers and reports of his own, instituted in 1955 THE JOURNAL OF IRREPRODUCIBLE RESULTS.

These beginnings originated as a few mimeographed sheets circulated to a few hundred fellow scientists who felt sufficiently secure in their own freedom from circumlocution and experimental jibberish to permit them to sit back and scoff at the antics of others.

Since Dr. Kohn was a research scientist in his own right he felt obliged by appropriate legend to distinguish those reports which were taken from the literature and were authentic and those which were contrived. Thus the readers at that time were able to enjoy the satire of the contrived articles, but laughed at the authentic ones with a "there but for the grace of God go I" attitude. This freedom of distinction suddenly changed in 1964 when publication was taken over by Dr. George H. Scherr, formerly Associate Professor of Microbiology at the University of Illinois and currently President of Technam, Inc. The sudden inability to distinguish contrived articles from authentic ones caused a near panic amongst the readers of the Journal and periodic flights to the library had to be made in order to satisfy what were becoming subjectively uncomfortable pangs of doubt as to how graceful God might have been!

The Journal boasts an editorial staff of highly competent representatives of their own discipline, all of whom serve without compensation to pass on the acceptability of contributed articles. The criteria of acceptance for articles are sufficiently stringent that approximately 75% of all submitted material is rejected.

Although printed exclusively in English, the Journal is circulated to subscribers and institutions in 55 countries.

If the wide circulation realized by the JOURNAL OF IRREPRODUCIBLE RESULTS accomplished anything, aside from providing relaxation by means of satire and critique principally involving scientific and related communities, the Journal hopefully has served to foster an image of the scientist that has best been expressed by *The Pelican;* "It is refreshing to see some scientists have a sense of humor. We imagined Teller to be the prototype, only laughing on the way down to his private bomb-shelter."

CONTENTS

Findings

that

could only

come from

highly

irreproducible

RESEARCH

A Mechanism for the Evaluation of the Importance of Research Results

MARCUS M. REIDENBERG, M.D.
Section of Clinical Pharmacology
Departments of Pharmacology and Medicine
Temple University School of Medicine
Phila., Pa. 19140

A problem requiring increased attention is that of evaluating the importance or significance, the quality, of research results rather than the quantity of results. Quantitative evaluation can readily be made by determining the number of papers published, amount of money spent, number of square feet of floor space a laboratory has expanded to occupy, etc. To make a qualitative evaluation of the importance of observations made is much harder. A new method is now proposed to establish a qualitative rating scale, capable of being used for self-evaluation, to be used to determine the importance of scientific discoveries.

When an investigator observes something new for the first time i.e., makes a discovery, he usually gets very excited. He then communicates this information to others in the lab and frequently to colleagues in adjacent laboratories. The number of people he informs of his discovery during this initial short time period after making the discovery is proportional to how excited the researcher is which in turn is proportional to how important he thinks his discovery is.

A custom in many labs, including our own, is to celebrate a new observation with a party that afternoon. We may buy some cake to have with the afternoon coffee in the lab. We may buy bakery donuts to share with everyone on our corridor at afternoon coffee. Sometimes we buy red wine and cheese when we get really excited. Once an afternoon champagne party was held.

Thus, empirically, one can observe that the number of people one tells about a new discovery on the day it is made and the cost of the refreshments served at the party to celebrate the new discovery within a day or two after it is made is directly related to the importance of the discovery in the judgment of the discoveror. Since the discoveror is more expert in the field of the specific discovery than anyone else, his judgment of its importance is probably better than anyone else's. His immediate judgment of its importance will be unbiased by financial, political, or other considerations and probably be a more valid scientific assessment of the discovery than can be carried out by other people or at another time.

Thus, we propose an evaluation of the quality of scientific discoveries on the basis of the immediate party the discovery causes. A discovery can be a coffee and cake discovery, a wine and cheese discovery, or a champagne discovery. One can develop finer gradations of the scale by subclassification. For example, a wine and cheese discovery can be subclassified into a domestic wine and cheese discovery or an imported wine and cheese discovery. One can further subclassify into a regionally bottled wine discovery or chateau bottled wine discovery, etc. Coffee and cake discoveries and champagne discoveries can be similarly subclassified.

A possible bias that can occur in this method of evaluating quality of research is for the investigator, knowing about this method of evaluation based on his own degree of excitement, to consciously fake more excitement than he really feels in order to upgrade the apparent importance of his discovery. A control mechanism to prevent this is an intrinsic part of this proposal. The discoveror naturally pays for the party. Thus, if a discoveror upgrades a coffee and donut discovery to a chateau bottled wine and cheese discovery very often, he will be penalizing himself only, since all his colleagues will enjoy the wine and cheese irrespective of the importance of the discovery. This should serve as a negative feed back function and cause most investigators to remain honest in their evaluation of their work.

13

SAGA OF A NEW HORMONE

NORMAN APPLEZWEIG

In recent months we've learned of the discovery of three miracle drugs by three leading pharmaceutical houses. On closer inspection it appears that all three products are one and the same hormone. If you're at all curious about how more than one name can apply to the same compound it might be worth examining the chain of events that occurs in the making of a miracle drug.

The physiologist usually discovers it first—quite accidentally, while looking for two other hormones. He gives it a name intended to denote its function in the body and predicts that the new compound should be useful in the treatment of a rare blood disease. From one ton of beef glands, fresh from the slaughterhouse, he finally isolates ten grams of the pure hormone which he turns over to the physical chemist for characterization.

The physical chemist finds that 95 per cent of the physiologist's purified hormone is an impurity and that the remaining 5 per cent contains at least three different compounds. From one of these he successfully isolates ten milligrams of the pure crystalline hormone. On the basis of its physical properties, he predicts possible structure and suggests that the function of the new compound is probably different from that assigned to it by the physiologist. He changes its name and turns it over to the organic chemist for confirmation of structure.

The organic chemist does not confirm the structure suggested by the physical chemist. Instead he finds that it differs by only one methyl group from a new compound recently isolated from watermelon rinds, which, however, is inactive. He gives it a chemical name, accurate but too long and unwieldy for common use. The compound is therefore named after the organic chemist for brevity. He finally synthesizes ten grams of the hormone but tells the physiologist he's sorry that he can't spare even a gram, as it is all needed for the preparation of derivatives and further structural studies. He gives him instead ten grams of the compound isolated from watermelon rinds.

The biochemist suddenly announces that he has discovered the new hormone in the urine of pregnant sows. Since it is easily split by the crystalline enzyme which he has isolated from the salivary glands of the South American earthworm, he insists that the new compound is obviously the co-factor for vitamin B-16, whose lack accounts for the incompleteness of the pyruvic acid cycle in annelids. He changes its name.

The physiologist writes to the biochemist requesting a sample of of his earthworms.

The nutritionist finds that the activity of the new compound is identical with the factor PFF which he has recently isolated from chick manure and which is essential to the production of pigment in fur-bearing animals. Since both PFF and the new hormone contain the trace element zinc, fortification of white bread with this substance will, he assures us, lengthen the lifespan and stature of future generations. In order to indicate the compound's nutritive importance, he changes its name.

The physiologist writes the nutritionist for a sample of PFF. Instead he receives one pound of the raw material from which it is obtained.

The pharmacologist decides to study the effect of the compound on grey-haired rats. He finds to his dismay that they lose their hair after one injection. Since this does not happen in castrated rats, he decides that the drug works synergistically with the sex hormone, testosterone, and therefore antagonizes the gonadotropic factor of the pituitary. Observing that the new compound is an excellent vasoconstrictor, the pharmacologist concludes that it should make a good nose-drop preparation. He changes its name and sends 12 bottles of nose drops, together with a spray applicator, to the physiologist.

The clinician receives samples of the pharmacologist's product for test in patients who have head colds. He finds it only mildly effective in relief of nasal congestion, but is amazed to discover that three of his head cold sufferers who are also the victims of a rare blood disease have suddenly been dramatically cured.

He gets the Nobel prize.

* President, Norman Applezweig Associates, Consulting Biochemists.

J.L. WINKELHAKE

W. VAN de STADT

E. FRANK

J.E. BERMAN
R.B. LOEWENSON
W.H. GULLEN

Formulation of Natural Law The Murphy's and Muench's Laws ... Entropy.

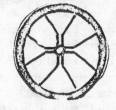

Editors Note: The subject of natural laws, Murphy's law, etc., has already been discussed in this Journal (Kohn: 1963, *11*, 58; Venegas: 1971, *18*, 46; Klipstein: 1970, *18*, 22). We feel, nevertheless, that a cooperative effort of 4 groups of scientists from the U.S.A. and Argentina is worth publication since it throws new light on this old problem.

Ever since the first scientific experiment, men have been plagued by the unceasing antagonism of Nature. No one knows why this should be so. It seems only natural that, of all things, Nature should be logical, organized and neat, but it isn't. The best teacher of all, Experience, turns out to be just the gradual acceptance of Nature's bullheaded eccentricities.

Over the years a series of laws and rules have evolved representing a distillation of the experience of thousands of experimenters. They are true because they have always been true, just like the Second Law of Thermodynamics. They have no derivation, however, no proof other than their sheer simplicity and beauty. They may be named the fourth principle of thermodynamics, or the equivalence principle (1-4).

The first enunciation of this Law is credited to Murphy: IF ANYTHING CAN GO WRONG WITH AN EXPERIMENT, IT WILL, (or in everyday language: "Everything happens so as to cause you the most trouble").

There is a host of attendant Laws and corollaries to Murphy's Law. They will not be listed here in detail, but some examples will be mentioned:

Attendant Law I: "No matter what result is anticipated, there is always someone willing to fake it or to misinterpret it."

Attendant Law II: "In any collection of data the figure that is most obviously correct, is the mistake. The most likely person to see it first, is your worst enemy."

Now, who was Murphy? From Klipstein (5) we know that his first name was Edsel Therefore, William Parry Murphy, born in 1892, who studied pernicious anemia, or William Lawrence Murphy (1876-1959), inventor of the folding beds cannot be credited with origination of the Law. The same applies to Arthur Murphy (1727-1805), an actor and dramatist of some renown, and John Francis Murphy (1853-1921), a painter. Moreover, it is simply inconceivable that the Humanities, could have produced intellects, of however high standing otherwise, with sufficient insight in matters scientific and technical to enunciate the law in question.

Finally we find John B. Murphy (1857-1916), a surgeon, inventor of the anastomosis button (related to the belly-button) and author of "General Surgery". Though many things in operating rooms are apt to follow the law, it seems somehow incongruous that a surgeon would find the spare time to stumble on one of the fundamental principles of applied science. So we are left with an enigma: Edsel Murphy's identity and the origins of his law are lost in antiquity.

Few attempts seem to have been made at quantifying Murphy's Law. We propose to introduce a unit to describe the smallest incremental measurable effect of the Law, the MURPH (abbreviated M). Since the Murphy is a measurement of chaos, it is related to the concept of entropy. We shall fix one Murph as some large factor above $10-23$ Joule per degree Kelvin, that quantity itself being immeasurably small. Undoing one existing Murph requires at least one counter Murph (CM); to score the first CM we choose the large factor mentioned above as 10^{+23}. Hence

$$1 M = JK^{-1}$$

or about 10^{23} basic bits.

A Murph can be regarded as a unit entropy generator: straightening out one Murph (i.e. one counter-Murph) requires an Entropy Sink. Scientists find themselves therefore as negative quantities vis-à-vis Murphy, i.e. M-sinks or CM-generators.

A Megamurph develops when many different drivers from different starting points decide to reach their respective individual destinations by passing at the same time on the same 4-lane highway, which has been ripped open to install a new sewer. Though only one man decided to install a sewer in that road at that time, the result of that one decision is extensive chaos. From this example it becomes clear that the energy expended in countering one Murph (decision to install sewer) is not necessarily linearly related to the causative Murph, i.e. $1M \neq 1$ CM, except in rare cases.

In general $1M = k \times CM$

wherein k, the proportionality factor, must be derived for each individual pair of M and CM. It is clear that k can be both logarithmic and probabilistic in nature, and generally is much larger than 1.

A mathematical formulation of Murphy's work has been developed by his close friend and colleague, Professor Finagle. Years ago when the Universe was relatively easy to understand, the Finagle factor consisted of a simple additive constant — sometimes known as the variable constant — which appeared in the equation

$$x^1 = K_f + x$$

where any measured variable, x, could be made to agree with the theoretical value, x^1, by the simple addition of the Finagle factor, K_f. As powerful as this adjustment was, later difficulties could not be solved so easily, so a Fudge factor, K_b, was introduced:

$$x^1 = K_f + K_b x$$

With the advent of World War II studies in servo theory came the need for still stronger influences. The Diddle factor, K_d was conceived as a result of this, and was used to provide a second order correction

$$x^1 = K_f + K_b x + K_d x^2$$

This second order adjustment was adequate until recently, when Dr. Cozen at Apollo Mission control found it necessary to account for discrepancies on the moon; consequently, the Cozen factor, K_c, was introduced:

$$x^1 = K_f + K_b x + K_d x^2 + K_c x^3$$

It is now felt that reality can be made to conform to mathematical theory with reasonable agreement on the basis of these four factors.

There is a different basic structure behind each of these four factors. The Finagle factor is characterized by changing the Universe to fit the equation. The Fudge Factor, on the other hand, changes the equation to fit the Universe. The Diddle factor changes things so that the equation and the Universe appear to fit without making any real changes in either. And finally, the Cozen factor doesn't change either the Universe or the equation, but instead changes the observer so that apparent disagreement between the Universe and the equation becomes an accepted fact, i.e. it incorporates Murphy's Law in mathematical form into the equation so that one can say that there is a limit to the accuracy of any experiment.

Although the Finagle factor K_f, the Fudge factor, K_b, the Diddle factor K_d, and the Cozen factor, K_c, are related to the proportionality factor k in the equation

$$M = kx \ CM,$$

they are not the same. The k factor is inherently coupled to the innate cussedness of inanimate (and sometimes animate) matter. It exists spontaneously, because Murph's exist per se.

Finagle et al. factors are properly used for fine adjustment of conceptual theories to allegedly observed facts. Since the facts are polluted by some Murphs, naturally Finagle type K factors are needed to balance the sought-after equality. Hence

$$K_f, K_b, K_d, K_c = f(M).$$

For example, the planet Uranus was introduced to the Universe when Newtonian Laws couldn't be made to match the known planetary motions. This is a good example of the Finagle's factor. Einstein's work leading to the theory of Relativity was strongly influenced by the observed facts about the orbit of Mercury. Here a Fudge factor was introduced. The photographer's use of a "soft-focus" lens when taking portraits of women over 35 is an example of the Diddle factor. By blurring the results, the photographs are made to match the facts in a far more pleasing and satisfactory manner.

The use of the Cozen factor is exemplified by the Heisenberg Uncertainty Principle which states that the product of the errors in two conjugate variables is always greater or equal to a constant; thus, the more accurately one variable is measured, the less accurately the value of the other variable can be measured (see also ref. 9).

Another known personage, who has made great contributions to the Murpheian Science is Professor Hugo Muench, retired Professor of Biostatistics at the Harvard Medical School. Professor Muench presented his knowledge in form of Postulates and Laws which bear on the design, conduct, analysis and interpretation of studies, especially in the medical - clinical field.

Muench's postulates are very simple:

P1. Everyone talks too much;

P2. Everyone writes too much;

P3. Nobody pays any attention.

On the basis of these postulates the following Laws have been enunciated (Muench's Laws):

L. I.   No full scale study confirms the lead provided in the pilot study.

L. II. Results can always be improved by omitting controls.

L. III. In order to be realistic, the number of cases promised in any clinical study, must be divided by a factor of at least 10.

These Postulates and Laws have induced the development of some corollaries:

P. 1. Corollary: Good talk can often substitute for good research, and is a lot easier.

Both Postulate 1 and its corollary are self evident and need no proof.

P. 2. Corollary: The length of a research report is inversely proportional to how well the investigators know what they are doing (Dr. Haggans). Proof: Current Contents.

The corollary of this postulate falls within the domain of Muench's three Laws.

Law I. Corollary:

a. When working toward a solution of a problem, it always helps if you know the answer,

b. provided, of course, that you know there is a problem (Werdin, DVM)

Law II. Corollary:

a. Double blind studies confuse the investigators.

b. The amount of monkeying with the data is inversely proportional to the quality of the data (see Finagle, Diddle, Fudge and Cozen's factors).

c. The more and more closely you look at the data, the bigger the trouble you are in.

The following additional practical precepts have evolved from Muench's Second Law:

"Experiments must be reproducible; they should all fail in the same way."

1. A record of data is useful since it indicates that you've been working.

2. In case of doubt, make it sound convincing.

3. Don't believe in miracles, rely on them (E. Kishon).

Law III. Corollary:

a. The difficulty of dealing with data may be expressed as
$$D = a + bt^{10}$$
where D is data, a and b constants bigger than 1 and t the time necessary to gather the data.

b. The administrative difficulties in research are 10 times bigger than the scientific ones.

By careful inspection of these mathematically based Laws, Postulates and Corollaries, one can discern the basic equivalence of different formulations, though the fields of validity are varying and restricted (6-8). The proof of this last Postulate is the fact of continuous rediscovery of things known half a century ago.

REFERENCES

1 *E. Frank and E. Frank* [+], Notes of the Zero Principle of Thermodynamics Never Published Paper Press (N.P.P.P.) 1970, p. 15

2 *Me & Me*, Notes on the First Principle of Thermodynamics, N.P.P.P. 1970, p. 27

3 *Me & The Co-Author Who Got The Money*, Notes on the Second Principle of Thermodynamics, N.P.P.P. 1971, p. 10

4 *E. Frank and E. Frank* [+], Notes on the Third Principle of Thermodynamics, N.P.P.P. 1972, p. 11

5 *Klipstein*, J.I.R. *18:* 22, 1970

6 P. Abeledo al Fadi: *Groundlessness and Causality*, to be published

7 A. Niunnoun Chientis: *Sleep as a source of new ideas*, Somnologia *126:* 105, 1970

8 E. Frank: *Philosophy and Physics* (How to publish useless papers) to be published

9 M. Epstein: *Uncertainty Principle in R & D*, J.I.R. *19:* 4, 1973

[+] They had the problem to decide who should be the first author.

HAROLD SCHULTZE
Assistant Professor

Viability of guinea pigs upon exposure to well defined experimental parameters normally associated with cessation of vital signs due to rapid crainial tissue contact with stainless steel in a cylindrical form.

A shot in the head
will make him dead.

FOURTH GRADE BIOLOGY EXPERIMENT   ·MR.HIGGINS   ANATOMY OF A FROG

PROCEDURE : The student shall dissect a frog and examine its
             internal organs.

Name of student . . . . E. MYRON FOGARTY

Labrotorie report on Cutting up a frog.

Plan. I will get a frog and a sharp nife, Wnich with I will cut
opin the frog whilst he is alive. I will studdie carfulley his
innerds, for the purpuss of gaining scientifik knolledge.

Part One. Mr. Higgens give me a frog, a nife, and a pan of
stuff like jello. I grapt the frog by his hine legs and I beet
his head on the edje of the lab bench so he wood not bight.
When he was woosie and ready for scientific investigathun,
I stuck thumtax in his foots and pinned him against the jello,
with his bellie in frount. Part Two. Soon the frog begun ones
agan to kick, and feering his eskape, I scientifikully rammer
the shiv in his stumak. There was a stickie dark red flooid
which ouzed out from whence I stabbed him. This was
kind of fun so I druv the shiv in him agan. I noted that
the more I stabbed him the more he kicked. Soon he begun
to kick less and less each time I stabbed him and finnalley

18

he kicked not at all. I went to Mr. Higgens and got a new frog. Part Three. I through what was left of the old frog in the wase basket. then put the new one in its place. I was determint to learn more from this frog by condukting a more scientifik experemint. I made too insessyuns akross his tummy and I peelt the skin away so I cood see better. It was kinda silverry inside so I cut deeper, and faund his innerds, which I scientifikully scoopt out with a spoon. - Part Fore. I got a woodin handil fork, upon which I put the frog. I turned on a bunsin burnur and held the frog, who kicked not much too terrible now, above it. Soon the smell of roastid frog filled the labb and Mr. Higgens made me share him with othur kids

Diagram of a frog which I learnt from this experiment.

DIAGRAM OF A FROG WHICH I CUT.

eyebull
other eyebull
lungs
glands
bones
guts
nose
more guts
tung
food comes out
essofigus
hand
innerds
Stumak
leg

Reprinted from JIR, 1963, 11, 65 from a reprint in Synthetic American, 1962.

19

THE TRIPLE BLIND TEST

R.F., M.D.

At one time, an investigator working alone could produce significant research. But the ever increasing array of electronic gadgets is making it difficult for one person to record objectively all his erroneous observations. Many irrational leads are thereby missed.

Since it is now virtually impossible for him to blunder blindly without help, teamwork has come to the rescue with a perfect solution: the double-blind study.

The value of the double-blind study was first illustrated by studies of the LD-50 (lethal dose for 50% of test subjects) of cyanide. In earlier experiments it was considered satisfactory to give, and not to give, the drug to alternate subjects. But now control subjects are given a placebo of exactly the same size, shape and color as the cyanide tablet. By doing the experiments in this way, the clinical impression that cyanide is lethal is verified by observations uncluttered by bias.

The accuracy of the double-blind test permits evaluation of a drug with far fewer subjects than heretofore; in fact, in some studies it has been possible to reduce the number of subjects to zero*.

In evaluating the precision of this method, researchers have made an unexpected discovery—the therapeutic effectiveness of sucrose and starch placebos. The diversified effects of these simple carbohydrates constitute a major discovery in medicine.

Of particular interest is the remarkable potency of starch in pathological pain, with no indication that it produces addiction. It is equally noteworthy that starch does not affect experimentally produced pain.

This observation has brought about the realization that analgesics should be appraised only in relief of naturally occurring pain since man may be the only species that imagines suffering.

A curious sex difference has also been demonstrated in that red placebos are effective in males, but only blue or pink placebos are effective in females. A report of two hermaphrodites who responded only to indigo-colored placebos should be verified.

Placebos are now available for the treatment of headache, rheumatoid arthritis and female ailments. In addition, they are as potent as ethanol either as "psychic energizers" in depressed states or as "psychic de-energizers" in overactive states. Work is now in progress to ascertain whether they act by blocking oxidative phosphorylation, cytochrome-c reductase or alcohol dehydrogenase.

Recently, there have been alarming reports about the toxicity of placebos. But these reports concern patients treated only with yellow or green placebos whose marked side effects may make it necessary to discontinue such treatment. In fact, a number of cases of agranulocytosis have occurred with the use of green placebos.

SERENDIPITY

Over the past few years, a new concept has arisen in medical research. Therapeutic nihilists now feel that the best chance of therapeutic breakthrough in mental disease, cancer and hypertension lies in experiments so completely unbiased and randomized that an accidental discovery of importance may turn up. This principle—sometimes called serendipity—is well recognized in mathematics: Sir Arthur Stanley Eddington said, "We need a super-mathematics in which the operations are as unknown as the quantities they operate on and a super-mathematician who does not know what he is doing when he performs these operations."

Applying the randomization principle to experimental medicine has led to the TRIPLE-BLIND TEST: The subject does not know what he is getting, the nurse doesn't know what she is giving and the investigator doesn't know what he is doing. Half way through the experiment, randomization is increased by a process known as turnabout—the patient administers the drug to the investigator, and the results are evaluated by a student-nurse. The famous mathematician, Lewis Carroll, may have had the randomization principle in mind in the phenomenon he described as Jabberwocky or "unknowable actors executing unknowable actions."**

The chance that triple-blind testing will produce something of consequence is calculated to be at least as great as that of spontaneous mutation. This probability is about one times 10 to the minus sixth power per generation. But considering the large number of chaotic investigations now in progress, the chance of a significant breakthrough in the next few thousand years is not improbable.

---

* A novel presentation of the theory of errors in small samples may be found in the recent book by B. L. Smith entitled *The Statistical Treatment of Vanishingly Small Samples and of Nonexistent Data.*

** Annals of *Alice in Wonderland* and *Through the Looking Glass.* A more precise description of Jabberwocky follows:

"Twas brillig, and the slithy toves
did gyre and gimble in the wabe;
all mimsy were the borogoves,
and the mome raths outgrabe."

20

THE PILL

MISS MARY SULLIVAN

(A sort of an autobiographical note)

I have been a laboratory technician for nearly twenty years now, so I think I can say, in all humility, that I really understand most of what there is to know on the practical side of the subject. Actually, it isn't complicated at all really; it's frighteningly simple.

Back in the 1930's, there were any number of people working on the effect of colchicine, studying its effect on mitosis, which it inhibits apparently by interfering with the spindle behavior. Cells treated with colchicine start to divide, the chromosomes split, they line up on the equatorial plate, and then something goes wrong: the cell stops dividing and goes back into interphase again, with double the usual number of chromosomes. In fact, that's how many tetraploid races of cultivated plants are obtained.

More recently, Mazia and his students at Berkeley have found that 2-mercaptoethanol interferes with spindles, too[1], though in a rather different manner (they think it's something to do with sulfhydryl bonds and sol-get conversions). Well, so much for the chemicals involved.

Now, over the past 15 years or so, while I've been working with Katsumi and Lindberg—first in Washington, then for a year at the Karolinska Institute and now here at the Rockefeller—we have been trying out these things on sea-urchin eggs.

The usual procedure has been to fertilize the eggs, and then test a variety of concentrations of various agents under various conditions on the first few mitotic divisions of the egg before it develops into a blastula. After the Lindbergs settled here in New York and started going to Woods Hole every summer, they tried a few other invertebrates, too, and even some frog-spawn shipped up from North Carolina, but the results were all much the same.

This did not stop them from publishing, of course, since luckily the details of concentrations and optimum pH values differed from one organism to the next.

Then we got a high-school student to help us one summer, and one morning he added one of the mixtures to sea-urchin eggs that had not been fertilized. I think the boy simply forgot to add the sperm first, but he said he did it just to see what would happen.

Well, between five and ten per cent of eggs started to cleave! When Lindberg heard about it, he (or maybe Mrs.

---

[1] Mazia D., Mitosis and the physiology of cell division. In: THE CELL, ed. J. Brachet and A. E. Mirsky, Acad. Press, N.Y., 1961, 77–394.

Lindberg, I forget now, since it happened three summers ago) changed the proportions of colchicine and 2-ME, and this raised the cleavage rate to almost 50%. When Katsumi got back from Heidelberg that fall, he had only a week at Woods Hole before starting it again with Kerberle in New York; so he naturally switched over to mice from the medical school colony there[2]. And the mice did the same thing! All he had to do was to add the colchicine and 2-ME mixture to the drinking water of unmated females, and, if they were in heat at the time, they just got pregnant—at least, a high percentage of cases did. When they littered, all the young were females, of course; and they were all identical with one another and with the mother, because the genotype hadn't changed. They were just as fertile, too. In fact, up till now we have raised some 18 generations, without benefit of a male of any sort, poor things.

Then Lindberg showed me how to remove uteri and wash out eggs at various stages, and I started one of the most boring and tedious parts of my job in my life. It was terribly frustrating. Much of the time my timing was wrong and I found nothing, or the eggs got lost among all the mucus and epithelial cells and stuff.

But slowly we began to build up a collection of eggs at different stages, fixed and stained nicely, so that Lindberg, when he got time off from teaching and committees, could study them carefully under a microscope. He found that they behaved just like the sea-urchin eggs. The details were published in four papers in Experimental Cell Research last year, and two more are still in press. They are all by Katsumi and one or both of the Lindbergs, and they included me in the authorship of the mouse egg studies[3] as they used to do in the 1950's when we were studying muscle fibers (Maybe this isn't worth mentioning).

Well, about that time my father died, and my sister came over from Connemara. (Mother had died in 1942, in one of the raids on Manchester). Poor soul Ellen has always been so cross-eyed that everybody was always sorry for her. But nobody does anything to help her; all her life she has been lonelier than any soul had ought to be on this earth.

So last fall I tried with some of the 2-ME mixture in her coffee, two mornings in a row, and she hardly noticed anything except a stale taste; then I gave her a bigger dose, about 400 times what we give to our mice—and it worked!

Ellen is a good woman, and she has been always quite a model of virtue, what with being more plain than most girls when she was young. But she has missed six months now and it's beginning to show. So I had to tell Katsumi about it. And that is when he started planning on the "P" pill, as the Lindbergs promptly called it.

And that's when I got worried. They all talk about it at every coffeebreak in the lab now. They say that meiosis is suppressed and the polar bodies are just resorbed into the egg nucleus, so that it becomes diploid again. They think that implantation is normal, at least in mice; so why not in other mammals? Lindberg, with Anderson, with whom he used to work in Stockholm, has taken out a patent. He is going to discuss it with somebody in Dairy Science at the Department of Agriculture in Washington at the beginning of next week, if he can get someone here to take over his anatomy class. But they don't talk about cattle all the time.

They say, too, that all sorts of women who want children can have them now without sinning, whether they happen to be married or not, because there are no laws against such pills. Katsumi has made up the fifth batch of the tablets, in three strengths, and he plans to give them away free after high-school graduation this coming June.

I don't know what to think; I have been wondering about all the mercaptoethanol that occurs naturally in garlic which people eat so much of in Mediterranean countries, and I've looked up *Colchicum autumnale* and found that it, like garlic, grows along the seashore in North Africa and Asia Minor. I don't know what to think now.

I started this story objectively, hoping to keep my personal involvements out of it, but I got carried away. I've been a good and virtuous woman these 43 years, and this is the first serious trouble I've got into. And now, what shall I do? My time is getting short, the Lindberg girls Elsa and Karen (home from Swarthmore for the vacation) can't keep their breakfasts down this week, and school will soon be out.

I hope I have done the right thing in writing all this.

[2] Kerberle, H. & al. 1965. Biochemical effects of drugs on the mammalian conception. Annals N.Y. Acad. Sci. *123*, 252.
[3] Katsumi, M., Lindberg, D., Lindberg, L. M. and Sullivan, M. 1965. Suppression of meiosis and restitution nuclei in mouse and hamster oocytes by colchicine and 2-mercaptoethanol. Exper. Cell Res., *28*, 567–581.

MOLESWORTH INSTITUTE REVISITED

Since 1956 there has existed in various locations in the United States a little-known, privately-supported, non-profit research organization known as The Molesworth Institute. Some of its earlier activities were reported on in the *ALA Bulletin*.[1] Since that time work on many of the important projects described there has continued unabated by our small staff of dedicated volunteer research workers. Some significant, albeit minor, contributions have been made by the institute in recent years.[2] Progress in general, however, has been somewhat slow and, in some areas, distressingly unspectacular, but we now expect at almost any time the kind of break-through in our project to microfilm all Braille books that will bring the Institute the recognition it so richly deserves.

As sponsored research elsewhere has turned increasingly to automation and information retrieval, as well as to other more significant areas, the Board of Directors of The Molesworth Institute has felt that the non-sponsorable research of its workers has fallen somewhat too close to reality and that a fundamental reassessment of the Institute's goals was long overdue. Consequently they recently decided to move the headquarters of the Institute to a more bucolic atmosphere; and, in conjunction with that move, they sponsored the Spring Hill Conference on the state of the art. As a result, the basic goals of The Molesworth Institute were reaffirmed. These goals are: "To foster the growth and development of Molesworth Studies in the United States, to combat the subversive and anti-human activities of the treens, to encourage the spread of general knowledge and raise the general standard of intelligence throughout the world, and to destroy the basic fabric of bibliography."[3] The goals were also broadened to include "the investigation and application of techniques being developd in other scientific disciplines to the world of books and libraries."[5]

In the few short weeks since this conference was held a number of significant new projects are already under consideration, and the work at The Molesworth Institute has developed a new atmosphere of intensive application, dedication, and rededication. As always one of the major problems is finding enough capable, dedicated research workers with a fundamental commitment to the basic goals of The Molesworth Institute. The Board of Directors has, therefore, contrary to its usual policy, agreed to announce the basic details of some of the new areas currently being investigated in the hopes that this will stimulate a number of people to become Fellows of The Molesworth Institute. We earnestly solicit applications from interested parties who feel that they possess the necessary qualifications.

One of our most significant new studies will be carried out in academic institutions as soon as enough volunteers can be found. It has often been said that "The library is the heart of the institution." To test this statement we now have a team of research workers investigating the possibility of heart transplants. We propose, for example, to move intact the library from a large ARL institution to a small college to see if the latter is suddenly rejuvenated and if the former can survive the shock. The prospects for transplants are numerous and only a few such exchanges should furnish much valuable information on the size of a "heart" which is needed to maintain institutions of varying ages, sizes, and natural conditions.

Another study involves the development of a non-citation index in which it is proposed to list regularly all scientific papers which have not been cited by another author.[6] This work may then be used either in identifying work that may be completely ignored since it has never been cited, or, by the more imaginative, in identifying important work that ought to be pursued further. Along somewhat the same lines we are considering the establishment of a number of NIGEL centers in parallel to the ERIC centers. The NIGEL centers (Negative Information on Godawful Educational Literature) will be concerned with the collection and destruction of educational reports and literature in a number of different areas. These centers will publish weekly bibliographic listings. Some consideration is being given to the possibility of the preservation for historical purposes only of the reports selected for destruction probably by publication in microfiche form at a reduction ratio far beyond the capacity of any reader now available.

Still another line of investigation concerns itself with the collection of picture postcards of libraries to assist in two projects. The first involves the use of a Hinman collator to identify the common features of library buildings in an effort to design the perfect library building. The second involves

*Norman D. Stevens is director of The Molesworth Institute and associate university librarian at the University of Connecticut. "Reprinted from the *ALA Bulletin*, 1975: 1969."

a consideration of the use of laser beams, and other advanced techniques in the field of microminiaturization, to develop programs for the solid state transmission of books and readers from one library to another.

Finally, one of our most important new studies is CRAM III (Clear and Readable Automation Manuals). Because of the urgent and difficult nature of the problem, the initial stages of Project CRAM and CRAM II were by-passed since our preliminary studies revealed that CRAM III is the first level at which any significant improvements are capable of being shown. Many of the details of CRAM III are, at the moment, either confidential or not fully worked out, but we can indicate that one line of research involves the mechanical translation of a number of automation manuals into treen.

Let me conclude simply by stating that The Molesworth Institute is now earnestly seeking research workers who wish to devote their energies to these, or similar research projects of their own making, vital tasks.

REFERENCES

[1]Norman D. Stevens, "The Molesworth Institute," *ALA Bulletin* 57: 75-76, 1963.
[2]See, for example, *Library Journal* 90: 2916, 1965; and 92: 945, 1967.
[3]*Op. cit.* p. 75. N.B., *Op. cit.* supersedes *Ibid.* see *Op. cit.* p. 76.
 In response to numberous requests from readers who have not seen *Ibid.* and whose libraries may not have complete files, I thought I might report here on one of the most significant accomplishments of The molesworth Institute which has previously only appeared in *Ibid.* That is, of course, the famous Molesworth Peason Universal Statistical Table.

Figure 1
The Molesworth-Peason Universal Statistical Table[4]

1	2	3	4	5	6	7	8	9	10
11	12	13	14	15	16	17	18	19	20
21	22	23	24	25	26	27	28	29	30
31	32	33	34	35	36	37	38	39	40
41	42	43	44	45	46	47	48	49	50
51	52	53	54	55	56	57	58	59	60
61	62	63	64	65	66	67	68	69	70
71	72	73	74	75	76	77	78	79	80
81	82	83	84	85	86	87	88	89	90
91	92	93	94	95	96	97	98	99	100
*	#	&	—	—	—	—	—	—	—

* Figures not available
# Latest figures — (e.g., 1938)
& Estimate based on sample of —% (e.g., 3.7)
– Users may provide their own symbols and notes for the remaining spaces

Special note: Through the use of these tables the researcher can immediately provide himself with any statistics he desires, and by properly quoting *Ibid.* can attribute them to any authority he desires. (e.g., The researcher first quotes a legitimate statement from Archer's book *Matableland Today*; he then states that the consumption of peanut butter in Matableland in 1965 amounted to 250 lbs. per person which statement he footnotes to *Ibid.*)
[4]Abbreviated version; for complete table and further explanation see *Idid.*
[5]Spring Hill Conference on the Future of The Molesworth Institute, December 9-13, 1968. *Proceedings*, p. 13.
[6]Our initial proposal was to list in the NCI works that had not been cited in another paper; our preliminary sample indicated that 97.3 percent of all authors cite their own works in later papers.

Short Communication

ACOUSTICS OF RESPIRATION DEFICIENT YEAST

C.U. Cumber and H. Gaisch

Rugin 7
2034 Peseux Switzerland

While pondering over profound biochemical problems concerning the interaction of cucumber salad and beer in humans, one of our associates heard distinct grumbling noises from a nearby rack of universal bottles containing:

    a. culture of respiration deficient yeast mutants
    b. culture of equivalent wild strain

By varying the position of his head he was able to locate the origine of the acoustic signals as being the rack of culture b. This points clearly to mitochondrial activities of high intensity in the wild strain. However, consequent investigations were interfered with by a high internal noise level. In order to overcome these extreme difficulties, the cucumber necessary to stimulate the metabolic activities of the observer was consequently sliced in the kryostat to 5″ thickness. This apparently reduced the general noise level in the laboratory but, unfortunately, the yeast had stopped grumbling as well. However, this is not in the least discouraging as it qualifies the observation for being reported in this Journal.

Great Flops I Have Known

A high point of the SJCC promises to be the panel on Lessons of the Sixties. At that time we can consider why Data Processing is a multi-billion dollar industry, but most people have so little to show for it. One of the reasons must be the enormous number of systems that are designed, programmed, debugged, tested, and documented—but never run. They don't go into production for a number of reasons:

- No real time is left for production.
- The system is dependent on a large data base which has never been assembled.
- The person who insisted on the system has been hired away by Cogar.
- The system was built as a package, but nobody bought it.
- The system cost so much to build that everyone involved went bankrupt.

and so forth.

I think it's possible that fully half of the systems built have never done anything. And there must be an elite corps of 5-year systems men who have never touched one that works.

It is interesting to consider a few case studies. For obvious reasons, the names have been omitted. The essentials are all true.

Case Study One: The project was an active management information system for a merchandise mart. The system would perform central billing for items purchased from 200 private wholesalers. At billing time, the buyer would undergo a credit check, a payment verification, and be assigned a time and location to pick up his combined purchases. The computer was to run an automated conveyor network that would move all purchases for a particular buyer from the various points of sale to the loading dock assigned to him and make them all arrive on time.

The conveyor together with its queueing and switching system had already been built but nobody knew what its capacity was. The project was begun in the faith that a 360/50 could run the conveyor at the necessary capacity. A simulation effort was begun at the same time. Midway through the development project, the simulation was completed, showing that the average day's purchases would take six days to deliver to the loading docks.

The project was cancelled for some convenient reason having nothing to do with the real problem.

Case Study Two: Twelve people began work on a management information system for a large conglomerate. The stated goal of the system was to permit the organization to be run from the top. All computing facilities were to be grouped into the one system to take advantage of Grosch's law.

A considerable amount of ecstatic hand waving was performed over the concept of the computer's modeling certain metal markets. This would enable the company to buy its principal raw materials at advantageous prices and alter its inventory policy to reflect coming changes.

After almost two years of work it was conceded that none of the acquired companies had any intention of giving up its own computer center much less operational autonomy. Furthermore, no one had the slightest idea of how to model the market.

Case Study Three: A medium-sized city with a severe traffic problem decided to install a reactive computer system to control stop lights. A complete simulation was performed. The simulation indicated that traffic flow would be eased by 15% (of something).

The system was put into effect and traffic stopped dead. The simulation was run again and used to prove that traffic couldn't possibly have stopped dead. The system was abandoned. The simulation lives on.

Case Study Four: Three bidders were paid to submit detailed proposals for a large industrial development project. The procuring organization (the Government, who else?) specified that the project should be managed with the aid of an on-line Management Information System.

Since the MIS would have to function from the first month of the project, each of the bidders was instructed to develop their own system. The contract was awarded and two of the three systems were junked.

Maybe you have a story to tell. Maybe you'll send it to me care of MODERN DATA. Maybe I'll start an abortion clinic.

Reprinted from MODERN DATA March, 1970 with permission.

QUOTES

R. P. Walton
RYPIN'S MEDICAL LICENSURE EXAMINATIONS, ED. II. p. 436
J. B. Lippincott Co., 1970
Ether is a widely used volatile anaesthetic and is probably the safest in the hands of the less experienced.
(Balasubramanyam, MBBS)

****

NATURE July 23, v. 232, 1971
"Laboratory studies of creep are often hindered by the length of time required for the test. This is particularly true at low stresses where a transient creep term dominates and the present of a small steady state creep may be masked.

****

Gesellschaft fuer Biologische Chimie.
MAMMALIAN REPRODUCTION
QP 251 G4 1970
J. M. Bedford (N.Y.)
THE SAGA OF MAMMALIAN SPERM FROM EJACULATION TO SYNGAMY, p. 124

****

9 contributors, 11 collaborating contributors, 9 Institutions and assorted grants
QUASARS REVISITED: TIME VARIATIONS OBSERVED VIA VERY-LONG-BASELINE INTERFEROMETRY, Science 173, 225, 1971 (July 16)
"New discoveries about Quasars deepen the agony as well as the joy of the theoretical astrophysicist . . . To test the reliability in a manner relatively free from the effects of the most likely systematic errors we performed sensitivity studies . . . These sensitivities show clearly, as does the least square solution that the declination components of the separation rate is the most poorly determined quantity. This conclusion is not surprising since the resolution of the interferometer determined by the projected baseline, is about 5 times greater in the $\Delta \delta$ rather then in the $\Delta \chi$ direction . . . We find that on the basis of our symetric double source model, the apparent separation velocity can be no less than about 10 - 3 times the speed of light! How can this startling result be understood? All in our nine suggested explanations may appear almost as dubious as the like number of lives of the proverbial feline . . ."
(Has the number of 9 contributors anything to do with the nine suggested explanations?)

H. Brauchli

****

D. Gould
NEW SCIENTIST p. 170 April 15, 1971
. . . the still too common view that science is some kind of sacred cult whose mysteries should be kept for the personal gratification of its properly ordained priests and their chosen acolytes" — is "dangerous nonsense. Science and things of science are no one's private property. They are a central part of the common heritage of modern man. And anyone who obfucates this truth is not only a traitor to his kind but a blazing idiot to boot.

****

Jordan, W. P. Jr.
Arch. Derm. 103: 85, 1971
A patient sought medical advice because he "was allergic" to his Volkswagen. Each time the patient washed his "Bug" he experienced an episode of hand dermatitis. The patient was found to be sensitive to N-isopropyl-N-phenvlaphenylenediamine (IPPD) an antioxidant used in the manufacture of automobile tires. IPPD, a potent sensitiser is not used in tires manufactured in the U.S. However, 80% of Volkswagens come equipped with rubber tires containing IPPD.

****

A. H. Maslow
THE PSYCHOLOGY OF SCIENCE
Harper and Row, 1966, p. 29
. . . science in general can be considered a technique with which fallible men try to outwit their own human propensities to fear the truth, to avoid it, to distort it.

THEORETICAL
ZIPPERDYNAMICS

HARRY J. ZIPKIN
Department of Unclear Phyzipics
The Weizipmann Inziptute

INTRODUCTION

The fundamental principles of zipper operation were never well understood before the discovery of the quantum theory[1]. Now that the role of quantum effects in zippers has been convincingly demonstrated[2], it can be concluded that the present state of our knowledge of zipper operation is approximately equal to zero. Note that because of the quantum nature of the problem, one cannot say that the present state of knowledge is *exactly* equal to zero. There exist certain typically quantum-mechanical zero-point fluctuations; thus our understanding of the zipper can vary from time to time. The root-mean-square average of our understanding, however, remains of the order of h.

ZIPPERBEWEGUNG

The problem which baffled all the classical investigators was that of *"zipperbewegung"*[3], or how a zipper moves from one position to the next. It was only after the principle of complementarity was applied by Niels Bohr[4] that

---

[1] H. Quantum: A New Theory of Zipper Operation Which Is Also Incidentally Applicable to Such Minor Problems as Black Body Radiation, Atomic Spectroscopy, Chemical Binding, and Liquid Helium. Z.I.P. 7, 432 (1922).

[2] H. Eisenzip: The Uncertainty Principle in Zipper Operation, *Zipschrift fur Phyzip*, 2, 54 (1923).

[3] I. Newton, M. Faraday, C. Maxwell, L. Euler, L. Rayleigh, and J. W. Gibbs, "Die Zipperbewegung" (unpublished).

[4] N. Bohr: Lecture on Complementarity in Zippers, Geneva Conference, "Zippers for Peace" (1924).

the essentially quantum-theoretical nature of the problem was realized. Bohr showed that each zipper position represented a quantum state, and that the motion of the zipper from one position to the next was a quantum jump which could not be described in classical terms, and whose details could never be determined by experiment. The zipper just jumps from one state to the next, and it is meaningless to ask how it does this. One can only make statistical predictions of *zipperbewegung*.

The unobservability of *zipperbewegung* is due, as in most quantum-phenomena, to the impossibility of elimination of the interaction between the observer and the apparatus. This was seriously questioned by A. Einstein, who in a celebrated controversy with Bohr, proposed a series of experiments to observe *zipperbewegung*. Bohr was proved correct in all cases; in any attempt to examine a zipper carefully, the interaction with the observer was so strong that the zipper was completely incapacitated[5].

THE SEMI-INFINITE ZIPPER

A zipper is a quantum-mechanical system having a series of equally spaced levels or states. Although most zippers in actual use have only a finite number of states, the semi-infinite zipper is of considerable theoretical interest, since it is more easily treated theoretically than is the finite case. This was first done by Schroedzipper[6] who pointed out that the semi-infinite series of equally-spaced levels was also found in the Harmonic Oscillator discovered by Talmi[7]. Schroedzipper transformed the zipper probelm to the oscillator case by use of a Folded-Woodhouse Canonical Transformation. He was then able to calculate transition probabilities, level spacings, branching ratios, seniorities, juniorities, etc. Extensive tables of the associated Racah coefficients have recently been computed by Rose, Bead and Horn[8].

Numerous attempts to verify this theory by experiment have been undertaken, but all have been unsuccess-ful. The reason for the inevitability of such failure has been recently proved in the celebrated Weisgal-Eshkol theorem[9], which shows that the construction of a semi-infinite zipper requires a semi-infinite budget, and that this is out of the question even at the Weizipmann Inziptute.

Attempts to extend the treatment of the semi-infinite zipper to the finite case have all failed, since the difference between a finite and a semi-infinite zipper is infinite, and cannot be treated as a small perturbation. However, as in other cases, this has not prevented the publishing of a large number of papers giving perturbation results to the first order (no one publishes the higher order calculations since they all diverge). Following the success of M. G. Mayer[10] who added spin-orbit coupling to the harmonic oscillator, the same was tried for the zipper, but has failed completely. This illustrates the fundamental difference between zippers and nuclei and indicates that there is little hope for the exploitation of zipperic energy to produce useful power. There are, however, great hopes for the exploitation of zipperic energy to produce useless research.

THE FINITE ZIPPER

The problem of the finite zipper is best treated directly, without reference to the infinite case. One must first write the Schroedzipper equation for the system:

$$(1) \quad H\,Z = -ih\,dZ/dt$$

---

[5] P. R. Zipsel and N. Bohr: Einstein Memorial Lecture. Haifa Technion (1956).

[6] E. Schroedzipper: "What is a Zipper," Dublin (1950).

[7] E. Talmi, Helv. Phys. Acta, 1,1 (1901).

[8] M. E. Rose, A. Bead, and Sh. Horn (to be published).

[9] M. Weisgal and L. Eshkol: "Zippeconomics." Ann. Rept. Weizipmann Inziptute (1955).

[10] Metro G. Mayer: "Enrichment by the Monte-Carlo Method: Rotational States with Magic Numbers" Gamblionics, 3, 56 (1956).

The solution of this equation is left as an exercise for the reader. From the result all desired observable information can be calculated.

The most interesting case of the finite zipper is that in which there are perturbations. For this case the Schroed-zipper equation becomes:

$$(2) \quad (H + H') Z = -ih \, dZ/dt.$$

Because of the perturbation term H', the original states of the unperturbed zipper are not longer eigenstates of the system. The new eigenstates, characteristic of a perturbed zipper, are mixtures of the unperturbed states. This means, roughly, that because of the perturbation the zipper is in a state somewhere in between its ordinary states.

One interesting case of zipper perturbation has been reported[11]. The zipper system in question was on the front of the trousers of a man sitting in a cinema. The zipper had been lowered to its lowest state when it was perturbed by the back of a dress belonging to a lady attempting to pass in front of the gentleman. The zipper immediately jumped into a highly perturbed state, and the zipper-dress coupling proved to be so strong that it was impossible to separate the variables by conventional techniques. It was necessary for the individuals concerned to leave the cinema, walking down the aisle in "a zippered embrace" with further perturbations from the light quanta of the usher's flashlight and intense sound waves from the audience. The separation was later achieved by "brute force," thereby rendering the dress unsuitable for further use and requiring payment of a fine by the owner of the zipper.

Another theoretical possibility of such perturbation was recently voiced by a lady who was considering buying a pair of trousers for her husband. She was offered a zippered type but she declined the offer. Her uncertainty principle was expressed in the following words: "I don't think such trousers would be good for my husband. Last time I bought him a zippered sweater, his tie was highly disturbed by the zipper perturbation."

---

[11] The Ithaca Journal, "A Zippered Embrace" (1939).

"OLD YELLER ENZYME"

INTRODUCTION

T. RAGLAND

"Old Yeller Enzyme" is important historically, if for no other reason*. It introduced the use of color to qualitate enzyme studies and made available for the first time an enzyme which could be thought of as a catalyst in a biochemical quagmire.

PURIFICATION

Nine pigs were Waring-blended and water-extracted according to the method of Baron von Lebedev[1]. Lead subacetate is added (400 ml of liquor plumbisubaceti i D.A.B. 6 per liter of Lebedev juice) and the mixture vigorously shaken with high-test anti-knock aviation octane (Stukka No. 3). The precipitate formed after 3 months at -20 centigrade is separated from the mother liquor by severing the umbilical cord and centrifugation. To the supernatant, which contains the enzyme, is added a half volume of dialysed Ramco No. 5[2]. After the viscous jel settles out, the "yeller" super is evaporated to dryness.

Step 2. 100 gr. of "ole yeller" is redissolved in chloroform and shaken in lusteroid Mickle disintegrator tubes for one week. The spray-ate, which has flown all over the walls and ceiling, is scraped off these fixtures and designated as "ole yeller" No. 3.

ASSAY

"Ole yeller", fraction 3 is scrubbed up in octanol and the co-enzyme "split" from the ape-o-enzyme. Upon the addition of DPNH, crude yeast extract (Canadian ale yeast, top variety, Hanson), and octanol sludge, a rapid bleaching occurs which is directly proportional to the intensity of the yellow color. Arbitrarily assuming that 5 Fisch Units catalyse 10 bleaches (assuming single hit kinetics) the fluorescence quenching may be calculated. One kg. of pig yields 3 mg of "ole yeller."

---

* As a matter of fact, *absolutely* for no other reason.
[1] Zeitschrift fuer Konigen, 12, 199.
[2] Available from Spitzungen and Schleicher.

The Semitruth about Semiconductors

M. A. VINOR
Department of Semistry
Institute for Advanced Anti-Semics

At present the research in the field of semiconductors is so heavily bombarded by mathematical artillery and so full of red herrings of new concepts such as traps, defects, holes, vacancies and the like, that one can hardly see the semiconductor for the holes. Therefore, we think that it is high time to revive the fundamental concepts and primary axioms and thus relieve the weary inquisitive reader of going through heaps of senseless papers which would be completely useless five years from now, anyway.

The First Dogma of the Semiconductor Creed is:

FOR ANYTHING WHATSOEVER ALWAYS PUT THE BLAME ON THE ELECTRON (its negative charge, its negative attitude to life, etc.)

Metals are exceptional in that they conduct electricity well. This is because they contain electrons on the loose and any bad influence, such as an electric field, pushes them to damnation.

Now, if you hang a piece of semiconductor (i.e. not exactly a non-metal) on a long piece of red tape in the middle of a conference hall, and if the people present argue hotly enough about it, then the sign of the current carriers in the semiconductor may be determined. This is known as the Hall Effect.

By applying the Hall Effect to many things it was found that some semiconductors had electrons as carriers, while others had positive carriers, which, evidently, could not be electrons since electrons are by definition always negative (see Dogma above).

The poor semiconductors were, therefore, divided into two classes:

1) Semiconductors of the *n* type (*n* = normal) in which the electrons misbehave as usual.
2) Semiconductors of *p* type (*p* = pervert) in which the electrons misbehave even more.

Now, solid state physicists could not assume the positive carriers to be some sort of positive electrons (positrons) because they have already been discovered by nuclear physicists and no original idea would be involved. Therefore, after many sleepless nights of beer (alco-hole) sipping, a new and very, very original idea was found. The Positive Carriers are HOLES!

If an electron jumps out of its place and goes, probably full of doubtful intentions, to Conduction Alley – then everybody is so glad that its vacancy is named Positive Hole. If another electron fills the vacancy – then it is considered good form to say (especially if ladies are present): "The Hole went away." And so, if you pump a German full of Holes, you don't get a sieve but a piece of *p* type Germanium.

A piece of solid is also full of other queer irrelevancies such as phonons, excitons, traps, etc. Electrons are always in the habit of getting pushed about by photons and phonons and falling into traps. This causes some confusion since nice people do not say that an electron came out of a trap, but say instead: "A Hole fell into a trap." This should not cause any misunderstanding if the true facts are borne in mind and point only to personal shyness.

We should also mention the Taboo of Semiconductors. By the ingenious definition above, Holes have negative masses. This is to mean that if you inject enough Holes into a semiconductor it should fly like a balloon. One usually finds that in conversation physicists evade or side-track the questions about this property. There are two reasons for it.

(a) They are embarrassed because this idea is not so very original; it was used long ago by the chemists who adhered to the Phlogiston theory (but do physicists know chemistry?).

(b) The whole subject is highly classified as this principle of annulling gravitational force is being secretly developed for guided missiles against guided missiles against guided missiles.

We hope that by laying bare before the reader the essential facts concerning semiconductors, we have shown that one can talk in a very learned fashion about them and never be exposed; one has only to observe two simple rules (one Dogma and one Taboo) and keep the face straight.

Good luck!

Semiconductors Are Not Equal Opportunity Employers

HAROLD MOTT
Electrical Engineering Department
University of Alabama

THE EQUAL EMPLOYMENT OPPORTUNITY COMMISION
1800 G Street, N.W.
Washington, D.C. 20506

Professor W. D. Radburn
Electrical Engineering Department
Wheat University
Galveston, Texas

June 18, 1973

Dear Professor Radburn:

I have been advised that you are in responsible charge of the Solid-State Laboratory in the Electrical Engineering Department of Wheat University. I have also been advised that this laboratory is concerned with the fabrication and utilization of certain solid-state devices called transistors, which I understand is some kind of portable radio. It is my further understanding that in the fabrication and/or utilization of these transistors you employ workmen having the job classifications of "minority carriers" and "majority carriers." I must tell you immediately that we here are gravely concerned about these job classifications. Even though we wish to give you every benefit of doubt, I must advise you that the existence of these titles appears to be *prima facie* evidence of discrimination, which is forbidden by Title VII of the Civil Rights Act of 1964 and Executive Order 11246, and is punishable by fines and/or imprisonment. Since the presumption of discrimination on your part exists I advise you to reply promptly and carefully to the following questions and directives.

. Is the ratio of minority carriers to majority carriers employed in your laboratory at least equal to the ratio, in the general population of your community, of individuals of the minority race to that of the majority?

. Is the average salary of the minority carriers equal to or greater than the average salary of the majority carriers? I suggest that you supply to me without delay a list of minority and majority carriers together with the salaries of each carrier.

3. Are there proportionally as many minority carriers in supervisory positions as there are majority carriers?

4. I understand that these carriers carry charges, and further that they carry charges of different sign. Are the charges carried by the minority carriers heavier than those carried by the majority carriers?

5. I understand that some of these carriers are said to "drift." I trust that you are not implying that any of the minority carriers drift aimlessly. This would seem to be an insult and is forbidden by Federal law.

6. What is this "diffusion" which I have heard about? You should keep in mind that while the maximum amount of integration is desirable, we will not tolerate talk about diffusion of minority carriers throughout the entire region.

7. I understand that your laboratory is involved with the development of devices called "integrated circuits." This is certainly a point in your favor, and we will keep it in mind as we review your situation.

In view of the gravity and urgency of this situation I am sure you will want to answer my letter quickly and completely. I await your reply.

Very truly yours,

W. E. McLiu

W. E. McLiu
Supervisor for Region III Compliance
The Equal Employment Opportunity Commission

WEM:ky

Anecdotal Evidence for the Existence of an Unfilled Niche

THEODORE H. FLEMING
Department of Biology
University of Missouri
St. Louis, Missouri

The question of whether habitats are saturated—contain the maximum possible number of animal species—is one which has intrigued ecologists for many years. The fact that introduced species often gain a foothold and increase in numbers in a new ecological setting seems to indicate that not all habitats are saturated (see review by Elton, 1958). The following set of observations, perhaps a perfect example of an unfilled niche, is offered as additional evidence for the unsaturated nature of certain habitats.

Materials and Methods

In hopes of attracting winter birds to my backyard, I set up a bird-feeding station in our backyard on November 15, 1968. The station consisted of a commercial "cone" of assorted "bird seeds" (Burpee & Co.) wired to two 9-inch aluminum pie plates (Jane Parker & Co.) that served as a top and a bottom for the station. The pie plates were supported by two pine slats 8 inches in length. The station was suspended by a wire from the west arm of our metal clothes-line pole.

The ecological setting of this bird feeder is the Backyard Biome (Dice, 1952) and consists of the normal garden variety of plants which includes lilac *(Syringa)*, dogwood *(Cornus)*, peony *(Paenonia)*, zinnias *(Zinnia)*, and strawberry *(Fragarus)*. One noteworthy feature is a stand of several 10-ft. tall *arbor vitae (Thuja occidentalis),* which serves to increase the privacy of our backyard. The overhanging boughs of one *arbor vitrae* protect the bird-feeder from possible damage by wind and rain. The area encompassed by our backyard is approximately 450 sq. ft. (0.10 a).

Since November 15, I have observed the feeder from my kitchen each day for one continuous hour at a time determined by use of a random numbers table (Steel and Torrie, 1960). In all honesty, I only observed the feeder for one-half hour if the designated time occurred at night. (At a distance of 40 ft., the station was extremely difficult to see in the dark). All observations were made using 7×35 binoculars. Biological observations and weather conditions (temperature, humidity, and precipitation) were recorded on IBM data sheets, and the data were transferred to IBM cards at the end of each week. Data included in this paper were analyzed on an IBM-360 computer.

Results

Between November 15 and February 25, I observed the feeding station for a total of 82.5 hrs., and in that time I failed to see a single bird utilize the food available there. Careful examination of the "cone" of seeds indicated that it had never been disturbed. This means that in the 2,448 hrs. that the food was available, no bird ever visited the feeder (Table 1).

The relationship between lack of feeding activity and temperature, humidity, and precipitation was analyzed by multiple regression. Results showed that none of the three variables was more important than any other in explaining the lack of results ($P > .05$).

Discussion

The lack of results was somewhat surprising and, frankly, very disappointing. I find it hard to explain why no birds were attracted to the feeding station. A paucity of birds in the immediate vicinity of our yard cannot be the reason because I observed English sparrows *(Passer domesticus)*, starlings *(Sturnus vulgaris)*, cardinals *(Richmondea cardinalis)*, and blue jays *(Cyanocitta cristata)* on numerous occasions not more than 50 ft. from the feeding station. There appeared to be nothing unusual about the bird seeds or the nature of our yard that might prove unattractive to birds.

The lack of results forced me to curtail the discussion somewhat as I had been prepared to compare my findings with the MacArthur "broken stick" model (MacArthur, 1957), with various measures of species diversity

TABLE 1. Number of hrs. of observation, number of birds seen, and average weather conditions during periods of observations of a backyard bird-feeder.

HOURS OF OBSERVATION	NO. BIRDS SEEN	NO. BIRDS SEEN PER HR. OF OBS.	AVG. TEMP. °F	AVG. HUMIDITY %	AVG. PPT. INCHES
82.5	0	0	30.5 ± 0.24	73.4 ± 2.5	0.13 ± 0.01

(reviewed by Hairstron *et al.,* 1968) and niche breadth (Levins, 1968), and Wynne-Edwards' (1962) theory of epideictic display. These comparisons will have to wait until observations become available.

Because no birds were ever observed to use my feeding station, I can only conclude that the feeder represents an unfilled niche. As such, it is intriguing to speculate on just what kind of bird could fill this niche. A more detailed description of the available niche will aid in deciding what kind of bird could take advantage of it. The "cone" of seeds consisting of hundreds of seeds that average 0.5 mm in diameter weighs 455 g. This biomass represents about 3,000 kcal of potential energy (Farmer's Almanac, 1968).

It is my opinion that this niche could support one very large, transient bird that might eat the entire feeder (including the aluminum pie pans) in one bite, or several small finch-like birds that might subsist on the seeds for several days. It seems clear that because the niche is rather ephemeral, any species specialized enough to fill it will become extinct very quickly unless it can find another niche with similar characteristics. The species will have to be a "fugitive" in the strictest sense of the word.

I am not undaunted by the lack of results so far and plan to continue observing this "unfilled niche" systematically in hopes of eventually discovering a species that can take advantage of this unusual energetic opportunity.

Summary

A backyard bird-feeder was observed from November 15, 1968, to February 25, 1969. In this period no birds were ever seen to feed there. I believe this represents a classic example of an unfilled niche.

LITERATURE CITED

Anonymous. 1968. Farmer's Almanac.
Dice, L. R. 1952. Natural communities. Univ. of Michigan Press, Ann Arbor.
Elton, C. S. 1958. The ecology of invasions by animals and plants. Methuen & Co., London.
Hairston, N. G., J. D. Allan, R. K. Colwell, D. J. Futuyma, J. Howell, M. D. Lubin, J. Mathias, and J. H. Vandermeer. 1968. The relationship between species diversity and stability: an experimental approach with Protozoa and bacteria. Ecol., 49: 1091–1101.
Levins, R. 1968. Evolution in changing environments. Princeton Univ. Press, Princeton.
Steel, R. G. D., and J. H. Torrie. 1960. Principles and procedures of statistics. McGraw-Hill Book Co., New York.
Wynne-Edwards, V. C. 1962. Animal dispersion in relation to social behavior. Hafner Press, Edinburgh.

THE UNZYME CONCEPT

HERBERT SAVEL, M.D.
Burlington, Vermont

Until the present time, the conversion of substance A → substance B by meat juice was considered to indicate the presence of an "enzyme" in the juice. However, it appears that there is an alternative explanation, which is the subject of the present communication.

It is commonly observed that when meat juice is added to substance A, substance B is most often *not* detectable after the appropriate incubation period. However, rather than leaping immediately to the traditionally negative explanation of absence of "enzyme," it may be affirmatively stated that A ↛ B is based on the presence of an "unzyme." By contrast, the less frequent A → B conversion would indicate the existence of unzyme inhibition. By virtue of the simple rule of economy of concept, it would appear that the unzyme hypothesis is more in harmony with underlying reality than is the enzyme hypothesis.

Our modest efforts to date have revealed instances of "competitive" and "noncompetitive" unzyme inhibition as well as evidence for the most complex of all interaction—allosteric unzymatic inhibition.

It is quite likely that other types of unzymatic kinetics will soon be uncovered by open-minded investigators.

An Overlooked (?) Basic Principle of Development and Personality*

F. NOWELL JONES
Department of Psychology
University of California

I should like to call the attention of psychologists to a basic principle of personality which has, most remarkably, been heretofore overlooked.

To begin with the history of the idea: Some months ago I visited Professor Harry F. Harlow's laboratory devoted to the study of infant monkeys. Many of the tiny little Ss were to be seen with thumb or finger in mouth, no doubt sucking. I was most struck, however, by one little fellow who was observing me with much manifest anxiety—a term readily defined operationally upon demand. Not only was this infant a thumb-sucker, he was also what we may call a tail-holder, for with the unmouthed hand he was clutching his tail and tickling his ear with the tip. The analogy to the blanket or towel or other object of similar shape which the infant Homo sapiens so often puts to similar use was dramatic and striking. Put bluntly, the human infant seeks a tail-surrogate, and I suggest that even in the adult a condition of tail-envy, as we shall call it, is embedded deeply in the unconscious. The universality of this new principle is emphasized by the remarkable fact that it applies to both sexes, a point which cannot be made for a rival concept which I shall not mention here.

This new principle of tail-envy explains many strange human behaviors. To mention but a few, consider dreams of such objects as snakes, or some persons' addiction to rope climbing—but why extend this list unduly? So important seemed the principle that I began an active search for positive, specific instances where it might be applied and have, after 20 months, found two. The first is the universal appeal *to adults* of the comic strip character of tender years whose life seems to revolve around his comforting blanket. So pervasive is this appeal that it can be based only upon some deeply embedded urge derived from our remote ancestors and transmitted through the unconscious—perhaps in unbroken line back to that ancient anonymous man-ape who first noticed that he had no tail and suffered trauma from this realization. The second instance is even more interesting because the appeal is completely adult and overlaid subtly with patina of modern sophistication. One airline advertises that "We really move our tail for you." How obvious can a principle be?

I cannot close without a brief comment designed to anticipate an expected immature objection to the new principle which will come from those threatened by it. The objection is, how can it be that 20 months have produced only two positive instances? The obvious reply would be that I have been too busy with committees to notice very much, but this is not, I feel, adequate. I should rather say that two instances per investigator for each two years is quite enough. If the active participation of only a few thousand psychologists can be enlisted, I am sure that the next few years will see many thousands of positive instances of tail-envy appearing in the literature. I am confident that once a sufficient body of examples has been assembled, the new principle will be difficult to overthrow, especially among those psychologists working in situations where one has to do something useful, not just play with facts in the laboratory.

* Reprinted, more or less by permission from The Worm Runner's Digest, 4:61 (1962).

On the Absolute Refractory Period in the Transmission of Information by Library Distribution of Scientific Journals

KENNETH H. REID
Department of Physiology and Biophysics
University of Louisville School of Medicine
Louisville, Kentucky 40201

ABSTRACT

A new syndrome, provisionally labelled "Acute Regional Bindery Block" is described. This syndrome, which appears to interfere with the transmission of scientific information, is characterized by the symptom complex:

URP DRP PUP ARP RRP rest

ULP RRP' *!! DRP PUP ARP RRP rest

Therapuetic measures and possible reactions are considered in the light of the physiology involved.

It is well known that most scientific journals are secreted at a steady rate (monthly, quarterly, etc.) which is quite independent of the amount of research being done in the field served by the journal under consideration. Equally well known is the fact that libraries reserve a finite amount of space for the reception and storage of current journals, and that this space does not differ greatly from one library to another. Consequently libraries find it necessary to excrete these accumulated secretions at regular intervals by transporting them to a distant place known as the bindery, where they are dehydrated, compressed, and eventually returned for dead storage in the library stacks.

From the point of view of the journal user, this physiological process has some unexpected side effects, which have not yet been discussed in the respectable literature. We will begin by dividing the secretary and digestive processes involved into periods, and will then describe selected ones of these in more detail. To begin with, we have the unpublished refractory period (URP), during which the data is unavailable to anyone except the referees reviewing the paper. Following publication we have the ditribution refractory period (DRP), which is the delay (from 1 to 8 weeks) between the publication date indicated on the journal cover and the date it actually arrives on the library shelf.

The arrival of the journal marks the beginning of the primary useful period (PUP), which terminates when the journal is either stolen or sent to the bindery. In practice, this period will be reduced, often considerably, by the user latency period (ULP), which is the time taken by the user to dicover that this particular journal contains something useful to him. The ULP will vary with the habits of the user; a monomaniacal literature scanner will read every journal the day it arrives in the library, and so will have a negligable ULP, but very sore eyes; readers of Current Contents will have reasonably short ULPs but will miss the vital articles in JIR; readers who rely on citation or other indexes will have relatively long ULPs , in some cases approaching the PUP.

A long ULP may not be the fault of the reader. Consider the following situation: an aspiring author submits his manuscript to a journal, commencing an URP. The editor sends the manuscript to a referee, who suggests (after some time) that the author should read a recent paper by A**** before drawing perhaps premature conclusions. The author attempts to oblige, and finds:

1) The reviewer read the paper by A**** during its PUP.

2) The PUP has now expired, and the paper in question is at the bindery.

3) Because of the constant secretion rate and the similar space allotments in different libraries, the PUP for the paper wanted has expired for all libraries within a radius of (approximately) 5,000 miles.

4) On writing to A****, the author finds he does not, as a matter of principle, send reprints to people at locations known to have good library service, but saves them for underprivileged scientists in distant lands (he collects stamps), and in any case he has no reprints left.

Clearly, the effect of physiological interest is the nearly simultaneous ending of the PUP over a very wide area. The following period, during which the published information is not available to anyone, will be called the absolute refractory period (ARP), by analogy with the corresponding phenomenon following excitation in nervous or muscular tissue. Following the ARP is (in many libraries) a period of relative inaccessibility, the relative refractory period or RRP, during which the bound journal may not be removed from the library. When the material has aged enough to be totally useless, it becomes freely available but inert. This is the resting state, which we will not discuss further.

The main excitation sequence is, as previously described, URP DRP PUP ARP RRP ending in the resting state, which is the same as the state of science before the work was done. To deal with the author-referee problem, we add the RRP' (referee reaction period), which is part of the author's URP, and note that failure of propagation occurs when the referee's ULP plus his RRP' exceeds the PUP of the paper he cites, thereby causing the author's search period to occur within the ARP of the paper sought. Diagrammatically:

URP DRP PUP ARP RRP rest

ULP RRP' *!! DRP PUP ARP RRP rest

Note the pronounced arrythmia, amounting to virtual block, resulting when the RRP' referring to the author's paper falls within the ARP of the paper cited. This pathological state, although only recently discovered, has already received 3 descriptors:

1. acute regional bindery block
2. primary retrieval block
3. %*x#!! syndrome

Therapeutic measures derive naturally from the physiology involved. The most sbvious approach is to shorten the ARP by application of the potent repolarizing agent $$$. The main objection to this approach is its relative high cost. More elegant is the suggestion (due to H. Poppenhymer) that the variance of the PUP be increased by varying the storage space available over the set of intercommunicating libraries. Even more elegant is the suggestion that the PUP be varied randomly and independently over:

1) the set of journals subscribed by a particular library
2) the set of libraries within a given region receiving a given journal

Although the result would undoubtably involve a substantial increase in interlibrary loans, and a slight increase in the ARP/PUP ratio (on the average) the procedure could reduce primary retrieval block to the negligable level that prevailed when libraries were considerably less organized than they are today.

Before abandoning the entire subject as a dead issue, one caveat is in order. Note that in the diagram the effect of acute bindery block on the author's work is to delay publication, and hence to extend the PUP, ARP, RRP, of his work, thus delaying its return to the resting state. Some authors may feel this is an advantage, particularly if it permits them to retire before their life's work is completely forgotten. If this is the case, attempts to introduce the therapeutic measures discussed above may meet determined, and not entirely disinterested, resistance. Perhaps things are just as well left as they are.

Musings of an aging "SCIENTIST"

RUSSELE de WAARD
Old Greenwich, Conn.

To an astute reader the title ("Scientist") is sufficient to set the mood for this document.

Ever since I can remember I have been insecure. When I was small I worried and worried that my slingshot would break and I would never find another tree branch to make a new one. This attitude has persisted until today. I get interested and work hard on something and it seems to me at the time that I have done a good job. The results of my work are printed and distributed among my peers. I go home that night quite satisfied and feeling good, but by the end of the next day I am concerned that I could have done a better job. By the second day I am convinced that most of what I wrote was wrong and I feel quite stupid. This is an example, which repeats itself over and over. I am quite convinced that I was apprehensive as a fetus. Although my failing memory doesn't confirm it, at that stage I probably worried about a kink in the umbilical cord.

I don't know whether to blame this deficiency on my genes, my chromosomes or my upbringing. But in the latter category, I have made a few observations. I have been taught to respect authority; when the Department Head says I am wrong, I am wrong. Since I did not go to MIT, I reason miserably, that Edgar Slack, my teacher at BPI, must have been wrong. On These occasions I take his book (Haussman & Slack) into the men's room to see if I might have misread it.

What one has to learn is that all the laws of physics are repealed by authority. Hence, if one speaks with authority, from a recognized box in the company organization chart, he is perforce believed. These things have only very recently come to me, but I don't know what to do about it. If I am lucky this draft will not be published and my discovery will go "undiscovered." My position is a bit like that of Galileo in the 15th century when his telescope told him beyond a doubt that the world was round and was rotating about the sun, but his friends told him to keep his big mouth shut or the Pope would feed him to the lions. I like to eat and to drink and not to rock the boat, so I think I'll do what Galileo did, unless tomorrow morning I ask Bobby to type this tape. The latter is unlikely since overnight my apprehension will return.

The funny part about all this is that when I go out on a sailing ship all my chicken-hearted propensities dissolve into the sea and I become a soul-mate of Captain Horatio Hornblower. The trouble is that none of the fellows in authority are along, and I curse at the wind and the waves to no avail.

If I keep on like I'm going, I might make three score and five, and if by that time I don't continue to spike my vodka martini with lemonade, I may have worked up enough gumption to say "no, I won't shut up, you sit down and listen for a change" to one of the fellows in the boxes.

Irreproducible

research

too often

leads to

GREAT

DISCOVERIES

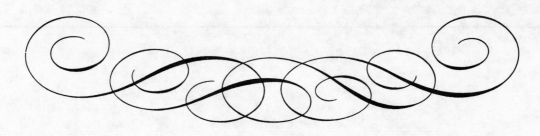

Quat-Quars* A Newly Discovered Phenomenon

R. KENNETH
TOM CABBIN
FELIX KLAUS
and TAB TAILOR

Introduction

Cats constitute a large percentage of the observable fauna in the township of Rishon-le-Zion. They have been found to outnumber human beings there by approximately ten-to-one, using the well-known methods of Ellenbogen.[1] It was noticed, however, by the senior author, that these incrutable animals are seldom to be seen in the evening hours, from the lowering of the reddening sun over the western horizon in a blaze of glory, till slumber-time for humans when they make their re-appearance, enlivening the night air with their gay antics and wassailing. The question was asked by the senior author, "Where do the critters go?" In fact, the question was not directed to anyone in particular, but the answer came from the vicinity of my knees, from my young son, who always looks up to his father, "Under parked cars, you fool!" After careful examination of his claims, and the wearing out of the kneecaps of two pairs of trousers, it was ascertained that he was fully justified in his conclusions. This phenomenon is designated as Quat-Quars.

One thing leading to another, a preliminary study was carried out, consisting of a survey on the habits, preferences and predilections of these beasts.

Materials and Methods

A hand-count was made of all cats present during daylight hours on a 200 meter stretch On the Street that I Live. This was accomplished by the baiting method,[2] using Grade A homogenized milk (kindly supplied from my neighbors' doorsteps in the early hours of the morning), poured in a straight line along the northern curb at the rate of one liter/10m. of curb. All cats answering this inexorable call were counted (and one can count on them to come, using a TAB electronic Quat-Quounter with a nine-life battery (Abercrombie & Fintch). Three assistants were employed to prevent cats from returning for second helpings, so it may be assumed that the figures are dependable. The count was replicated (three different hours). The results were: 160,15**, 140, with an average of 150, which turned out to be a nice round number to work with.

On seven consecutive evenings, careful counts were made of numbers of cats under cars, at different hours. The full details, together with statistical analyses, are presented in five other papers being submitted elsewhere. In this paper, we will suffice by summarizing the more important findings, and trust that the reader will understand that all the results were statistically very significant, as is the importance of the findings.

Results in Brief

1. Of the cats counted during the day, 98.5% are bedded down under automobiles during evening hours. Of the others, 1.2% were still up trees and afraid to descend, and the rest (0.3%) were found to be trapped in garbage cans whose lids had fallen down (Isn't there a better way for me to earn a living than this?).

2. For some reason still not fully understood, no more than one cat may be found under a single car. We believe that this could be linked to the "ecological exclusion principle", and also to Gresham's Law which states "Bad cats drive out good".

---

*Quat-Quars: (kăt'-kărz), n. (< Sanskrit).

**Deleted from our calculations — The sudden appearance of Mrs. Strauss' poodle upon the scene during the second count, seems to have had a catalytic effect (Webster: Kat-a-līsis (>Gk. a losing), causing what may henceforth be called the "Quatar-disappearance phenomenon", in which trees suddenly become populated by the creatures to the detriment of the street level. Catalysis and autolysis have been found to have no connection whatever; the latter describes the situation whereby a car gets lost, in theft.

3. The peak hour for sub-vehicle resting is from 2200-2300 hours, there being approximately twice as many felines present there as during 2000-2100 or 2100-2200. The number of parked cars present, however, during 2200-2300 hours are considerably more than earlier in the evening, due to the return of the theater crowd, so that the number of cats in proportion to that of cars is about the same during all hours under investigation.

4. It was ascertained that there is no car relation whatever between the size or age of the cat and the make or size of the automobile under which it seeks repose.

5. The color of the cat, as regards the color of the car was examined. Although it is true that at night all cats are gray, the problem of color differentiation in late evening was solved by the elegant procedure of cruising my car (senior author, Cadillac Fleetwood, 1970 Model), with full headlights, up and down the street to bring out color highlights particularly the black. This, unfortunately had to be discontinued after the senior author received a black eye from an irate motorist. However, it was found that the eye (black or otherwise) becomes accommodated to the dark, and various shades could eventually become distinguished (see Fig. 1).

FIG. 1. Black cat under hearse at 2330 hours.

The results show that there is no car relation between color of cat and that of automobile, and that color is only fur deep.

6. There is a definite car relation between the variety of cat and the size and make of the automobile. Unexpectedly, it was found that Siamese and Persian cats prefer small cars of any make to large ones, leaving the Cadillacs, Chryslers and Lincolns on the Street that I Live (!) to the more plebian breeds. This was shown by us to be a matter of "noblesse oblige".

7. Cat sex and cars:
   a. Female cats, as a rule, prefer dainty cars, such as the "deux-chevaux". Male cats prefer female cats.
   b. The female cat of any variety or breed seems to be perfectly willing to yield its place under any make or size upon the approach of a male, as a matter of courtesy. Strangely enough, the male seldom takes advantage of this generosity but usually follows her, calling out[3] that the gesture was not necessary, as he was just strolling by, taking in the night air. Females, however, have seldom been persuaded to return to their rightful place.[4]

8. Cats do not sit at any and every place under automobiles. Being agoraphobic, they react to thigmotactic stimuli under the car and generally gravitate to a car tire, snuggling up to it and calling out with delight. This is known as caterwauling (next to the senior author's car's tires of course, it is caterwhitewauling).

[1] Ellenbogen, K. 1937. Methods for the estimation of populations, carried out on Sundays at Coney Island. Jour. Applied Math. 7 (11) :32.
[2] Whittington, R. 1422. On Cats and Queens. J. Gutenberg Press, London & Mainz.
[3] Doaks, J. 1960. My brother talks to cats. Sat. Eve. Post. January 10.
[4] Millett, K. 1970. Women's Liberation. Juno Press, Manaos, Amazones.

Acknowledgments: This research was supported by the Ecological Foundation, the S.P.C.A., the Ford Foundation and the Volkswagen Foundation.

LETTERS TO THE EDITOR

October 29, 1973

Dear Dr. Kohn:

It is ironic that the lead article in the June issue of the Journal, "Vide-Infra," which deals so eloquently and authoritatively with the subject of footnotes should be accompanied in the same document by another paper that reports on an investigation (Quat-Quars* A Newly Discovered Phenomenon; R. Kenneth et al) that leads to certain conclusions, but tangentially and somewhat infraentially seeks to posit the existence of a phenomenon (not referred to in the article title) in, of all places, a footnote!

From the reported facts one might well deduce that the "Quatar-disappearance phenomenon" is based upon hasty conclusions derived from only superficial observances and, in fact, little or no car relation exists. Catalysis is not the operative effect in the situation involving "the sudden appearance of Mrs. Strauss' poodle upon the scene during the second count. . . ." (op. cite; ibid.). That the trees suddenly became populated to the detriment of the street level is a clear and demonstrable parallel to the charged particle field effect phenomenon reported by Coolidge, Bragg, Eigen, Rutherford and every other physicist who has worked at sometime or other with atomic nucleii.

It is clearly established that when a high energy, freely moving, charged particle (poodle) is placed within the field of a system having a circumscribed boundary (as defined by Kenneth et al) with all the occupants of that system at a static state of activity but possessing great potential, the energy of the introduction particle is radiated to the occupants causing a triggering in their discrete systems, heightening their activity rate, making available their kinetic energy and causing what might at first glance be thought of as a random scattering (or, randoms cattering as known in some quaters).

But the scattering is not random. It will be noticed that within the field there are stable poles or nodes. These poles (trees, for example) are not themselves charged but do support a charge at an elevated level. In this regard, unaffected as they are by this field effect scattering phenomenon, they are known as catalytic agents within the bounded field. It is upon these stable elements that the occupants are catapulted from a lower level to a higher level.

It is to be noted, however, that the impinging charged particle that was the initiating cause of the scattering loses much of its energy in the transference process. It does not have the capability to rise to the higher level attained by the Quat occupants; witness the fact that poodles are not normally found in trees in their natural state. The impinging charge rather, remains at street level solitary in a depopulated state, not completely entropic, but undoubtedly dejected.

In summation, this reported situation is quite analogous to electron scattering, and it is no new or strange disappearance phenomenon at all. This is a problem in existence theory that deserves better treatment than being squeezed into a footnote.

It may be fair to theorize that if, in addition to the acknowledged supporters of the reported research, a grant had also been obtained from the High Energy Division of the National Science Foundation, the importance of the field effect phenomenon would not have been overlooked.

Sincerely yours,
H. M. Sarasohn
Director of Engineering Communications

CSCMOETM TIMER

A CONTRIBUTION TO THE PHILOSOPHICAL BACKGROUND OF, THE BASIC AND APPLIED THEORY OF, AND AN APPROACH TO THE PRACTICAL AND ECONOMIC UTILIZATION OF THE Cyclic Self-Correcting Method of Exact Time Measurement.

O. SJAASTAD
SEACON A/S, Oslo, Norway

B. N. MAEHLUM
CSCMOETM-Lab., Oslo, Norway

SUMMARY:
The authors claim that the accuracy with which time can be measured and recorded is the factor that governs progress and inventions in science, technology and in economics. The authors claim that all funds and all efforts spent on research and development are wasted, and that all efforts should have been concentrated on the problem of accurate time measurement, since the results here would immediately lead to the desired progress in other fields of science, technology and economic life. The claim has been proved, using a digital computer, and has been verified by a practical test with a new device called the CSC-MOETM-timer® which is described in this article.

1. INTRODUCTION

The state of the art of time measurement and recording was fairly low when Adam and Eve were forced to leave Paradise. The only record of the event states that apples were fit for human consumption, which leads to the suggestion that the error could be as high as $\pm 5 \times 10^6$ seconds. The level of technology must have been very low, even the textile industry was not developed. The gross national product and, hence, the level of atmospheric pollution must be assumed to have been negligible.

A remarkable result of improved time measuring methods can still be seen in Egypt. The Egyptian KLEPSYDRA reduced the error below the value which has been necessary to unveil the mystery of civil engineering, commencing the period of pyramidization.

Experience shows that when a certain threshold in accuracy is attained, an important invention is automatically the result. Early achievements of mankind cannot, with great certainty, be plotted on an error-vs- innovatibility chart. The bulk of available data is too small to justify the use of an electronic digital computer, and the job could only be done by using manual thinking and common sense. Such a chart would consequently lack the scientific approach, and would sacrifice confidence in the results which a computer would give.

An important event took place in the town Schaffhausen, Switzerland, in the year 1903. This is the first event where the authors have been able to analyze the effect of time measurement on technological progress. The Swiss watchmaker Rüzli Grossklein was, in the summer of 1903 well underway with the construction of a temperature compensated clock, which he expected would have an accuracy of $\pm$ 0.8 seconds in 24 hours. A successful testrun, of 24 hours duration, was terminated on December 17th, 0839 UT. The clock had gained approximately $\pm$ 0.78964 seconds in 24 hours. It is not a coincidence that Wilbur and Orville Wright were able to fly their airplane on this very day. Mr. Grossklein had been able to surpass the error threshold which would enable man to fly. The credit for the successful flight should certainly be given to Mr. Grossklein, and not to the Wright brothers. The flight was the result of Mr. Grossklein's efforts, and would have taken place on this very day anyway, by someone somewhere. Weather reports show that the temperature in Schaffhausen was about 11° C above the average. Later tests with the Grossklein clock showed that the clock was slightly overcompensated with regard to temperature. The error would probably have been 0.82 seconds if the temperature had been down to the average, and an air crash (the first in history) would have been inevitable.

It is interesting, and disappointing, to note that the enormous funds spent on space research are wasted. The achievements in space technology are the result of improved methods of time measurements and recording, not of the activities within the field of space research. The same results would have been obtained if a development proposal of a small group of scientists in one of the major industrial undertakings had not been rejected in 1946. If these scientists had been successful, man would have put his foot on the moon in the year 1949 (perhaps with the expression "In one small side-step by the clock-man, that's one giant sweep for mankind".)

2. THE CSCMOETM-timer®

2.1 Basic philosophy.

The authors have invented a device (the CSCMOETM-TIMER®), which measures time exactly. An error of $\pm$ 0 seconds will yield an infinite increase in production of every possible and impossible matter and will make unlimited economic resources available to everyone. The authors were certainly not prepared to bear the responsibility for a testrun on this invention, and a testrun was conducted after introducing an artificial (man made) error of controlled magnitude. The test was thereafter reversed, to restore the pre-test conditions. The test was conducted on November 16th, 1971, 140020 UT to 140030 UT, and reversed the same day 140035-140055 UT. This testrun should, according to the authors' estimate, give a temporary, 25 seconds, enhancement in production, and a subsequent drop back to the original level. The enhancement is estimated to:

Increase in gross national product:	7.32%
Increase in personal income:	4.4 %
Increase in income tax:	18.2 %
Production of everything:	6.4 %

Reports about these irregularities will be highly appreciated, giving a valuable contribution to the processing of the results of the testrun.

The CSCMOETM-TIMER® is based on the principle that a defective watch, which is not in operation, displays correct time ($\pm$ 0 sec.) (Universal as well as Local) twice a day. Although this means a tremendous improvement over a working watch, which never shows exactly correct time, we admit that the time resolution of the defective watch (12 hours = 43200 sec.) is inadequate for some applications. The time resolution for exact timing may be improved by rotating the hands of the watch anti-clockwise and, hence, increase the number of correct time interceptions.

2.2 Technical description.

The first prototype of the CSCMOETM-TIMER® (Mk 1) is presented in Figure 1. The rotation is produced by a handcrank. During our testrun, the time resolution was as good as 100 msec. at 0900 LMT, increasing to 670 msec. after local noon.

Faster engines have been utilized on the more recent models (Mk 2 and 3), and we anticipate that the time resolution may be improved to some 600 ± 13 nanoseconds within the end of this century (see Figure 2). This is, of course, a significant step forward relative to the existing crude time-monitors like the cesium standard, by which the exact time can never be obtained, and which is too complicated and too expensive for most domestic purposes.

2.3 Future development.

If small, inexpensive, fast engines and high precision gears become available within the next few years, we expect to present the prototype of the Volks model of the CSCMOETM-TIMER® (called the VS-T®) to the scientific community by 1980, whereas the production model for electronic laboratories will be ready early 1983. A smaller *cscmoetm-timer®* for sports use will be offered by 1992, depending on the future production of small engines.

Note added during proof reading: We appreciate the comments by one of the referees, who drew our attention to the fact that a stroboscopic light source slaved to the timer is needed for recording the exact time. This unit is now being developed at our laboratory, and it will probably never be completed.

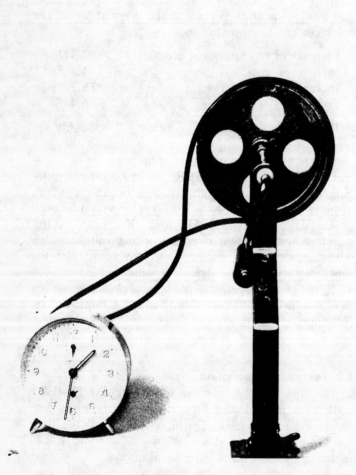

FIGURE 1
CSCMOETM-TIMER® (Mk 1). Note the twisted driving belt
(Patent pend.)

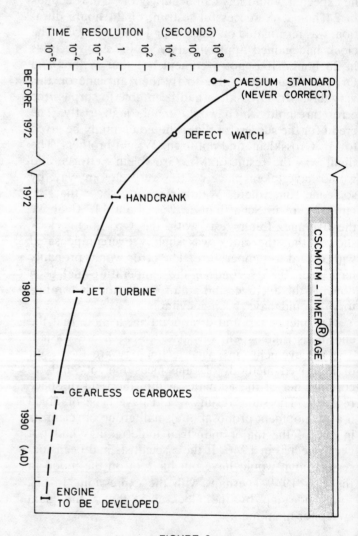

FIGURE 2
Prognosis of improved accuracy in time measurements.

New linear accelerator to take wing?

COLONEL SANDERS
Montana State University
Bozeman, Montana

At a time when physics is faced with funding crises everywhere, it is reassuring to find that some research projects can still be run on mere chicken feed. In this regard, we call attention to the recent announcement, by the National Research Council of Canada, of the successful operation of a new linear chicken accelerator, or LCA (see *Chemical and Engineering News*, 2 November 1970, page 56). The LCA, which is capable of accelerating a four-pound chicken to speeds of 620 mph, is currently being used as a flight-impact simulator in an engineering study of airplane-bird collisions. But we believe it may have application as a basic research instrument, since — in more familiar terms — it has a rated energy of 5×10^{14} GeV, which makes the LCA the most powerful accelerator of its kind in the world today.

A careful study of high-energy chicken-chicken collisions, with due attention paid to the production of virtual chickens (i.e., eggs), could lead to a resolution of an age-old question of causality, namely, which came first, the chicken or the egg? At somewhat higher energies, one could look for the production of the intermediate vector chicken, or hawk, and in general study the problem of rooster-hen coupling. At yet higher energies, the scattering would of course be discussed in terms of the Pomeran-chicken trajectory. Crossing symmetry would be important here, and one could hope to discover why, or even whether, the chicken crosses the road. By simply replacing the chickens with ducks, one could undoubtedly establish a threshold for the production of quacks.

Although group-theoretical cacklations based on the eightfowled way can be expected to establish a pecking order, a really comprehensive theory would be based on an apprropriate egghenvalue equation. Quantization would then naturally proceed by introducing the "capon," with appropriate truncation. It should be noted that capon-chicken coupling may be assumed to be very weak to all orders. A clue as to the correct form of the egghenvalue equation might be provided by noticing that Coop(er) pairing is obviously described by interactions such as $*R$, where R is the propagator, or rooster function. Owing to a lack of bilateral symmetry, it seems clear that operations such as $R \cdot$ probably do not occur naturally, if at all. These theoretical difficulties obviously leave us with nothing to crow about.

Yet much can be done. The LCA should be used to measure breast masses and farm factors. A determination of Rooster's angle would probably help to establish the correct egghenvalue equation. Coherent production of chicken-anti-chicken pairs could be investigated by analogy with the well known dove-hawk interaction, which quickly produces a state of incoherence and annihilates to a large number of put-ons. In this regard, we might ask whether the beautiful picture of an elementary particle that appeared on the cover of the 27 November 1970 issue of *Science* is really a put-on or a capon? We suggest that a Feather's analysis be carried out immediately. Who knows: there may be a Pulletzer prize in all this. We have only scratched the surface!

From *Physics Today*, 1971.

THE PARADOXICAL NATURE OF REALITY

GEORGE MELHUISH

In order to define reality adequately, we must turn away from dogmatic ideas to a discipline wherein the representation of the finite world as a selectivity implies actuality, only in consequence of the representation of the infinite world as a non-selectivity.

If that's the case let's define obscurantism.

From *New Scientist*, 2 May 1974.

A photomicrograph of a "question mark" photographed in the electron microscope and enlarged here to 38,000x. The subject is in fact a platinum-carbon replica of a polishing scratch in the epoxy resin embedding some grains of moon rock from Apollo 12 (sample number 12057). When studying these replicas this clearly fortuitous and irreproducible punctuation mark was quite appropriate as I was pondering the structures in the mineral grains themselves.

Kenneth M. Towe, Geologist
Nat. Museum of Natural History.

NATIONAL GEOGRAPHIC, THE DOOMSDAY MACHINE

Pollution of many types and kinds is currently paramount in the public mind. Causes and solutions are being loudly proclaimed by all of the media, politicians, public agencies, universities, garden clubs, industry, churches, ad infinitum. Pollution runs the spectrum from the air we breath, the water we drink, the soil we till, as well as visual and audio pollution, and in recent years, pollution of outer space from junk exploration hardware. These threats to our environment, our health and our mental well being are real and with us, but not nearly as immediately catastrophic or totally destructive as the disaster which imminently faces this nation and which has gone unheeded, unheralded and ignored for over 141 years. The insidious consequences lurking in this menace of monstrous proportion bode national, even, continental disaster of proportions likened only to the entire country resting on a gargantuan San Andreas fault. Earth-

quakes, hurricanes, mud slides, fire, famine, and atomic war all rolled into one hold no greater destructive power than this incipient horror which will engulf the country in the immediate and predictable future.

This continent is in the gravest danger of following legendary Atlantis to the bottom of the sea. No natural disaster, no overpowering compounding of pollutions or cataclysmic nuclear war will cause the end, instead, a seemingly innocent monster created by man, nurtured by man, however as yet unheeded by man will doom this continent to the watery grave of oblivion.

But there is yet time to save ourselves if this warning is heeded.

PUBLICATION AND DISTRIBUTION OF THE NATIONAL GEOGRAPHIC MAGAZINE MUST BE IMMEDIATELY STOPPED AT ALL COSTS! This beautiful, educational, erudite, and thoroughly appreciated publication is the here-to-fore unrecognized instrument of cosmic doom which must be erased if we as a country or continent will survive. It is NOT TOO LATE if this warning is heeded!

According to current subscription figures, more than 6,869,797 issues of The National Geographic Magazine are sent to subscribers monthly throughout the world. However, it would be safe to say that the bulk of these magazines reach subscribers in the United States and Canada, and it is and never has been thrown away! It is saved like a monthly edition of the Bible. The magazine has been published for over 141 years continuously and countless millions if not billions of copies have been innocently yet relentlessly accumulating in basements, attics, garages, in public and private institutions of learning, the Library of Congress, Smithsonian Institute, Good Will, and Salvation Army Stores and heaven knows where else. Never discarded, always saved. No recycling, just the horrible and relentless accumulation of this static vehicle of our doom! National Geographic averages approximately two pounds per issue. Since no copies have been discarded or destroyed since the beginning of publication it can be readily seen that the accumulated aggregate weight is a figure that not only boggles the mind but is imminently approaching the disaster point. That point will be the time at which the geologic substructure of the country can no longer support the incredible load and subsidence will occur. Gradually at first, but then relentlessly accelerating as rock formations are compressed, become plastic and begin to flow; great faults will appear. The logical sequence of events is predictable. First will come foundation failures and gradual sinking of residences and public buildings in which the magazine has been stored. As these areas depress the earth, more and more structures will topple and sink until whole towns and cities will submerge, then larger and larger land masses. This chain reaction will accelerate until the entire country has fallen below the level of the sea and total innudation will occur.

The areas of higher subscription density, affluence and wealth will be the first to go, followed by institutions, middle class, urban and ghetto areas in that order, with the relatively unpopulated plains and mountains finally sinking into the sea.

We have been warned of this impending calamity by a seeming increase in so-called natural disasters throughout the country as well as isolated occurrences striking areas heretofore immune to natural destruction.

Increase in Earthquake activity in California has been triggered by population growth and the subsequent increase in National Geographic subscriptions and accumulations of heavy masses of the magazine. This gradual increase in weight has caused increased activity along the San Andreas fault.

Earthquakes in the Denver area were not caused by pumping of wastes into wells at the Rocky Mountain arsenal, but by accumulation of National Geographic magazines by more and more people as the population increased over the years.

Sinking of several coal mining towns throughout the country can only be attributed to the increase in workmen's benefits and pay increases allowing them to subscribe to and hoard National Geographic.

Mud slides in California which have brought destruction to hundreds of homes built on the hillsides were triggered by the final straw in the form of the last mail delivery into these areas of National Geographic subscribers and hoarders.

The list is endless, the warnings are clear.

The time grows short and we must act at once if this calamity is to be averted. The National Geographic must cease publication at once, if necessary, by Congressional action or Presidential edict.

From the National Aeronautics and Space Administration (NASA) letter on procurement policy.

PAGE 2 NASAHQ 285 UNCLAS

"THE PURPOSE OF THIS MESSAGE IS TO PROVIDE CLARIFICATION, ON AN INTERIM BASIS, TO BE FOLLOWED UNTIL SUCH TIME AS PRD 70 - 15 IS FORMALLY REVISED, NOTE THAT THIS INTERIM GUIDANCE ON THE CONDUCT OF DISCUSSIONS IS NOT REPEAT NOT A CHANGE IN POLICY OR CONCEPT, IT IS SOLELY CLARIFICATION, AND SHOULD BE SO CONSTRUED. WHILE THE CLARIFICATION IS PRESENTED IN THE FORM OF A PARTIAL REVISION OF PRD 70-15, THIS DOES NOT NECESSARILY MEAN THAT FORMAL REVISION WILL FOLLOW THE SAME FORMAT OR COMPOSITION; BUT RATHER IT IS SO PRESENTED SO THAT IT MAY BE READ IN CONTEXT WITH 70-15, WHICH, OF COURSE, REMAINS EFFECTIVE. THE AFFECTED PART OF 70-15 IS PARAGRAPH III. D(2) COVERING CONDUCT OF DISCUSSIONS IN COST-REIMBURSEMENT TYPE CONTRACTS AND ALL R & D CONTRACTS."

Editor's Note: This is not, repeat, not the formal policy?

May 24, 1974

Dear Editor:

It was with mixed feelings that I pondered George H. Kaub's "National Geographic, the Doomsday Machine," J. Irr. R., March 1974, P. 22, since similar thoughts had passed through my mind on occasion. Especially hitting close to home was the discovery in a previous home that my Living Room putting practice was quite sour due to tilt of the house because of unsymmetrical attic storage (hoarding, if you insist, Mr. Kaub) of my copies of Life Magazine over a mere 35 years; the earth below, as well as my spirits, was definitely suffering depression. However, it would have been unseemly of my scientific mind to extrapolate so local an incident to a global catastrophy after once having formerly been caught in an error of judgment on a much grander scale, namely the State of Texas.

A compatriot in my army outfit it was, who put me in my place. He was a short-statured Texan, who, I had earlier thought, was also short in cranial content. But, like so many Texans who engage in hyperbole in all matters dealing with that state, this one bragged about the fact that Texas rests on a sea of oil, whose enormous monetary value supports all the affluence attending not only the medical profession, but even the lowliest gandy-dancer in that state. I retorted with exaggerated smugness that his privileges were to be short-lived because, as that wealth of oil was withdrawn from beneath his great state of Texas, his great state is going to sink out of sight and mind. But imagine my chagrin for having overlooked the well-documented answer, when, some days later, he accosted me with that victorious air and declared, "Your prediction is impossible. I looked it up and found that the oil is pushed out of the ground by brine which is pumped into the ground. Therefore, no void is created and Texas won't sink."

Thus, I must raise the point that George Kaub is alarming us unduly, despite the apparent legitimacy of his thesis. There must be a compensating factor which is not obvious at the moment.

Yours Truly,
Joseph G. Koosman
54 Brookside Terrace
North Caldwell, N.J. 07006

NATIONAL GEOGRAPHIC: Doomsday Machine or Benefactor? A Vindication

L. M. JONES

Department of Geology
University of Georgia
Athens, Georgia 30602

Response to "National Geographic, The Doomsday Machine," J.I.R., Vol. 20, No. 3, p. 22.

An attack on the National Geographic Magazine is an attack on a venerated American tradition, one as American as apple pie, Watergate, Pogo, and pizza.

The cry for the immediate termination of publication and distribution of the National Geographic Magazine cannot go without challenge. Kaub (1974) has not only created an aura of hysteria for the future of the earth, but he has also imparted an unnecessary sense of guilt on anyone who inasmuch reads an issue of National Geographic, let alone anyone who would sequester an issue in an attic or garage.

Kaub (1974) contends there will be disasters of continental proportions due to the indestructiveness of the National Geographic Magazine. He suggests that localized accumulations of the National Geographic are responsible for earthquake activity in areas such as the San Andreas fault and Denver. He also would attribute directly to the Magazine other natural disasters such as mud slides and subsidence. Kaub (1974) further knells the doomsday bell, by predicting that continued storage of the magazine will result in massive subsidence of buildings, cities, and finally, inundation of the entire country by the sea.

Nonsense.

It is such erroneous expoundings as Kaub's that have created undue panic among the populace on other occasions. For example, movement along the San Andreas fault has been interpreted to mean that California will soon fall into the sea!

And now the National Geographic! Is nothing sacred?

Let's examine this problem calmly and logically. First, ten issues of the National Geographic Magazine were selected from the collections of the author and a colleague. These issues were weighed and measured; these data are given in Table 1, in addition to calculated values of area and density for the Magazine.

To simplify the following calculations, it was assumed that erosion of the landmass was negligible, as well as other geologic factors. The only geologic process that would be operative is isostasy, which is the approach of crustal masses to a flotational equilibrium. Other assumptions that were made include the following:

1. the density of the upper mantle is 3.3 g-cm^{-3}, which represents a lower limit;
2. the monthly circulation of the National Geographic is that as given by Kaub (1974), 6,869,797, and remains constant;
3. distribution of the Magazine is restricted to the conterminous 48 United States (with no offense intended to Hawaii, Alaska, or any country; Hawaii and Alaska were excluded on the basis of relatively small area and small population, respectively);
4. the Magazine is evenly distributed over the 48 United States;
5. the area of the 48 states is 7,954 x 10^3 km^2 (Showers, 1973);
6. area of the oceans is 362,033 x 10^3 km (Showers, 1973);
7. no issues of the National Geographic Magazine will be destroyed;
8. the average thickness of the ten issues in Table 1 is representative (0.719 cm).

Taking the predictions of Kaub (1974) at face value, the height of a column of National Geographic Magazines necessary to depress the continental land mass by 100 feet (30.48 m.) was calculated. This would be a vertical stack 82.33 meters high, equivalent to 11.45 x 10^3 magazines. This depression of the land mass would produce a rise in sealevel due to displaced mantle material. Assuming the effect is confined only to the ocean basins, a net depression of

100 feet (30.48 m) would be due to an actual depression of the land of 29.82 meters and a resultant rise in sealevel of 66 cm.

There would be a notable change in the coastline with a net depression of 100 feet. These changes are shown in Figure 1. While there will be little change in the outline of the west coast due to the steep slope, that of the east coast will change markedly. It is readily seen that many urban problems will be solved by inundation, saving vast amounts of urban renewal funds. The Atlantis legend will be recalled with the flooding of cities such as Boston, New York, Washington, D.C., Baltimore, Savannah, Miami, Houston, and New Orleans. Of course, unexpected benefits would be realized by other communities. For example, Yazoo, Mississippi would become a major seaport; certainly a possibility that had not been dreamed of by town officials, even in their wildest imagination.

No matter how beneficial the results of this crustal depressing might be, there is the question of time. Assuming even distribution of the National Geographic over the present surface, it would take 17.94×10^{13} copies of the Magazine to cover the 48 United States with one thickness. If the National Geographic Society continues to publish the Magazine at 12 issues each year, it will take 2.176×10^6 years to deposit one thickness over the United States. The time it would take to accumulate a thickness of the National Geographic sufficient to depress the crust 100 feet would take 24.92×10^9 years. Since this length of time is several times greater than the present age of the earth, it should be obvious that we or future generations have little to fear from the National Geographic Society.

If Mr. Kaub is still distressed about the weighty threat by the National Geographic Society, perhaps he should consider taking up lighter reading.

TABLE 1. DIMENSIONS, WEIGHT, AND DENSITY OF TEN SELECTED ISSUES OF THE NATIONAL GEOGRAPHIC MAGAZINE.

	Thickness, mm	Weight, g	Width cm	Length cm	Area cm^2	Density, g-cm^{-3}
June 59	7.73	402.15	17.33	25.34	439.1	1.185
August 61	7.02	370.28	17.49	25.39	444.1	1.188
May 62	7.70	408.72	17.51	25.35	443.9	1.196
October 62	7.27	388.50	17.48	25.44	444.7	1.202
May 63	7.58	396.15	17.43	25.32	441.3	1.184
April 66	7.985	422.60	17.55	25.35	444.9	1.190
July 71	6.52	342.72	17.36	25.31	439.4	1.196
November 71-I	6.95	371.49	17.54	25.48	446.9	1.196
November 71-II	7.05	373.71	17.51	25.50	446.5	1.187
January 73	6.05	324.75	17.49	25.38	443.9	1.209
ave.	7.19				443.5	1.193

REFERENCES

Kaub, G. H., 1974, National Geographic, the Doomsday Machine: Jour. Irreprod. Results, v. 20, no. 3, p. 22-23.

Showers, V., 1973, The World in Figures: John Wiley and Sons, New York, 585 p.

FIGURE 1.

The eastern coastline of the conterminous United States. The present-day coastline is indicated by the dashed line. The heavy, solid line represents the coastline following depression of the continental landmass 100 feet (30.48 m.) upon extensive accumulation of the National Geographic Magazine.

NATIONAL GEOGRAPHIC: DOOMSDAY MACHINE REVISITED

VICTOR MILSTEIN, Ge. 01
Academy of Appurtenant Analyses

Kaub's excellent article (JIR, 1974, 20:22–23) was the first organized warning of imminent disaster. Unfortunately Jones' recent response to this is quite erroneous and dilutes the efficacy of the alert. The same issue of the Journal (JIR, 1974, 20, No. 4) contains a letter by Koosman (page 31) which reports a directly validating experience of Kaub's hypothesis but then goes on to deny the generalizability of it.

Allow me to dispose of Koosman's ready acceptance of this Texan's explanation first. Texas will sink (sic) and is in fact sinking (sic) at present. The reason for this has nothing to do with the accumulation of the magazine Kaub described as beautiful, educational and erudite, since these qualities usually are not considered in relation to oil in Texas. While it is true that the oil that is being pumped out of the ground is replaced by the brine pushing it out, this will not save Texas. Everyone knows that oil floats on water; even salt water. (Remember the oil-soaked gulls and other birds after the oil-spills in the Gulf of Mexico and along the Atlantic and Pacific Coasts?) This means that the light oil that Texas is floating on is being replaced by brine. This heavier brine will compress the material under it and sink deeper into the earth. *Quod erat demonstrandum,* Texas will continue to sink (sic).

To return to Jones' whitewash of the impending catastrophe. He makes eight assumptions in arriving at his conclusion that it will require 24.92×10^9 years to depress the crust of the United States 100 feet. Of these eight assumptions, two are completely incorrect and three are irrelevant (numbers 1, 3 and 6). The two crucial, incorrect assumptions are numbers 2 and 4. Number 2 assumes that the monthly circulation of National Geographic will remain constant. Since the population of the United States and especially the population of children in the U.S.A. is increasing, it is clear that the monthly circulation of National Geographic will also increase since the magazine is subscribed to mainly for school children. (The initial subscription is taken out with the intent of allowing the child to cut-up the magazine. However, the beauty of each issue is such that parents never permit such sacrilege.) Thus, since the population of the United States is increasing, the monthly circulation of the Magazine will also increase. This will be a lower bound estimate since both standard of living and degree of pretentiousness have been increasing at a more rapid rate than the population of the United States. This pretentiousness is an important motivating factor in subscribing to National Geographic.

The other critical assumption, namely number 4, is that the magazine is evenly distributed over the 48 states is false. In truth, the 23 states comprising the Eastern one-fourth of the country in land area (in fact 23.8%) comprises more than half (56.4%) the population. Thus, it is clear that more than 50% of the density of the increasing numbers of the magazine is accumulating in less than one-fourth of the land mass.

These figures necessitate a recomputation of the ultimate effect of accumulation of National Geographic Magazines. The most likely result, taking account of the increasing population density of the West Coast as well, is that subsidence will occur at both the East and West Coastal ends of the United States. The probability is that both coasts will sink, and the West Central portion of the United States (with the exception of Texas, as noted above) will be raised up an average of 217 meters. And, Jones to the contrary, this will take place in much less 24.92×10^9 years. It will occur in 457.247×3^7 years! Clearly Kaub's warning must be heeded if we are to avoid disaster.

PROPERTIES OF THE BOLONIUM ION*

CARL TRINDLE

Department of Chemistry,
Yale University, New Haven, Conn.

Abstract: A review of the current knowledge of the classical and nonclassical bolonium ions is presented, with some reluctance. Definite conclusions are avoided.

The bolonium ion has played a major, if largely unappreciated, part in chemical and physical theories for many years. For example, many of the theories of chemical combination promulgated in the period 1840-1920 can be seen in retrospect to be rooted in the properties of the classical bolonium ion. More modern theories of the chemical bond, derived primarily from inaccurate solutions of a crude approximation to the Schroedinger equation, are firmly based on the quantum mechanical view of the bolonium ion. For these reasons, extensive study of the bolonium ion is essential.

The exact structure of the bolonium ion is not known precisely. This is due in part to its great reactivity; few preparations of organic compounds are free from traces of the ion. Furthermore, although most compounds of the bolonium ion B^+ with any substance S are remarkably stable, and have an incredibly long shelf life if kept away from the light, these compounds decompose upon analysis, sometimes explosively. Generally only the original substance is recovered, usually quite battered and blackened. The process may be summarised:

$$BS^+ \xrightarrow{\text{hz}} B^+ \uparrow + S + \triangle \text{ (heat)}$$

Physical-chemical studies of the bolonium ion have produced a great mass of highly irreproducible data. Briefly, the molar volume of the bolonium ion is strongly dependent on the external pressure. Active research at the Haight Institute of Gray Physics has established that it behaves like, man, a real gas. Conductivity studies indicate that the ion is usually highly charged, either positively or negatively, depending on your attitude. It is often found associated with radicals, although no political group has taken out a patent.

Recently semiempirical quantum mechanical calculations on the bolonium ion have been performed at this laboratory, with a complete lack of success. Nevertheless, the following conclusions can be made, since they were accepted before our calculations were done:

1. the stability of the bolonium ion and its compounds is enhanced by resonance, and other oratorical tactics.
2. hyperconjugation is not present in the stable bolonium ion; on the other hand, traces of bolonium are deemed essential for conjugal stability. (It apparently acts as an inhibitor.)

No discussion of the bolonium would be complete without a word about the medical uses of the ion. Many researchers have prescribed ordinary aqueous solutions of bolonium ion (usually its extortionate salt) with great success, at least financially. Numerous instruments producing little other than flashing lights and bolonium ion have been used to treat any ailment you might name. Unfortunately, the fact that the bolonium ion is quite unstable under analysis (who isn't, after all?) has rendered evaluation of its therapeutic value difficult.

I hope this brief review will interest more researchers in the opportunities in bolonium ion research. Its industrial application promises to be enormous, and the government already has an active program in operation. It has been said with great truth that the bolonium ion is the philosopher's stone of the twentieth century.

I acknowledge the help of John Morris, and the example of Baron Munchausen.

---

* This study was performed without the knowledge of the National Science Foundation.

The Biopump Solution

THOMAS A. EASTON, Ph.D.
Director
Center for Independent Research

The force of peristalsis is used by all the higher members of the animal kingdom for the movement of liquids, slurries, and small solid fragments, but this force has hitherto been tapped commercially only in the design and use of small peristaltic pumps for biomedical applications. These mechanical pumps, however, suffer from the two drawbacks that they (1) handle only small quantities (a maximum of less than three liters per minute),[1] and (2) require a continuous energy supply apart from that required to maintain their operators.

Each of these drawbacks may now be defeated with a new device,[2] henceforth called the Biopump, which can achieve flow rates of well over three liters per minute[3] and which requires no external energy input. The latter benefit is of particular significance during these days of an energy shortage and means that use of the Biopump will not be affected by brownouts, blackouts, or strikes. It also means that use of the Biopump will not adversely affect the ecology of any region in which it is used.

The Biopump consists of a flexible, thin plastic tube, one end of which is equipped with an input hose fitting and one end of which expands into a bulbous reservoir with a second hose fitting placed to one side. The latter fitting couples the reservoir to a tube of a heavier gauge plastic tube which ends in an output hose fitting. Each of the components is made of biologically inert materials.

To prepare the Biopump for use, the thin plastic tube is threaded through the human esophagus and the input fitting is mounted through the cheek in such a way that an input hose may be coupled to it. The reservoir is placed in the stomach with its hose fitting traversing the stomach wall in such a way and position that the second, more rigid hose may connect the reservoir to the last hose fitting at the navel, where an output hose may be attached. Once in place, as shown in Figure 1, the Biopump forms a continuous path from cheek to navel by which the operator can propel, by swallowing and the consequent esophageal peristalsis and stomach churnings, liquids, slurries, and small solids from one vessel or level to another. Several Biopumps arranged in parallel can transport virtually any quantity of material. Arranged in series, they can transport material over virtually any distance. And, if their operators stand on their heads, they can even be used to transport materials up hill, for peristalsis is independent of gravity.

There are no constraints on the materials that the Biopump can transport other than those of consistency, for the Biopump effectively isolates its operator from toxic or corrosive substances. The only influence that crosses the plastic barrier of the Biopump is that of the muscles of the operator's alimentary system.

Because the Biopump is made of a thin, flexible plastic, when not in use the esophageal tube and the reservoir will collapse into a thin layer against the walls of the esophagus and stomach. It will thus not interfere in any way with its operator's ingestion of food and drink, although its operator must, as a simple safety precaution, refrain from all those foods, such as popcorn, nuts, and boney fish, which might tear, puncture, or otherwise impair the integrity of the Biopump. The operator should also, of course, have those teeth nearest the Biopump's input removed.

The applications of this device should be immediately obvious. Eminently portable, it will allow motorists, at a moment's notice, to siphon gasoline into their automobiles. Inexpensive to produce and virtually maintenance-free, it will give graduate students new assistantship opportunities as their professors seek new ways to eliminate their dependence on outside energy supplies and equipment suppliers for moving their solutions about. It will give industry new ways to employ persons of little education or skill. And it will allow ecologically disruptive pipelines to be replaced by lines of thousands of government bureaucrats and oil company executives, each one equipped with a Biopump.

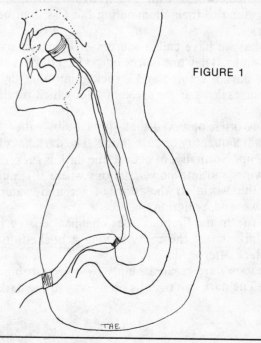

FIGURE 1

---

1 See, for example, the pumps produced by Harvard Apparatus.
2 It has not yet been built, but anyone who wishes to try may feel free to do so, and patent it as well, if he wishes, as long as he makes the proper acknowledgments.
3 Estimate based on the observation that I can swallow 200 milliliters in 4 seconds.

THE AGE OF ENLIGHTENMENT ENDS

KIRK R. SMITH
Environmental Health Science
Warren Ha
University of Californi
Berkeley, 9472

There is no such thing as light. What there is in the universe is dark.[1] It is obvious from simple observations that this is so.

What we call light is merely the absence of dark. Dark is continually created. As fast as it is whisked away, more fills up the space.

We can easily establish these facts long hidden by the tenaciousness with which light-headed scientists have clung to their illuminating but less than brilliant theories.[2]

What we have called sources of light are in reality dark-sinks. They are places into which dark is sucked. More dark is created and is sucked into the "light". It, of course, flows at the speed of dark which is relatively fast.

It is often observed that "light bulbs" after failure contain a quantity of dark inside. The dark has clogged them up. Normally, of course, the dark is sucked down the wires and into power stations where it is put back into the world in the form of air and water dark (smoke and pollution).

A fire in the fireplace uses chemical energy to pull the dark out of the room leaving a bucketfull in the fireplace afterwards.

Shadows are created simply by objects being in the way. The dark can't get by on its way to the dark-sink.

I suspect that a physicist, being conservative by na ture as well as by law, will not accept this radical nev theory without flaring up.

"What about 'light pressure'?" he will grumbl darkly.

Simple: When dark is sucked away, new dark i created to take its place. This new dark is created a in pair-production. The new piece of dark (darkton travels backwards with equal velocity and momentun as the darkton being pulled away. When it strikes a object it exerts a pressure. (See Figure I) Since be hind the object being pushed there is no new darl being created, there is no push from behind. The push is all on one side and results in an effective pressur away from the dark-sink.

The photoelectric effect? Merely the darkton hittin an electron on its way to the sink or after being newl created.

Colors? Different shaped darktons. See Figure II fo most probable shapes. We are able to see differen colors because of these shapes. For example when th newly pair-production created darkton is yellow i shape it fits into the enzymes in our eyes as in Figur III. As we have seen in molecular biology texts en zymes come in the appropriate designs to detect al possible color-shapes.[3]

This is by no means a revelation to be treated lightly. Our view of the world will be markedly changed. "As the sunrise empties the valleys of dark" will become precise scientific description instead of poetic vision. Basic philosophy will have to be transformed.[4] "Let there be dark-suck"? But first there had to be the dark. Perhaps we should alter the old adage and, applying ourselves directly to the source, we should, indeed, curse the darkness.

---

[1] R. R. Lyrae, "Speaking in Variables" Journal of Microwave Astrology 11:45 1963

[2] The first clues leading to this line of reasoning developed from meterological research done at the botanical gardens. Following the method of multiple-hypotheses in pursuing the possible connections between trees and wind, it was found that, in fact, the wind is caused by the fan-like action of forests. In no case was there observed wind without the trees waving.
S. Maizlish, "Observing the Forest in Spite of the Breeze" Ohio Journal of Forensic Forestry 12:31 1945
[3] "Photo" synthesis is just the reverse.
[4] D. Koch, "The Real Thing" Turn-on Delight Monthly 7:25 1955

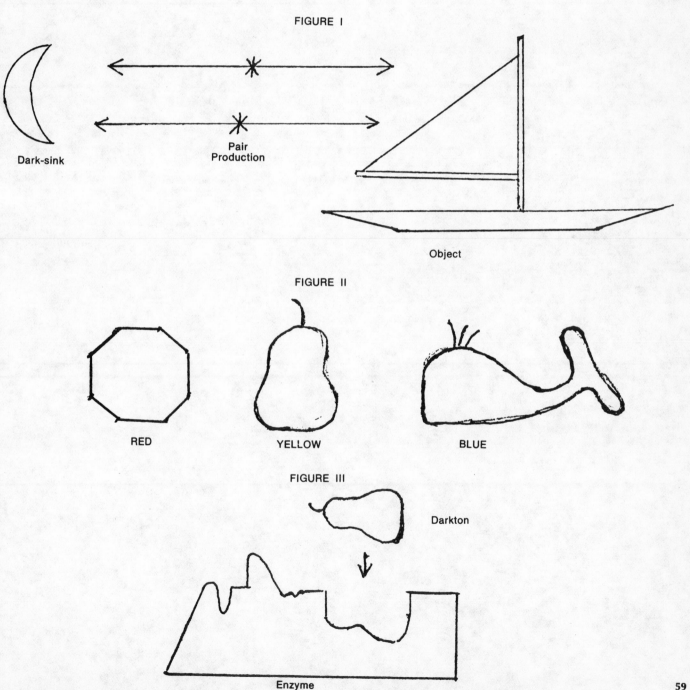

FIGURE I

Dark-sink

Pair Production

Object

FIGURE II

RED   YELLOW   BLUE

FIGURE III

Darkton

Enzyme

Irreproducible

great

thoughts

concerning

RELIGION

AND THE

COSMOS

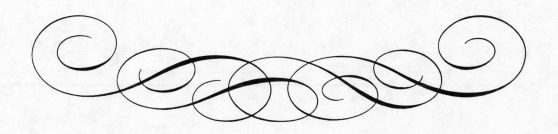

The Creation Clarified

or
a Simple and Straightforward
Treatise to Explain the Hither to Complex
Study of the Creation of the Universe

It seems that we have to deride
Our experts who often have tried
To explain in terms terse
Our complex universe —
They have tried, but no facts could provide.

By focusing brains that are trained
The secrets of life are unchained;
All the puzzles dissolve
How the world did evolve —
The complexities now are explained.

ALBIN CHAPLIN
15362 Grandville
Detroit, Michigan 48223

The creation of the universe has been under perpetual discussion since man first learned to speak, and out of a multitude of ideas three major ones have come to the forefront, but up to the present time no one has been able to satisfactorily substantiate any one theory and dismiss all the others. This treatise is therefore presented to clarify this discrepancy, once and for all.

The three possible theories of the creation of the universe are well-known to all and are as follows: Firstly, that the universe is stable; secondly, that the universe has a beginning, and by implication, an ending; thirdly, that the universe is pulsating and is without beginning or ending. Any other theories are so highly conjectural as to have no place in a discussion of this type.

Let us consider the first proposal, that of the stable universe.

A stable universe means a changeless universe. This is a universe that has always been here and always will be here. In this kind of universe nothing can be created or destroyed. This suits the first law of thermodynamics, but in a changeless universe there can be no progress and no evolution. There can be no Garden of Eden, no Adam and Eve, it cannot progress and it cannot run down, and this is where it contradicts the second law of thermodynamics.

Since simple observation points to the fact that the sun is running down, novae are bursting out here and there, gal-

axies are receding, then we may conclude that we are most certainly not a part of a stable universe.

If we were to plot the amount of matter in a stable universe at any given time, we would obtain the graph as shown in Figure 1.

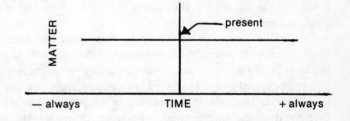

FIGURE 1

From Figure 1 it can be readily observed that there are no changes for better or for worse, and likewise there is nothing going on. This obviously is not the case, for in our universe, and especially in our planet, there is always something going on.

We can conclude that we are not living in a stable universe.

The second theory is not by any means as simple as the first theory. This theory supposes that the universe has had a beginning and therefore must also have an ending.

In this type of universe, a beginning implies that before the beginning there was nothing, absolutely and categorically nothing — just a vast emptiness of space. This is very difficult to imagine; as a matter of fact it is impossible to conceive of such a state of things, or as one may more aptly put it, such a state of nothings.

From this nothing we are suddenly plunged into a vast universe, all in an instant, with a big bang, so to speak, and this is often called the Big Bang Theory.

If we can for the moment conceive of this universe starting instantaneously with a big bang, and we plot matter against time, we will have a graph of the creation of the universe as shown in Figure 2.

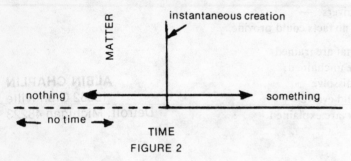

FIGURE 2

At some given time, although we cannot conceive that time exists and matter does not, a dot will appear on the graph representing x atoms of matter created in zero units of time. At the same time, or moment, if you please, time will begin, and it will flow inexorably forward in one direction, since it is unidirectional, and it will continue to flow unto the end of time, and not one moment beyond.

This is the beginning of the universe; a clock has been created and at the same moment, or time if you wish, it has begun to beat time to measure the life of this newly created universe, created in a condition of low entropy, from which it wiii relentlessly run down according to the second law of thermodynamics, like a child, who upon emerging from some mystical and formless womb, is undeniably faced with the prospect of death.

However, long before the entropy has increased to its maximum, the universe is doomed to disappear in, can we say, a blinding flash? But no, for a flash implies the conversion of matter into light and heat which is just another form of energy. Therefore the universe will disappear into an unblinding nothing, suddenly, and incapable of being observed. The eye, no matter how it strains, will not be able to see anything, for there will be no eye to see. All the light waves which stretch for septillions of miles into space in all directions will suddenly be overcome, and these light waves will be overtaken instantaneously and converted into nothing, and this of course is entirely possible, for nothing travels faster than light.

The graph of the annihilation of the universe would appear as in Figure 3.

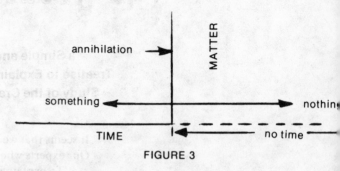

FIGURE 3

To show clearly the graph for the existence of the universe we can combine the graphs from Figures 2 and 3, enlarge the dot representing instantaneous creation, split it in two for clarity, and we have the result as in Figure 4.

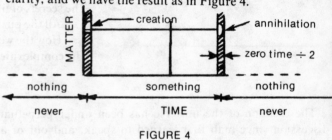

FIGURE 4

Note that the vertical lines which pass through the semi-dots, although in reality having no width, have been widened to conform with instantaneous occurrence, and with instantaneous annihilation.

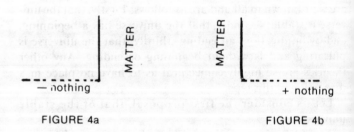

FIGURE 4a   FIGURE 4b

Figures 4a and 4b are added for further clarification. They show the graphs of matter against time to the right and to the left of the "time" portion of Figure 4. Of course there is nothing on the graphs proper since time does not exist, and nothing therefore takes the place of time in the abscissa. The plus and minus values should be self-explanatory.

Now we come to the second version of the second theory, wherein the universe was created over a period of time, in the place of instantaneously, whether that time be six days or six microseconds. A graph plotting creation of matter against time is shown in Figure 5.

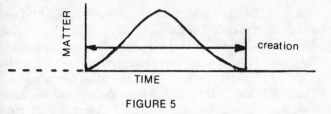

FIGURE 5

The area under the curve represents the total amount of matter in the universe. Time starts with the creation of matter and continues as long as matter exists. This is an excellent example of the Big Bang Theory where the universe is created in a finite time.

We still have to contend with the annihilation of the universe, where matter and time cease to exist. Once we have assumed that it takes time to create the universe, then ipso facto it follows that time is consumed in destroying the universe. This is the big bang in reverse and this is shown in Figure 6.

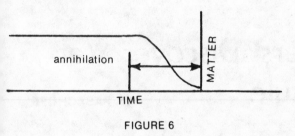

FIGURE 6

Combining Figures 5 and 6, we have the complete story of the universe according to the Big Bang Theory, version two, and this is shown in Figure 7.

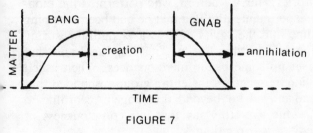

FIGURE 7

Thus we see, according to this theory, that the universe is created with a fantastic BANG, continues for a whole eon (an indefinite period) and then it disappears in the same amount of time that it took to create it, with an unheard of GNAB, or a tremendous SCHLLP, which is pronounced while sucking in wind.

Considering the two versions of the second theory, although this type of creation does lend itself to graphical analysis which can readily be comprehended by the layman, and it can simply be interpreted and plotted, yet it defies the first law of thermodynamics, which states that matter or energy can neither be created nor destroyed. Furthermore it also runs afoul of the second law of thermodynamics which states that the entropy in a closed system is increasing, whereas the sudden creation of the universe implies a sudden decrease in entropy from a condition wherein no entropy existed. This whole occurrence is a once-only phenomenon, and it is not within the ordered realm of science to draw a conclusion or formulate a law from one partially observable event. It follows here that we must look askance at the second law of thermodynamics, and I fear that this law must be subjected to further critical and unbiased examination.

These observations on the second theory, versions one and two, would lead one to conclude that the universe did not materialize with a big bang and will not dissolve with a gnab (schllp, while inhaling).

The third theory maintains that the universe always has been here and always will be here, and furthermore it is a pulsating universe, which consists of matter and energy, constantly converting one into the other, the total supply remaining constant, in deference to the first law of thermodynamics, but in dispute with the second law of thermodynamics, for this pulsating universe requires that entropy be pulsating and not be increasing, and a slight revision of the second law of thermodynamics is hereby in order.

A graph describing the pulsating universe is shown in Figure 8.

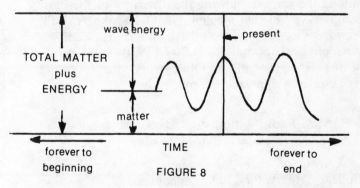

FIGURE 8

Time is always considered to flow one direction but no one has yet come up with a direction in which time flows. However, there is a simple way out of this dilemma. If Figure 8 is plotted on a sphere, time then can flow in any direction through curved space (ref. Einstein) and it will be noted that minus always on the graph will always meet plus always, and time can be considered to flow in all directions, somewhat in the same manner as light flows in all directions.

This whole theory of the pulsating universe is akin to a baseball being unraveled, while the end of the string is fed back into the core, leaving the baseball continuously the same size as it was at the beginning, if any, and as it will be at the end, if any. The pulsations, of course, would be evident if the string in the baseball were pulled out hand over hand, and this is evidently what occurs in the universe where great globs of matter are converted into energy, and this energy is gathered or forced into a core where it is reconverted into matter.

Another favorable point, and a veritable cornerstone of the pulsating universe theory, is that it answers all questions, such as, "When did the universe begin?", the answer being "Never" or "Minus always", and to the question, "When will the universe end?", the answer being "Never" or "Plus always"; keeping in mind this important factor that "Minus always" and "Plus always" are the beginning and the ending, and when plotted on a sphere representing curved space, the beginning and the ending will meet and become one and the same at some point, dependent, of course, on exactly where we start, if that is of any importance, and vice versa.

In conclusion we may state that this concept of the pulsating universe is the most plausible description of the universe, and it has been pulsating from the very beginning of time, and it will continue to pulsate unto the very end of time, barring any unforeseen catastrophe, such as World War III.

I sincerely hope that this treatise will clear up what has been in the past a very confusing situation regarding the creation of the universe.

Harvard Radio Astronomers Discover Yet Another Interstellar Molecule

JAY PASACHOFF

Astronomers have recently been discovering more and more complex molecules existing floating in space among the stars. Following the discovery of the most complex yet, methyl alcohol, CH_3OH (John A. Ball, Carl A. Gottlieb, A. E. Lilley, and H. E. Radford, Astrophysical Journal *162*, L203 (1970) by scientists at the Harvard College Observatory, the following mock release appeared anonymously:

Press Release
Harvard Radio Astronomers Discover yet another
Interstellar Molecule

A team of radio astronomers from the Harvard College Observatory today announced the detection of the most complex interstellar molecule yet — $C_3H_4NH_3OHCOOH$ — "mescaline". When asked about the significance of this stunning discovery, the astronomers responded with a general euphoria. "Far out," said Professor A. E. Lilley, leader of the group, "compared to this, the methyl alcohol was a bummer."

At a sherry party held in their honor by the Professor of Theoretical Physics (curiously, the radio astronomers were not interested in the sherry), the Director of the Observatory observed that astronomy is becoming more relevant than ever before. Reaction of local citizens at the Cambridge Common was enthusiastic.

The critical scientific breakthrough that lead to this discovery actually occurred in the radio astronomy laboratories. Harry Radford, who performed the pioneering experiment, admitted that he had been dropping mescaline into the cavity of his wavelength measuring equipment from time to time "just for fun," and that it had set up some beautiful resonances. When asked about line frequencies, the entire group responded that they had moved far beyond that stage. According to Lilley, "One can truly say that our consciousness of the medium is expanding."

This discovery bodes well for continued support of astronomy. NASA is moving with immediate plans for a new manned space flight program, encouraged by the advice of the Harvard group that rockets are no longer necessary. Applications by local youths for the new astronaut program are pouring in, despite the restriction to Sagittarius only.

There were, however, some reservations expressed. One astronomer remarked, "Excuse me, but I would prefer to reserve comment until I consult with somebody absolutely first rate," and returned to his afternoon tea.

Proof:

How Many Angels Can Dance

Upon the Head of A Pin?

JEFFREY A. BARACH

Ever since the middle ages, scholars have wondered how many angels could dance upon the head of a pin, without a satisfactory solution.* Finally, an answer to this medieval question has been found. The answer is none. The reasoning follows.

The great mistake of the medieval scholastics was to think that the size of an angel was the key variable, when it is not. Size cannot only be factored out of the equation, but it confounds the solution. Since size is a terrestial, exact, real concept without strong moral overtones, its logical type (or level and character of abstraction)** is inappropriate for use with the concept of an angel in the context of a logical proof.

An angel is a metaphorical, anthropomorphic concept with moral overtones. That is its logical type, or level and character of abstraction.

In the same logical typology, we do not even need the aid of the works of Sigmund Freud to know that "to dance upon the head of a pin" is blatantly salacious.

Given the sexually repressive character of early Christianity,* no angel — either male or female — could dance upon the *head* of a *pin*. Q.E.D.

What is particularly fascinating is that the ancient scholars did not pose the problem upon another miniscule object, but rather chose the head of a pin and asked the angels to enjoy the pleasure of dancing upon it.

One reason for the fascination of this exact formulation of the problem and for the delayed discovery of the solution until the 20th century may be that the highly devout scholars of the Middle Ages could not answer it because of the "double bind"** placed upon them by the sexual connotation. If they had thought of the solution — perish the evil thought — they might have repressed it. Had they not repressed it, it would have approached heresy to articulate it, and implied the carnal sin of all who posed or pondered the question itself, including the one who claimed to have solved it.

Thus, the riddle remained, wrapped in the enigma of mismatched logical types, confounded by an extraneous variable (*Clupea harengus rubens*), and sealed in silence, binding by its nature anyone from leading his mind towards its solution and sealing his lips should he stumble upon it.

Only with the advent of a secular and sexually freer academic community could the bind be lifted, and by then, the matter was of insufficient interest to warrant the serious attention necessary to solve it.

Vide William Duranti (Durandus), 1237-1296, *Rationale diuinorum officiorum*. Mainz: Fust and Schoeffer, 1st ed., 1459.

**Vide* Gregory Bateson, Don Jackson, Jay Haley, and John Weakland, "Toward a Theory of Schizophrenia," *Behavioral Science*, I, #4 (October 1956), pp. 251-64.

*E.g., "Sex and marriage always involves sin, partakes of sin, since it inevitably involves bestial movements," St. Augustine; "Sex in marriage has only one positive value, it can produce virgins," St. Jerome.

**Bateson, *et al, op. cit.*

Some Preliminary Notes on FASEG*

LAWRENCE M. JANIFER
FREDERICK W. KANTOR

One of the problems involved in doing basic research on the properties of spirits is that spirits, in great majority of cases, are incoherent. This incoherency may be compared to the incoherency of light emitted from a normal light bulb. One of the most difficult technological problems to be solved, therefore, before further experiments might be performed was the problem of producing spirits which were coherent—for example, the comparatively simple area of work in which this research group has become interested: producing coherent fairy godmothers.

References in the literature, in most cases literature of a certain antiquity and standing, point out that the natural pumpkin is, in fact, a ground state of many other objects—for example, carriages. It is possible to state with some certainty that the pumpkin is converted into a carriage by the absorption of a fairy godmother, the carriage being an excited state. Presumably, the carriage decays after a certain period of time to the original state of a pumpkin, emitting one fairy godmother.

We know that the fairy godmother is absorbed, because after the carriage is created she no longer appears in the story. It appears, moreover, a reasonable presumption that the fairy godmother must be emitted on return to the ground state because of conservation laws covering the total available number of fairy godmothers, and also the fact that the fairy godmother is available for another story later.

Now, beginning with these basic principles, it was realized that, although it is possible to produce the excited state (carriage) in a statistically small number of cases by absorption of an available fairy godmother, it might also be possible to produce this excited state by modern methods of production and technological media, so that we will have an abundant supply of carriages.

Our most successful experimental model to date involves a large original supply of carriages, arranged into a latticework, very closely packed in relation to each other, and placed between two flat untenable positions.

In this particular experiment, the untenable positions utilized were Sin and Lechery. Sin, as the literature shows us, is perfectly reflective for fairy godmothers. Lechery, on the other hand, is in some cases apparently justifiable, and, for this reason, provides a finite probability of a fairy godmother tunneling through it, appearing on the other side and racing off in the form of propagating waves suitable for scattering experiments and the other basic experiments of spiritual physics.

The carriages being arranged in a laboratory, we remained as observers until, at the stroke of midnight, the first of the carriages decayed from its excited state into the ground state (pumpkin), emitting one fairy godmother. The fairy godmother oscillated rapidly back and forth between our two flat untenable positions, in one of the normal modes of the cavity, stimulating the emission of further fairy godmothers and the decay of the entire lattice of carriages into the ground state (pumpkins). As we had hoped, a known percentage of this accumulation of fairy godmothers tunneled out through our flat untenable position of Lechery, and appeared in the form of a coherent beam. For the first time in history, we have been able to produce, in a laboratory setting, a quantity of coherent fairy godmothers.

Further results are expected from our outlined series of experiments in the problem of elf consistency. (We are awaiting for this work a foundation grant-in-aid.)

---

* (Fairy Amplification of Stimulated Emission of Godmothers)

Some Refinements In FASEG[1] Theory

RAY D. LLOYD
ROGER L. AAMODT
WILLIAM W. WAGNER
Department of Spiritual Physics
Ethereal Institute
Transylvania

L. M. Janifer and F. W. Kantor[2] report their observation of the fgm decay of the carriage excited state under controlled conditions in the reaction

$$Cg^* \rightarrow Cg + fgm \qquad (1)$$

where

Cg^* = carriage (excited state)
Cg = pumpkin (ground state)
fgm = fairy godmother particle

Their article contended that a pumpkin is raised to its excited state (carriage) by the absorption of a single fgm particle and that the excited state decays to the ground state by the emission of a single fgm particle (fairyon). A careful search of the literature cited as the basis for their study reveals that in every case reported, collision of the fairyon with other particles in a definite order always precedes its absorption by the pumpkin. In the most clear-cut and accurately reported tabulation, the fairyon was observed to collide with six mice, a dog, a horse, and a collection of rags before its absorption by the pumpkin was possible. Each of these particles was also raised to an excited state as the result of the transfer of finite quantities of energy. These reactions were

$$mur + fgm_0 \rightarrow mur^* + fgm_1 \qquad (2)$$
$$can + fgm_1 \rightarrow can^* + fgm_2 \qquad (3)$$
$$equ + fgm_2 \rightarrow equ^* + fgm_3 \qquad (4)$$
$$fab + fgm_3 \rightarrow fab^* + fgm_4 \qquad (5)$$

and finally

$$Cg + fgm_4 \rightarrow Cg^* \qquad (6)$$

where

mur and mur^* are, respectively, the ground state (mouse) and excited state (horse) of the mouse particle (muron)

can and can^* are, respectively, the ground state (dog) and excited state (footman) of the dog particle (canion)

equ and equ^* are, respectively, the ground state (horse) and excited state (coachman) of the horse particle (equon)

fab and fab^* are, respectively, the ground state (rags) and excited state (gown) of the fabric particle (fabron)

fgm_0 is the fairy godmother particle (fairyon) of full energy, and $fgm_1, _2, \ldots _4$ are degraded or scattered fairyons of lower energy.

This observation has been interpreted by other workers[3] as evidence that the absorption of a fairyon by a pumpkin is a resonance phenomenon and occurs only within a narrow range of fairyon energies. It has also been reported[4] that quantum considerations demand that the degraded fairyons $fgm_1, _2 \ldots _4$ each lie at energy levels which are integral multiples of $h/2\pi$ below the unscattered particle fgm_0.

Some investigators consider the two particles mur^* and equ to be identical, but recent work[5] has shown them to be mirror images of eath other because of a difference in parity.

In most cases, the energy difference of the incident and scattered fairyon ($h\nu_0 - h\nu_1$) exactly equals the difference in energy of the ground state and excited state of the struck particle ($E_{mur}^* - E_{mur}$). Since the reaction involves two colliding particles and two diverging particles, momentum is conserved. The single exception appears to be the final absorption of the fairyon by the pumpkin. Clearly a third particle must be involved in this reaction to conserve momentum. There has been some speculation that the cinderon, or maiden particle, is requisite for this reaction to proceed, but vector analysis of the momentum shows that after the absorption of the fairyon by the pumpkin, the cinderon and carriage do not move apart as in the classical situation, but they move together, and the cinderon becomes loosely bound inside the field of the Cg^*. Moreover, the cinderon seems to be periodically emitted and reabsorbed by the carriage until the final decay process occurs. At this time, it is almost certain that the cinderon and fairyon are emitted in cascade. The order and orientation of this double decay are not known with certainty, and it is suggested that Janifer and Kantor repeat their experiment using an array of cinderon detectors *inside* their untenable position shield. Unlike the fairy godmother particle which cannot penetrate sin but has a finite probability of tunnelling through the lechery barrier, the cinderon is totally reflected by both surfaces and cannot be detected outside the shielding. A suitable detector for the maiden particle is Pc I (Km) (Kingium-activated Princium Iodide) in a pressurized, hyperthermal pure carbon (diamond) annulus.

The application of a strong magnetic field perpendicular to the axis of the untenable position shielding might enable the investigators to determine the order of the double decay as well as the spins and orientation of the emitted particles and their conditions of isotropy. This could be accomplished if separate readout devices are connected to each fgm-cinderon detector pair which has been wired in delayed coincidence.

Another variation would be to cool the entire apparatus to liquid nitrogen temperatures to see if the time between the emission of the two particles can be increased, thereby enabling the direct observation of the hitherto unknown short-lived intermediate state lying between the excited state (Cg^*) and ground state (Cg) of the pumpkin. We expect that the experiment will show the fairyon to be emitted first, since the temporary release of a virtual cinderon from the carriage for periods exceeding 10^{23} sec apparently is not associated with the triggering of the fairyon-cinderon cascade.

Suitable diffraction gratings placed outside the shielding will enable the investigators to determine the energy of the emerging fairyons. If any are observed to possess energies near the maximum (fgm_0), the question must then be put in terms of energy conservation in that somewhere, the excited states of the other particles equal in number to those originally involved must also have decayed to the ground state in reverse order for all of the energy to have been released. This observation could prove to be of tremendous importance in explaining the scattered reports of the spontaneous transformation of horses into mice, etc.

Note added in proof:

Our wives have been complaining that they frequently find upon opening their clothes closets, some of their expensive, beautiful clothes have been transmuted to rags.

[1] Fairy Amplification by Stimulated Emission of Godmothers
[2] *Analog*, VOL. LXXVI, No. 3, pp. 66-67 (Nov. 1965) and J. I. R. 15:3, pp. 65-66 (April 1967).
[3] B. Abbott and L. Costello, J. Spiritual Phys. *3:*10, p. 1931-1943 (1957)
[4] A. Onestine, *Nutritional and Metaphysical Science* 141:2, pp. 810-931 (1905).
[5] B. von Frankenstien, in *Textbook of Spiritual Chemistry* (Harper and Fathers: New Amsterdam), p. 14 (1651).

"Clearly, the most challenging aspect of the problem from the point of view of potential for improved morality is the group of patients who die too suddenly to receive medical care."
Stuart Bondurant: Circulation Supplement IV, Vol. 40 (5), page IV-2, November 1969.
Well, that's one way to ensure that they won't sin no more.

Confess: A Humanistic, Diagnostic-Prescriptive Computer Program to Decrease Person to Person Interaction Time During Confession

KENNETH MAJER
Institute for Child Study

MICHAEL C. FLANIGAN
School of Education
Indiana University

Recent Vatican interest in the effect upon laymen of the shortage of professional priests (PP) and the decreased seminary enrollment of potential priests (P'P) has led to the development of Computerized Operations (Non-retrievable) for Expediting Sinner Services (CONFESS). This program provides a viable alternative to traditional confession procedures by listing penance requirements (by sin) on a private print-out to confessees appropriate to the sin committed. This eliminates one problem which frequently occurs where the confessee, because he is under extreme duress, may forget the original penance. In addition, the program provides a probability estimate of the consequence of not completing the penance associated with a given sin; for example, number of years in purgatory. Thus, full freedom of choice is given to the participant/user (PU). The program requires no PP involvement and hence frees PPs to engage in more pressing activities. It is hoped that by providing PPs with more time for critical theological activities, P'Ps will consider the priesthood a more socially conscious and relevant profession, causing an increase of P'P enrollment in accredited seminaries.

Program Description

CONFESS is available in three natural interactive languages, COURSE WRITER III, BASIC and TUTOR and can be programmed for most other natural languages such as interactive FORTRAN. The program has been developed utilizing on-line computer terminals linked to an IBM 360 for data input, but could be modified to operate in batch mode on almost any third generation configuration given the willingness to sacrifice immediate feedback.

The computing procedures for CONFESS are as follows: The present sins input (psi) yields the graduated penance accrual (GPA) as a function of present sins (ps) plus frequency of confession visits (fcv) times completed penances (cp) divided by recurring sins (rs). Hence, GPA is a function not only of the immediate sins reported but also a partial function of the reciprocal relationship of recurring sins to completed penances by frequency of confession visits. The relative penance, then, is increased by the inclusion of recurring sins.[1] Mathematically, this can be represented as follows:

$$\text{psi} \rightarrow \quad \text{GPA} = f \quad \left\{ \text{ps} + \text{fcv} \left(\tfrac{cp}{rs}\right) \right\}$$

Therefore, each present sin yields a specific GPA that is stored until all GPAs have been computed. At that time, punishment and its maximum likelihood of occurrence[2] should the GPA not be completed, are retrieved from core storage and printed out for the individual GPA prescription.

Validity and Reliability

A study to establish the validity of the CONFESS program was conducted. The procedure included a sample of 243 actual confessions stratified across low, medium and high socio-economic income brackets with non-significant differences in proportions of black, white and Spanish speaking PUs. Fourteen priests were used in the study from seven different cities.

The actual sins confessed and penances prescribed in the confessional booths were tape recorded without the confessor or confessee's knowledge to insure absolute authenticity of confessor-confessee interaction.[3] The tapes were further analyzed and penances were rated on a scale of 1-10 where 10 = maximum severity.[4] Then ratings were made by the seven cardinal evaluators identified by Stake (AERA, 1972). The interrater reliability was .949.

The 243 sin sets taken from the taped confessions were then entered into the CONFESS program via remote terminal. A Pearson product moment correlation was computed between the actual PP penance prescriptions and the CONFESS PGAs. A correlation of .971 was interpreted to provide sufficient concurrent validity for CONFESS confidence.

A further series of small studies to determine the reliability of the CONFESS program were conducted as follows:

Study I: External Latency Reliability. The mean wait for confessional booths with PPs (where there were 2 booths/church) was 7.12 minutes while, in comparison, the average wait for a CONFESS bo (one installation per church) was only 1.72 minutes This difference in out-side wait latency is significan at the $p < .01$ level.

Study II: Internal Latency Reliability. This stud examined the latency from the last sin confessed unt the PP or CONFESS program provided the penanc or GPA, respectively. Again, the CONFESS latency was significantly shorter than the PP latency. Th means were 1.31 minutes (plus an average of 9.3 hea shakes) for PPs, and 6.1 seconds for CONFESS.

Study III: Computer Breakdowns vs. PP Rest Breaks In this study the CONFESS program was monitored for computer breakdowns and don't-understand-not-compute-either (DUNCE) loops. During the 243 CONFESS program runs (a total of 517 minutes), n breakdowns were reported and only one (1) DUNCE loop was reported. The DUNCE loop was in the case of one PU who was previously excommunicated from the church; however, the CONFESS program has been modified and will now process excommunicated PUs as well as non-excommunicated PUs. PPs, on the other hand, showed an average of 1 rest break for a mean of 12.3 minutes every hour and one-half.

Study IV: Consistency of PP penance vs. GPA. In this study, the 243 confession tapes were re-heard by the same 14 PPs. Each PP re-heard the same confessee's albeit on tape and without hearing the end of the tape which contained the penance he gave. In 241 cases, the PPs did *not* give the same penance and, in fact, in 191 cases the penance severity changed at least one degree (e.g., from a severity rating of 7 to a severity rating of 8). Although no speculation for causality is made here, it is important to compare the CONFESS consistency. In all 243 cases, the GPA was identical.

The results of these four studies are sufficient to provide confidence in CONFESS program reliability.

Procedures/Output

Being a natural language program, the procedures for CONFESS are extremely simple. The following steps describe the PU procedures.

Step 1: Enter the CONFESS box,⁵ and kneel on cushioned kneeler in front of the type-writer/console. Type in your personal PU identification code.

Step 2: The typewriter will type your name and the elapsed time since your last CONFESS session (CONFESSION). Following the request for present sins, type in all sins since your last CONFESSION.

Step 3: Press the "enter" button and silently repeat the short form of the ACT of Contrition. (Given the average latency for GPA, 6.1 seconds, this is usually reduced to "I'm sorry").

Step 4: Remove the CONFESS personalized GPA printout.

Sample Printout

CONFESS   GPA PRINTOUT   JOHN POPE Age 29

TIME SINCE LAST CONFESSION = 3 WEEKS

PRESENT SINS	TYPE	GPA	PUNISHMENT	PROBABILITY THEREOF
1. SECRETLY ENVIES BOSS	VENIAL	10 OUR FATHERS. PRACTICE SMILING AT BOSS	1 YEAR IN PURGATORY	.98
2. SWEAR AT WIFE	VENIAL	10 HAIL MARY'S. PRACTICE SMILING AT WIFE	1.73 YEARS IN PURGATORY	.84
3. COVET NEIGHBOR'S WIFE	MORTAL	ONE ROSARY/DAY FOR ONE WEEK. PRACTICE SMILING AT WIFE.	ETERNAL DAMNATION	.91

ONLY *3* SINS THIS TIME *MR. POPE.* YOU'RE IMPROVING. YOU HAD *14* LAST CONFESSION. NICE GOING. KEEP UP THE GOOD WORK. LET'S SEE IF YOU CAN MAKE OUT A LITTLE BETTER WITH NUMBER *3* IN THE FUTURE.

Availability

The write-up, listing, and source deck can be obtained from Dr. Kenneth Majer or Dr. Michael Flanigan, School of Education, Indiana University, Bloomington, Indiana 47401.

[1] Notice that updated past history records are necessary to compare previous sin records to present sin input in order to compute an up-to-date GPA. To insure confidentiality between confessor and confessee, a private code number is given to each PU and no master record is kept to identify the PU. This is the Non-retrievable aspect of the CONFESS program. Only by preceding the CONFESS session with his private code can the PU receive a GPA. Social security numbers are suggested as possible PU code identification numbers.

[2] This probability estimate taken from *Rome's Actual Transgression Sentences* (RATS) edited by Pope II. Randomness, Inc., Rome, 12 A.D.

[3] It should be noted that *ex post facto* permission to use the tape recordings was obtained from each confessor and confessee prior to use of the data. Hence, the sample of 243 represents a sub-sample of non-refusals from confessors and confessees. The original sample was 12,409.

[4] It may be of interest to the reader that 4 Our Father's and 4 Hail Mary's received a unanimous severity rating of 1 while 2 Rosaries per day plus mass each day for 2 months was rated unanimously as 10.

[5] The CONFESS box is patterned after the Skinner experimental box/chamber described in *Schedules of Reinforcement* by C. B. Ferster and B. F. Skinner, Appleton-Century Crofts, Inc., N. Y., 1957, 14-19. Although the present study does not address itself to the question of recurring sins and reinforcement/punishment contingencies, this question is currently under investigation by the authors.

REFERENCES

Ferster, C. B. and Skinner, B. F. *Schedules of Reinforcement.* Appleton-Century Crofts, Incs. New York, 1957, 14-19.

Rome's Actual Transgressions (RATS). Ed. Pope II. Randomness, Inc., Rome, 12 A.D.

Stake, Robert. *The Seven Cardinal Evaluators.* A paper presented at the National American Educational Research Association in Chicago, 1972.

ASHES TO ASHES

H. J. STEVENS
Alfred University
NYS College of Ceramics
Alfred, New York 14802

During the last two years we have been involved with studies on lunar glasses and their properties under the sponsorship of NASA Contract No. 33-187 (001). In the course of our work we analyzed the composition of several glass spheres[1] extracted from four half gram samples of lunar soil 1mm in depth (Samples 12070,38; 12057,61; 12033,25; 12001,74). Sample 12033,25 was taken from a depth of 15cm. The range of the major analyzed compositions is given in Table I.

Table I
Lunar Glass

Oxides	Wgt. %
SiO_2	38.8 – 48.8
Al_2O_3	9.8 – 27.3
FeO	3.52 – 19.4
CaO	9.0 – 13.55
MgO	5.8 – 12.8

A new research project on fly ash sponsored by a local electrical power company revealed an interesting correlation between fly ash, the residue from coal combustion, and our analyzed lunar spheres.

Fly ash and bottom ash are the residue left from the combustion of coal in the power plants. The fly ash is collected from the stack through a series of collectors. It is then generally shipped to suitable land fill sites. The bottom ash is that material which settles to the bottom of the furnace, and is removed from there as a glass, often spherical in form. It is also used for land fill.

The chemical composition of fly and bottom ash is given in Table II.

Table II
Fly & Bottom Ash

Oxides	Wgt. %
SiO_2	41.9
Al_2O_3	27.6
Fe_2O_3	16.1
CaO	3.1
MgO	0.8

Chemically, it is very similar to the analysis of the lunar glass that we reported. The appearance of the fly and bottom ash is also very similar to lunar fines in regard to color and flow characteristics. Particle analysis of lunar fines[2] showed

57.5% thru 200 mesh   .074 mm.
45.4% thru 325 mesh   .044 mm.

The fly ash particle size analysis varied slightly from the lunar fines with

87.0% thru 200 mesh
77.5% thru 325 mesh

The similarities between the two materials immediately evoked discussion among the members of our research staff and various theories about the origin of the lunar fines were projected.

The theory that our power companies were secretly shipping waste fly ash to the moon was ruled out because of two factors: 1) The fly ash has iron in the form of Fe_2O_3, whereas the lunar fines are mainly FeO. This would indicate that the original formation occurred in a more reducing atmosphere than that which occurs on earth, i.e., the moon's atmosphere. 2) Since the particle size of the lunar fines is slightly larger than the fly ash, formation on the moon is indicated. The moon, having a lower atmospheric pressure and gravity, would permit larger particles to be blown through the stack.

The slight differences in composition also indicates another raw material source.

All of these observations point to one inevitable conclusion: Sometime in the history of the moon, large power generating stations covered the landscape. In the quest for more and more power, the warnings of the ecologists were ignored and alas the moon buried itself with its own fly ash!

REFERENCES

[1] Greene, C. H., Pye, L. D., Stevens, H. J., Rase, D. E., and Kay, H. F., *"Compostions, Homogeneity, Densities and Thermal History Of Lunar Glass Particles,"* Proceedings of the 2nd Annual Lunar Science Conference, Vol. 3, pp. 2049-2055, The M.I.T. Press (1971).
[2] Frondel, C., Klein, C., and Ito, J., *"Mineralogical and Chemical Data On Apollo 12 Lunar Fines,"* Proceedings of the 2nd Annual Lunar Science Conference, Vol. 1, pp. 719-726, The M.I.T. Press (1971).

Nothing

can be

more

irreproducible

than

NATURE STUDY

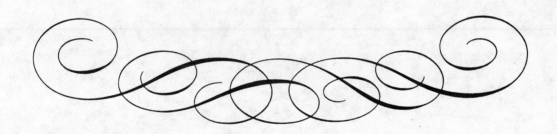

The Reconstruction of "NESSIE" The Loch Ness Monster Resolved

JOHN C. HOLDEN

NOAA, Atlantic Oceanographic Laboratories
901 South Miami Ave., Miami, Florida

FIGURE 1.
Sketch of the Loch Ness monster according to information supplied from an eye witness. Due to the trauma of the experience many details of this reconstruction may be in error, though gross morphology is considered valid.

INTRODUCTION

In recent years there has become available to science an increasing amount of important data concerning the existence of a hitherto undescribed animal residing in the body of fresh water known as Loch Ness in northern Scotland. It is now possible to reconstruct a close facsmile of this enigmatic organism based on three types of data: (a) direct factual information obtained by scientific inquiries on the subject, (b) rumors and hearsay about such a creature and the characteristics ascribed to it by local residents and (c) inductive logic consistent with the geological, paleontological, and biological requirements of the situation. Within the limitations of the above constraints, it is now possible to place the species commonly known as "Nessie" into the scheme of contemporary taxonomy and once and for all establish the scientific reality of the Loch Ness monster.

According to a recent report by the Loch Ness Investigation Bureau[1] sonar signals were recorded from hydrophone experiments in Loch Ness. These noises, from as deep as 300 feet in the Loch, consist of sonic vibrations of variable intensity and frequency. Some 25 miles of recording tapes still await interpretation. Scientific activity on the Loch Ness monster is of fairly recent origin. The legend of the monster goes back much farther, however. In general, first hand observers have described Nessie as a slithery or undulating object breaking water. These data are usually gained at night, especially on foggy or other evenings of low visability attesting to the animals keen shyness to being too closely scrutinized. One source[2] has described his personal encounter to the author which is here summarized in figure 1. There are undoubtedly some errors in the sketch as the witness was highly excited during the interview. It is interesting to note that during the Second World War the German High Command had sufficient confidence in the reality of the monster to actually drop bombs in Loch Ness with the intent of destroying the creature and, thereby, damaging British morale[3].

In this paper, most of the emphasis is placed on the inductive logical parameter mentioned above. With this data a realistic interpretation concerning the nature of Nessie can be made in keeping with the observations and being at the same time consistent with taxonomic and geologic theory.

Two animal types are good candidates for the alleged monster: one, Cetaceans (Porpoises and whales) and two, plesiosaurs, a thought-to-be-extinct group of marine reptiles. The Cetaceans can attain "monsterous" size and are known to have developed complex sonar systems. We must rule them out, unfortunately, since according to Marshall[1], the noises in Loch Ness are unique. The plesiosaurs, on the other hand, are a fruitful avenue of investigation. First, they show no paleontological evidence of ever having developed sonar signals. Therefore, should they have done so it would be unique. They also have the additional advantage of being more naturally monsterous looking than the friendly cetaceans. The plesiosaurids were large reptiles and though not related to dinosaurs were of comparable size and must have been the dragons of Jurassic-Cretaceous seas.

CLASSIFICATION AND SYSTEMATIC DESCRIPTION OF THE SPECIES

Taking the basic plesiosaurid shape, which has been aptly described as threading a snake through the body of a turtle[4] as a guide, it is possible to make the appropriate changes and reconstruct what Nessie probably looked like. The important features of the re-construction include: (a) a well developed sonar organ, (b) loss of eyes, (c) elongation and narrowing of the snout with the forward migration of the nostril, enabling the animal to breath inconspicuously without exposing very much of its body, and finally, (d) basic modifications of the body morphology from the muscular, trim, streamlined ocean going model to the lethargic, flabby, freshwater type. The following formal description is a convention required by the International Congress of Zoological Nomenclature.

Phylum .... CHORDATA
Class .... REPTILIA
Order .... SAUROPTERYGIA
Suborder .... PLESIOSAURIA
Superfamily .. PLESIOSAURIDEA
Family ...... PLESIOSONARIDAE new fam.
Genus ...... PLESIOPHONUS new gen.
Species .. HARMONICUS new sp.

Plesiophonus harmonicus new gen., new species

Figs. 1, 2, 3, 4b

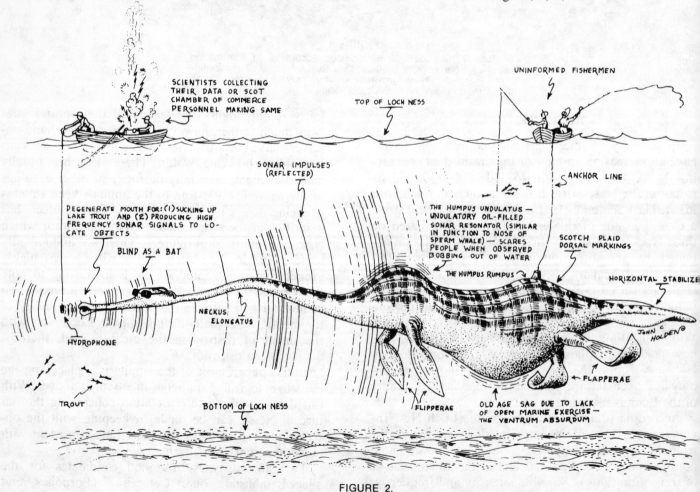

FIGURE 2.
Reconstruction of **Plesiophonus harmonicus** in its natural habitat in Loch Ness. The specimen is shown using its sonar for locating a hydrophone. Other organisms indigenous to the area are also shown for scale.

Description. Body size: large. Appendages: the *flipperae* and *flapperae* are typically plesiosaur-like; *neckus elongatus* long, sinuous, scary; *tailus terminus* with horizontal stabilizers. *Humpae* of various types new to science (see especially fig. 3): A *humpus undulatus* in the shoulder region housing oil-filled sonar resonator sensitive to self emitted sonar frequency signals. This organ is extremely repulsive and strikes fear into those observing it bobbing out of the water on dark nights. Dorsum shifted posteriorly to form the *humpus rumpus* counteracting the anteriorly situated mass of the *humpus undulatus* and maintaining the animal's center of gravity. Prominent *ventrum absurdum* holds vital organs, developed as a result of the species languishing listless loch life lacking proper open marine exercise. Head region (see especially fig. 4b); highly specialized. Teeth and eyes absent. Anterior cranial parts elongated, forming snout-like mouth for sucking up lake trout and emitting sonar signals. Skull bulbous to accommodate increased I.Q. necessary for (a) acoustical higher mathematics, (b) keeping away from people, and (c) responding to ever more sophisticated electronic apparatus placed into Loch Ness by curious scientists. Markings: Dorsum covered with scotch plaid color pattern, naturally.

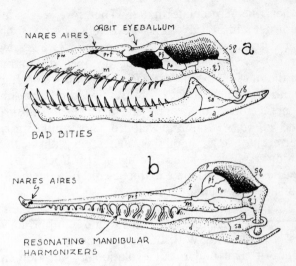

FIGURE 4.
Contrasting skulls of the extinct plesiosaurs (4a above) and closely related **Plesiophonus** (4b below) from Loch Ness. In the latter the teeth are no longer needed and have disappeared through disuse. Similarly, the **orbit eyeballum** is gone with the concommitant enlargements of the **postfrontal** (pf), **postorbital** (po), and **frontal** (f) skull segments. The **maxilla** (m) is modified into a series of tuning forks that enable a wide range of unique sounds utilized in sonar emission. The **prefrontal** (prf), **maxilla** and **dentary** (d) are elongated to form a prominent snout.

NATURAL HISTORY OF THE LOCH NESS MONSTER

Loch Ness is the body of water occupying a very ancient and fundamental geological rupture known as the Great Glen Fault. This fault is a tectonic juncture within the crustal Paleozoic and older rocks comprising the basement of northern Scotland. The fault is very ancient as so must be the loch. In fact, Wilson has suggested that it is contiguous under pre-continental drift reconstruction with the Cabot Fault in the Bay of Fundy, North America.[5] This makes the loch greater than 220 m.y. old. The plesiosaurid great reptiles existed after the basin was already in existence in the Jurassic and Cretaceous (180 to 65 m.y.b.p.) so probably inhabited the narrow seaway that extended into the Great Glen Fault. At the end of the Cretaceous the basin was closed to the sea and gradually became freshwater. Most of the entrapped marine fauna became extinct except for some plesiosaurs which adapted to the new freshwater conditions and decided to remain there. Today they tittilate the curiosity of visiting scientists, scare the local Scots, and bolster the national economy with visitors from all over the world waiting for a glimpse of something new.

In order to adjust to the new freshwater conditions, the entrapped reptiles had to learn to live in the murk of a freshwater body which lacks, by definition, the sodium cations so helpful in flocculating clays and

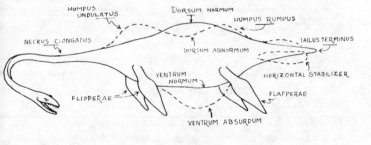

FIGURE 3.
The generalized body of **Plesiophonus harmonicus** compared to the basic plesiosaurid type. The typical plesiosaurid body is shown in solid line; that of **Plesiophonus** in dashed line. The single **dorsum normum** of the plesiosaurid gives way to two **humpae**, an anterior **humpus undulatus**, and a posterior **humpus rumpus.** Also, the **ventrum normum** typical of the Jurassic-Cretaceous reptiles atrophies into a **ventrum absurdum** in the Loch Ness monster.

other fine particulate matter. Therefore, early in the monster's life history Nessie evolved a highly sophisticated sonar organ. As this happened the eyes degenerated by disuse. Competition dropped off markedly in the new environment as *Plesiophonus* found himself there alone. This lack of exercise produced phylogenetic muscular atrophy and the *ventrum absurdum* and *humpus rumpus* developed (not unlike in other vertebrates, e.g., hominids, under easy physical conditions). In the sleepy refugium of Loch Ness the species did not become extinct as did his cousins in the harsher ocean environments.

For more than 65 m.y., small changes withstanding, the species remained in homeostatic equilibrium with its environment. With the appearance of man on the scene it then underwent evolutionary saltation in response to intolerant and meddling hominid behavior. Due to specialized prejudicial activities of early man along the banks of Loch Ness, Nessie was induced to evolve a coloration pattern mimicking the traditional scotch plaid. Undoubtedly, nonconformists were

selected against violently. During this time the nares aires migrated anteriorly along, and to the end of the elongate snout thereby enabling the species to always keep most of its head submerged.

It remains only a matter of time until one of the specimens of Nessie is captured. Motivation is now supplied not only by a desire for the scientific knowledge to be gained by a face to face encounter but also by a monetary reward. $1,000 (U.S.) has recently been offered for the capture of the "'monster".[6]

LITERATURE CITED

[1] Marshall, N. B. (*In*: Nichol, D. M.), 1970. "None can say Nessie has lochjaw": Miami Herald, Fri., Dec. 4:3-G.
[2] Prof. Samual P. Welles, 1971. (personnal communication).
[3] Dr. Robert S. Dietz, 1970. (personnal communication).
[4] Romer, A. S., 1968. The procession of life. World Publ. Co., New York, 195.
[5] Wilson, J. T., 1962. Cabot Fault, and Appalachian equivalent of the San Andreas and Great Glen Faults and some implications for continental displacements: Nature, *195*:135-138.
[6] Sneigr, D., 1970. "Miamian offering $1,000 for best 'monster'": Miami News, Wed., Dec. 9:7-G.

The Demise of
Escopeta blanco

RICHARD HANSIS
Department of Geography
Pa. State University

The growing interest in environmental quality and the concomitant concern for the preservation of endangered species has led to a deluge of articles and books, some of which have caught the public fancy. The publication in newspapers of various endangered species listed by conservation organizations and the well-publicized disappearance of some species, e.g. the passenger pigeon, has neglected one lowly creature, the skeetbird, *Escopeta blanco*.

The slaughter of this hapless species has reached alarming proportions under what could hardly be called sportsmanlike conditions. As a domesticated bird, raised entirely in captivity, it is in little danger of immediate disappearance. However when released from their breeding grounds, they are immediately hunted, with the majority of them being killed outright by the pursuing hunters. The ones that manage to

escape this deadly barrage are unable to survive in the wild owing to their complete dependence on man for sustenance. With more data becoming available, empirical models based on complex linear flows should be able to forecast future populations.

Another shocking part of this story is the complete disposal of the carcass after being shot. Lead pellets render the skeetbird useless for eating. Utilization of the unharmed bird is possible, however. Cutting the skeetbird in half would produce two frisbees, a vital item in contemporary America, or a manual popcorn popper or even a pair of hubcaps for a small car. Multipurpose use would have two main benefits: it would lead to a more rational harvesting of the skeet population and would conserve scarce resources. This type of enlightened self-interest needs to be encouraged.

THE INFLUENCE OF HYDROGEN REPELLENTS ON THE GENETIC DETERMINATION OF FEEDING HABITS OF MOSQUITOES ON RABBITS

MICHAEL BAR-KEV-KEVES
Israel Substitute for Entomological Research

It has been long known that some insect repellents have repelling effect on mosquitoes[1]. These substances were, therefore, widely used in tropical and semitropical areas by civilians and military personnel, who did not possess sufficient olfactory acuity to make the substance repellent to themselves.

In view of the fact that most of the commercially available repellents have a large part of their molecular volume occupied by hydrogen*, it was desirable to test the repelling effects of hydrogen itself on mosquitoes, as well as to find whether the feeding habits developed by such repelled mosquitoes (the frustration complex) would be genetically fixed.

METHODS: A solution of hydrogen was injected intravenously into a series of rabbits, which were being prepared as a substrate for the mosquitoes. Live animals rather than artificial membranes were used since anyway "special defeathered or defurred young bird or animal skins have to be used for successful blood feeding. They must be prepared by the investigator and cannot be purchased commercially"[2].

At this stage of hydrogenation of the rabbits a surprising phenomenon was observed: the injected rabbits developed negative gravity and tended to collect under the ceiling of the laboratory. This phenomenon was studied elsewhere in a mathematical study by Wolyniec[3] and a formula was developed:

$$\lim(R + H) = Ce$$

here R represents rabbits, H hydrogen, Ce ceiling or

any other horizontal impermeable surface above the rabbit.

Since we were not interested in rabbits but in mosquitoes, and did not want to embark upon teleological experimentation, the phenomenon of negative gravity was not pursued any further.

In all successive experiments the rabbits were simply securely tied to tables before the injection of hydrogen. The problem of introducing a sufficient quantity of hydrogen into the blood circulation of the experimental animals was solved by injecting first an aqueous suspension of micronized zinc into the ear vein, and following this after a few minutes by injection of concentrated hydrochloric acid into the vein of the second ear. The buffering capacity of blood versus the acid was measured beforehand and the amount of acid injected was sufficient to produce the desired generation of hydrogen.** The exceptional rabbits that survived this treatment (hereafter called hydrogenated rabbits) had a satisfactory saturation of blood with hydrogen.

Mosquitoes. The breeding and the genetical selection of mosquitoes was done by the method of Maire Yassat and O. Sex[4].

RESULTS: Carefully numbered mosquitoes were anaesthetized by CO_2, whereupon their palpi and antennae

---

* Chlorohydrocarbons.
** No representative of Soc. Prev. Cruelty to Animals was permitted to be present in the lab during this stage of preparation.

TABLE 1.
FEEDING OF NORMAL AND ANTENNA-LESS MOSQUITOES ON HYDROGENATED RABBITS

	TOTAL NUMBER USED	NUMBER FEEDING ON HYDRO-RABBITS	NUMBER FEEDING ON NORMAL MOSQUITOES
Normal mosquitoes	100	44	99*
Antenna-less mosquitoes	100	28	31

were surgically removed. As soon as the mosquitoes woke up from their anaesthesia and resumed normal activities, they were introduced into the cage containing hydrogenated rabbits. As controls served undamaged mosquitoes. Table 1 shows the results of a typical experiment.

When antenna-less hydrogen-fed mosquitoes were introduced into a chamber containing oxygen and platinum sponge, they exploded. Normal mosquitoes did not show this effect. We attribute the explosion to leakage of hydrogen from the cut surface at the base of antenna.

A very interesting finding was obtained with the hydrogen-fed normal mosquitoes. They were shown to be able to communicate the information about the presence of hydrogen in a rabbit by a complicated movement of their antennae. This movement was cinematographically recorded through a stereoscopic microscope. Exposure of unfed mosquitoes to cinematic screen (suitably diminished) displaying these recorded movements was sufficient to prevent the viewers from approaching hydrogenated rabbits.

SUMMARY: Hydrogenated rabbits are dangerous to mutilated mosquitoes and repellent to normal mosquitoes.

REFERENCES
[1] W. F. King, Resistance Studies, vol. I., Burgess Publ. Co., 1958, pp. 83–89.
[2] F. W. Fisk, Feeding and Drinking Methods, in RESISTANCE STUDIES, vol. I. Burgess Publ. Co., 1959, p. 114.
[3] G. Wolyniec, Mathematical and statistical interpretation of negative gravity I. Floating of hydrogenated rabbits, J. Irrepr. Statistics, 1958, 3, 10.
[4] Maire Yassat and O. Sex, Finger-printing as Means of Determination of Genetic Identity of *Culex* and *Anopheles* in Middle East and in Africa (not to be published).

* The remaining mosquito, which did not feed, was found to be a male. This male was inadvertently included in the batch of females by one of the technicians, who was under a self-treatment with saccharomycetin (C_2H_5OH).

Maternal Behavior In The Domestic Cock Under The Influence Of Alcohol

Abstract. *When normal male domestic chickens were given a single dose of grain alcohol and then exposed to newly hatched chicks, they assumed maternal behavior. The same behavior can be elicited by the administration of prolactin, but the results of these experiments suggest that maternal behavior in the cock is not exclusively dependent on hormonal mechanisms.*

We were led to the investigation of this phenomenon by an old custom, prevalent among Hungarian farmers, of transferring newly hatched chicks from the hen to a "drunken cock." The farmers justify this transfer by the argument that: (i) the cock is better than the hen at defending the chicks from predators; and (ii) such transfer frees the hen for returning to the commercially desirable egg-laying cycle.

Joseph K. Kovach
Menninger Foundation
Topeka, Kansas

From *Science*, Vol. 156, 5/12/67.

15. SEX BEFORE AND AFTER SUBSTITUTION
Count of Persons Before Allocation

By: Before and After Substitution (2)   By: Sex (2)

Before substitution and allocation:
  Male
  Female

Substituted persons:
  Male
  Female

From *1970 Census Users' Guide, Part II*, U.S. Department of Commerce Maurice H. Stans, Secretary.

A SOCIOLOGICAL AND BIOLOGICAL STUDY OF POOL LIFE

S. FLOWERS
Rehovot, Israel

This research was carried out in two locales: Berkeley, California, and Rehovot, Israel. Certain similarities were noted in both pools, the various forms of wild life being identical; only the cries they uttered and the mating calls showed basic linguistic differences.

The pool has a total area of 1234 square feet and contains 1,300 gallons of water; 13.297 gallons of that water have been drunk by aspiring, perspiring and expiring swimmers; the maximum depth of water is 3.5 meters and is the only place where a scientist can go off the deep end without hurting anyone's feelings (unless he lands directly on someone), x families are members, y people are willing to pay for visitor's tickets each summer, and at least z people were unwilling to pay and tried to get in by other means. Such facts can easily be ascertained from the Royal Institute of Statistics or by using one of the many computers on the campus at either Berkeley or Rehovot.

There are two species of pool users—male and female. The females can be tabulated thus:

near misses	(aged 0 – 13)
misses	(13 – 18)
someone's dear missus	(18 – 80)

These divisions are not always clear-cut and there are exceptions to the above classification. It is more difficult to classify the males. They can be roughly divided into boys and men. The only trouble is that the boys try to act like men and the men try to act like boys. The easiest way to differentiate them is that the boys have hair on their heads, while the men have it on their chests.

Apart from the horizontal division above, we may also perform a vertical division into the following categories:

a) The monostroke
b) The polystroke
c) The sunstroke

A rich variety of wild life has appeared in this habitat in an amazingly short space of time. Among the many new species the following have been observed:

HIPPOPOTAMI (Hippopotamidae) puff and pant as they swim around clumsily.

ELEPHANTS (Elephantidae) trumpet and spout water over anyone within range.

TURTLES (wrongly known as tortoises; chelonia), are slow and sure as they do their daily kilometer or more.

SEALS (Phocidae) swim gracefully and effortlessly, their sleek heads breaking the smooth surface only for air, and they are capable of covering vast distances.

TADPOLES (Ramidae) are those plump bright-eyed little creatures that flash in and out of the paddling pool. It is usual to find a croaking frog or ungainly stork in the vicinity.

PORPOISES (Odontoceti) are easily recognized. They resemble children as they frolic and splash all over the place.

POOL LIZARDS (Lacertidae) are those languorous brown creatures seen stretched out around the pool. They are usually the female of the species. A noted anthropologist informed me that this is perhaps due to the fact that the males of the species are too busy studying the few perfect female specimens and are therefore more likely to be found slithering in and out of the pool.

(Gourmets please note: lizards are particularly succulent when cooked. Those that have been slowly broiled, after having been basted in good quality cream or oil, look more attractive and have a better appearance that those fried in cheap oil. They also tend to burn when roasted too quickly.)

QUOTES

G. H. E. Hopkins and Miriam Rothschild
AN ILLUSTRATED CATALOGUE OF THE ROTHSCHILD COLLECTION OF FLEAS
British Museum, London 1962, 168 s.

* * *

G. Olsson
SELF-INCOMPATIBILITY AND OUTCROSSING IN RAPE AND WHITE MUSTARD MODE
OF FERTILIZATION
I. RAPE
Hereditas, 1960, *46*, 241.

* * *

K. E. Goard
INFECTION BY *Leptospira Pomona* CONTRACTED FROM PIGS BY MOUTH-TO-MOUTH
RESUSCITATION.
Med. J. Australia, 1961, *1*:897 – 898 (June 17).

* * *

J. B. Graham & al.
HUMAN DOUBLE CROSS-OVER
Nature, 1962, *195*, 834.

* * *

D. Waugh and E. van der Hoeven
FINE STRUCTURE OF THE HUMAN ADULT FEMALE BREAST
Lab. Invest. 1962, *11*, 220 – 228

"The fine structure of the resting and of the pregnant breast in the human female is similar to that described in the virgin, resting and pregnant mammary gland in the mouse, rat and cow."

* * *

New Yorker, June 20, 1959 quoting *Leominster Daily Enterprise*:

"*The proceeds will be used to purchase Hi-Lo beds for the hospital. These beds are constructed so they can be manually raised and lowered to accomodate both patients and nurses.*"

* * *

Paul Weiss (Rockefeller Institute)
EXPERIENCE AND EXPERIMENT IN BIOLOGY
Science, 1962, *136*, 468–471.

"We see bewildered youngsters composing research projects like abstract paintings: picking some colorful and fashionable words from recent literature, and then reshuffling and recombining them into another conglomerate, yielding a stew of data, both undigested and indigestible. We see narrow specialists lavishing their pet technique on reconfirming in yet another dozen ways what has already been superabundantly established to everybody's satisfaction.

"The hallmarks of dilution of research effectiveness: irrelevance, triviality, redundancy, lack of perspective, and unbounded flair for proliferation."

* * *

N. S. Kline
YOU CAN'T GET THERE FROM HERE
Indian J. Psychiatry, 1959, 1, 18–25.

". . .a researcher is a paranoid, noisy, obsessive, compulsive long-shot gambler who simply doesn't know when to leave well enough alone."

* * *

Donald Mazia (University of California, Berkeley)
A.I.B.S. Bulletin, February 1962, p. 5

"In common language, we described the nucleus as the administrator of the cell. It shares two attributes with more familiar administrators: it tends to perpetuate its kind, and it defies so successfully all efforts (by outsiders) to learn what it is doing that only by trying to get along without it can we satisfy ourselves that it is working at all."

* * *

Editorial, Lancet, July 1, 1962

"The differences between male and female in man (as in most species), however conspicuous or however important in practice, are not really profound."

* * *

Eder, P.
Brit. J. Med. Psychol., 1962, 35, 81

"We are born mad, acquire morality and become stupid and unhappy. Then we die."

A Portable Laboratory for the Unobtrusive Observation of Animals in their Natural Habitat: The Pachydermobile[1]

TERRY MAPLE
Department of Psychology
University of California at Davis 95616

Tracking wild animals is, at best, an arduous and sometimes hazardous task. It is necessary, of course, if the animals in question are to be properly understood. But wild animals are wary of human observers, as well they should be. How then does a scientist wishing to study animals in their characteristic milieu get near enough to really see?

The answer to this question is not found in the use of traditional apparatus. Blinds constructed to conceal the human form or allow for long-distance viewing are not mobile. A lot of what an animal does with its time cannot be observed without mobility on the part of the observer. How about the trusty Land Rover? Nope. Many animals have learned to associate the vehicle with hunting or capture. Also, the Land Rover is noisy and conspicuous. In this writer's opinion, the best way to study wild animals is to become a familiar part of the beasts' environment. For many African species, what is more familiar than an elephant?

Construction of the Pachydermobile

A diagram of my portable laboratory is presented in Figure 1. It is best constructed of genuine elephant hide stretched over a steel shell. Naturally, the hide should be obtained from reputable authorities who will guarantee that the animal expired from natural causes.

The engine is designed to run on methane (derived from local animal fecal material) and should be of lightweight construction. I recommend that the recording apparatus and internal controls of the vehicle be carefully constructed from modern and sturdy materials. Such material may be obtained from the writer's brother-in-law for a small honorarium.

Advantages of the Pachydermobile

The Pachydermobile has many obvious advantages, many of which I haven't thought of yet. Some of these came to me in a vision, others remain to be discovered through use of the lab-vehicle. Consider the following:

1. The Pachydermobile not only looks like an elephant, it also smells like one due to three external pheromone outlets. These outlets secrete enough fluid to convince even the most suspicious animals.

2. Its prehensile trunk allows the scientist-operator to collect scats for ecological analysis and — via the methane converter — utilize these stool samples as fuel.

3. The Pachydermobile is capable of emitting a variety of elephant vocalizations and heavy panting sounds in order to further diminish the minimal engine noise, and enhance its authenticity.

4. The Pachydermobile is a four-wheel drive vehicle equipped with tough knobby tires, capable of traversing the most difficult terrain. It also floats and for a small sum can be altered to propel itself through water.

5. The Pachydermobile can operate by night through the use of its infrared sensing equipment.

6. The tough elephant skin of the Pachydermobile covers a strong bullet-proof shell which should discourage potshots by illegal elephant poachers.

A final note

It is recommended that the Pachydermobile be used for the study of animals other than elephants. Most African species are not afraid of elephants and will tolerate the presence of a lone animal. However, due to the lab-vehicle highly effective disguise, an elephant herd may not accept such a stranger. While they may be inclined to attack, a more likely result is that courtship may ensue. The emergency semen receptacle (R) is designed to take advantage of any romantic advances by curious bulls. Resistance is always dangerous and at such times, it is best to "ride-it-out" with the beast.[2] Semen may be analyzed at the appropriate time.

While the advantages of such a device as the Pachydermobile are many, the disadvantages are comparatively few. Amorous bull elephants are a potential hazard as are persistent hunters. The most serious difficulty, however, may well be the high cost of construction. These problems may be circumvented by the construction of a miniature version of the Pachydermobile. Such a scaled-down version would require a small fraction of the expenditure for a larger model. An additional advantage is that only the most deviant of poachers and/or bull elephants would be attracted to a *young* Pachydermobile.

---

[1] This research is possible through generous grants from the membership of the Davis Geographical Front and the International Society of Educated Beasts.

[2] It is recommended that the operator of the Pachydermobile wear a gorilla suit should abandonment of the vehicle be required.

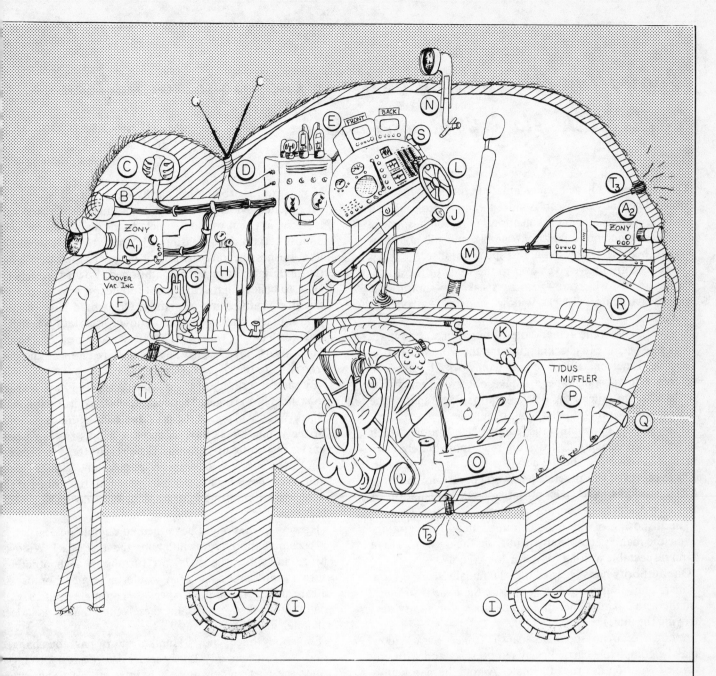

FIGURE 1: COMPONENTS OF THE PACHYDERMOBILE

A_1 A_2	TELEVISION CAMERA	K	GEAR BOX
B	INFRARED HEADLIGHTS	L	STEERING WHEEL
C	SOUND MICROPHONE	M	SWIVEL SEAT
D	ANTENNAE	N	PERISCOPE
E	TELEVISION RECEIVER—TAPE DECK	O	ENGINE
F	VACUUM TUBE (prehensile remote-control trunk)	P	MUFFLER
G	STOOL ANALYZER	Q	DUAL EXHAUST PIPES
H	METHANE CONVERTER	R	EMERGENCY SEMEN RECEPTACLE
I	KNOBBY TIRES	S	MASTER CONTROL PANEL (adjustable)
J	FOUR WHEEL DRIVE SHAFT	T_1 T_2 T_3	EXTERNAL PHEROMONES SECRETION OUTLETS

Increasing Abnormality in the Sexual Behavior Pattern of the Male Black Widow Spider

W. HENRI KREICKER, D. E.
1005 South Country Club Dri
Warsaw, Indiana 4658

Over the years I have been an amateur entomologist, as a hobby. The study of insects is indeed a fascinating subject. There are almost countless genuses. One could spend a lifetime studying butterflies, for example, and still not know all that there is to know about this species of insect.

More recently I have given over to the study of the arachnids or spiders, which are — strictly speaking — not insects, and in particular, Black Widow spiders (Latrodectus mactans).

I have made some remarkable observations. I say, remarkable because in checking through the works of Fabre, Gertsch, Emerton, Bristowe and Comstock, I found no reference to the phenomena I have observed, which has to do with the male of the Black Widow spider family. The male is considerably smaller than the female.

It is generally known that the female Black Widow, which is venomous, usually destroys the male immediately after mating. Frequently she devours the male after killing it. I have observed this practice on several occasions. Authorities on spiders have given no satisfactory explanation of this androcidal tendency, nor have I one.

The disposing of the male is immediately after mating, while the male is completely spent from the orgasm. There is no respectable waiting for the ardor to cool.

One authority has suggested that the female Black Widow is invariably disappointed in love, since the male is so much smaller, and exhibits her utter contempt by promptly destroying the male.

Another researcher speculates that the female Black Widow may be completely carried away with ecstasy and with unbridled emotion destroys the male. Among human beings the saying, "I love you so much I could eat you", is not uncommon. The annals are replete with cases of teen-agers so-called necking wherein what practically amounts to mayhem was perpetrated, frequently stitches having to be taken.

Kucharov has suggested that the female Black Widow may be completely emotionally unstable and as a result is filled with mistrust. Fearing the peregrinations of the male during her gestation period she may put her mind at ease by destroying him, then cozily hatching her brood.

A French authority has suggested that the female Black Widow may be likened unto Shah Jehan of Agra, India, who commissioned the Taj Mahal to be built and upon its completion destroyed the builder so that he could never construct anything more beautiful than the Taj Mahal.

However, this explanation hardly seems plausible.

It is quite obvious that the libido of the male Black Widow is strong or else it would not yield to the mating instinct wit almost certain death staring it in the face. This would b uxoriousness beyond the line of duty. On the other hand the male may have been conditioned, down through th ages, to believe that death is not too dear a price to pay fo the utter gratification of mating. One would have to mat with a Black Widow spider to know for certain whether i was worth paying with one's life. It would appear exorbitant The Italians, however, have a saying, "See Florence and die" (referring to the city, of course).

By careful scrutiny of the minute creatures I have learne that there is a growing tendency upon the part of the mal Black Widow to weigh the pros and cons of mating. Som of the young bucks have adopted a "fools rush in wher angels fear to tread" attitude. As a result, there is a lessen ing of the Black Widow spider population. This is favor able since they are dangerous to mankind, their bite (of th female)often resulting in death, albeit it is decreasing study material.

However, what might be termed an unbiological situatior is becoming more prevalent among the male Black Widows More and more the males are turning to each other fo sexual gratification, in what would be termed homosexu alism among the human species. The male spiders with palpi interlocked, as in a Japanese kendo match, is indeed an amazing sight.

Somebody once said, "Human nature has not changed since the first human." Likely spider nature has not changed since the first spider. But, it is interesting to conjecture whether on some far distant tomorrow the (1) species will become extinct (like the Great African Scaled Sloth which was too indolent to mate), the (2) female will see the error of her ways, and — superinduced by the dread of being a spinster — will adopt a policy of "live and let live", or the (3) male will adroitly develop a "touch and go" procedure, leaving the female with murder in her heart as he rapidly departs after mating with an "it was fun while it lasted" attitude, or what passes for an attitude among spiders.

Perhaps some observer in 5000 A.B. (After the Atomic Bombing) will know the outcome of the erstwhile precarious love-life of the male Black Widow and the Black pre-Widow too.

---

* Distinguished Exterminator

THE BATTLE OF THE TEAT*

MICHAEL KELLY, M.D.

The Australian kangaroo, like other marsupials, is born in an immature state. After birth it crawls up its mother's belly into the pouch where it firmly grasps the nipple with its jaws. There it remains fixed for many weeks until it can fend for itself.

These facts have been known for 150 years, but a contrary belief has been cherished by many people in the Australian outback. In 1924 Frederic Wood Jones, then Professor of Anatomy in Adelaide, spoke in a public lecture of the birth of the kangaroo. He was assailed in the press by a number of selfstyled "practical men" who pitied the ignorance of the theoriest but recently arrived in Australia. Wood Jones did not reply, but another scientist took up the challenge and showed six of the bushmen a specimen of a kangaroo embryo *in utero*. They laughed this to scorn as a fake, and invited Wood Jones himself to prove his theory; but at first he ignored the challenge.

One of the six men offered £100 to the Children's Hospital if he could prove his case. Wood Jones was tempted. He got together a large number of specimens, and put on a complete and convincing demonstration in the Anatomy Lecture Theatre. The demonstration was well publicized, and a large crowd — mostly of medical students and bushmen — turned up. We third-year medical students were on duty as demonstrators. But the bushmen were not convinced. Every argument of Wood Jones was met with a "practical" reply starting with "all this theory . . ." Wood Jones' patience was sorely tried, and in the end he made a few mildly sarcastic remarks. The following account of this occasion is taken from the *Adelaide Medical Students Review* of Nov. 1924.

"The story of the Gallant Six will go down in history. They will be immortalized in legend, for the manner in which they resisted the futile attacks of science. The University had been haunted for weeks by strange bearded men who carried small bottles in their hip-pockets. One carried an apple from which grew a wart-like protuberance; he proclaimed: 'If apples grow like that then kangaroos do.' Another had personally shot and skinned 10,000 kangaroos in 12 months and had never seen an embryo except upon the teat.

"On the fateful afternoon a mighty army of Practical Men turned up to do battle. One of them exclaimed audibly as he entered the hall: 'Me for the teat.' Respectful silence greeted the efforts of the Theorist; some of the 'stoodents' thought him victorious. But no; the Six were still untouched. At the first word ('All this theory . . .') it was evident that no impression had been made — that no risk had been taken when the offer was made to the Children's Hospital.

"One Practical Man drew from the Theorist the admission that the embryo when first seen on the teat was fully formed. The practical man had seen them on the teat 'half-formed, aye, and quarter-formed; no longer than a grain of wheat.' This, he said, proved that the embryo flowed out of the nipple like milk, solidified, and then shaped itself into a recognizable animal. But another member of the Practical Clan admitted that he had often seen, just before delivery, congealed drops of a "milky substance" (colostrum) on the nipples of mares. It is strange that foals do not grow on the teat.

"One keen observer claimed that he had often seen in the kangaroo a tube from the ovary, running through the belly wall to the teat; on one occasion had observed an embryo working its way along the tube. He was shown a specimen of the belly wall of a female kangaroo, cut into serial sections: it possessed no tube. His reply was: 'the belly wall's very thin, and if the embryo gets up against it, God will do the rest.' One Practical Man expressed his contempt for the despised 'stoodents,' who 'had never seen an adjectival kangaroo in all their sanguinary lives . . . Lot of hoodlums; I wouldn't let 'em touch me dorg if it was sick.'

"One of the strongest supporters of the teat theory had a private interview some days later with the specimens. He came away convinced. However, he had never before seen the inside of a kangaroo, though he had shot and skinned a great number!

"And so the battle of the Teat ended. Victory crowned the practical men. Patriotic Australians could not allow the foreigner within their shores to insinuate that the Australian kangaroo was less than it seemed. Secure behind a safe shield of ignorance they laughed in their beards at the vain theories of university 'perfessors' and all such cranks."

---

* from A MEDICAL BULLETIN vol. IX No. 1.

A BIOLOGICAL LASER

MICHAEL E. FEIN
and DIANE C. MILLER

One of the authors recently invested several years of his life in the development of a laser that ran on hot air,[1] only to find out that the job had been done earlier and far more effectively by a classified military-funded research program.[2] Despondent, the author turned to drugs and communism. As a result, we are able to report here the first achievement of population inversion by a biological system. This also appears to be the first recorded realization of coherent radiation from a population of completely incoherent radiators.

It will become apparent to the reader that this investigation required resources that could only have been provided by the People's Republic of China. The cooperation of the Chinese was most generous, but the delicate nature of diplomatic relations did require delaying the publication of these results until the present. If not for a hitherto-unpublicized side trip to Peking by a well-known American labor leader ostensibly enroute to North Vietnam, this publication might still be impossible.

The essential process utilized was the hyperactivation of luciferase by lysergic acid diethylamide. The experiment was performed in a large population of common fireflies,[3] which were placed on their heads by immersion in an aqueous solution of LSD-25 (.0001M), coactivated by dimethylsulfoxide (.001M). Since preliminary measurements had indicated that the inversion thus achieved is exceedingly weak, approximately 2×10^6 fireflies were required.[4]

The fireflies were aligned near the optic axis of a ten-thousand meter unstable resonator by stretching a fine wire between the mirror centers[5] and placing the fireflies on the wire. It can easily be shown that the cycloidal shape assumed by the stretched wire approximates very closely the normal to the constant-phase surfaces of the principal cavity mode, so that if the fireflies could be aligned with sufficient accuracy to the wire they would all radiate into the principal mode. The desired standard position of a firefly relative to the alignment wire is indicated in Figure 1.

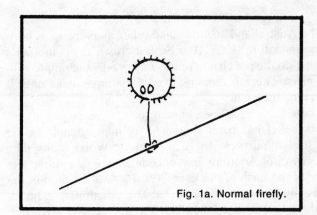

Fig. 1a. Normal firefly.

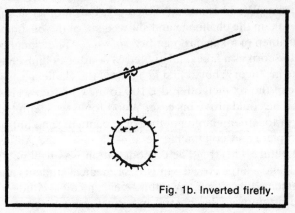

Fig. 1b. Inverted firefly.

The mean lifetime of fireflies in the inverted state was found to be approximately thirty minutes, after which they usually fell off the wire, so that it proved to be difficult to align all two million fireflies with sufficient speed. This difficulty was overcome by enlisting the cooperation of 20,000 members of the People's Institute for Glorious Anti-imperialist Technology. Each cooperating scientist was responsible for processing and aligning 100 fireflies. Several of the scientists who were insufficiently prepared in Mao's thought became themselves inverted, but after elimination of these side reactionaries it was possible to achieve adequate alignment.

The exact length and spectrum of the output pulse achieved is uncertain, as the spectrometer and photodetector were vaporized, but the well-cooked state of the fireflies makes it evident that the laser threshold was exceeded. Figure 2 is a reproduction of the far-field pattern sketched by one of our Chinese colleagues from a persistent retinal afterimage (the observer described this image as a "way-out picture", which nearly resulted in our misunderstanding his true meaning).

Fig. 2. Far-field pattern.

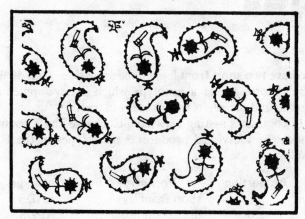

The authors are pleased to report that researchers in the People's Republic are just as concerned as are American scientists with the maximal use of natural resources. Appendix A is ample testimony to their success.

Finally, we wish to express gratitude to Peter and Margot van Schaick of Toledo, Ohio, who raised the fireflies in their basement.

Note added in proof: We are informed that Dr. Michael Craigie of the University of Illinois Department of Quantitative Electrosemantics has recently demonstrated a fruit fly laser, which required the alignment of a large number of white-eyed *drosophila*

upon the teeth of a brilliant orange zipper. Measurements taken with this apparatus are expected to answer the question: "If time flies like an arrow, what do banana flies like?"

APPENDIX A

Sweet Plum Firefly[6]

2000 pre-cooked fireflies
2 crushed cloves garlic
1-2 teaspoons ginger sherry
pinch each salt and MSG
2 shakes pepper
2 teaspoons beaten egg
2-3 tablespoons self-raising flour
deep peanut oil
For plum sauce:
   2 tablespoons canned plum sauce
   3-4 tablespoons hot chicken stock.
   1 tablespoon dark sugar crystals
   1 tablespoon hot water

Place the fireflies in a bowl. Add the garlic and then the sherry and seasonings. Work them well into the individual fireflies. Next add the beaten egg and work it in too. Discard the garlic. Dip the fireflies in the flour and shake off excess. Work the flour well into the fireflies.

Meanwhile have the oil heating to 375°F. Drop the fireflies into it and cook to a golden color, separating the fireflies during cooking if necessary. Drain, place on a heated serving dish, and hand the hot sauce separately.

To make the plum sauce:

Blend together the canned plum sauce and stock. Dissolve the sugar in the hot water and add it. Heat together, then rub through a sieve.

[1] Applied Physics Letters *14*, 337 (1 June 1969).
[2] E. T. Gerry, IEEE Spectrum, Nov. 1970, pg. 51.
[3] The rain
tries without avail
to quench your lamp
and the rushing wind
but makes it glow
the more.

I believe
that if you flew
up to the sky
you would twinkle   Li Po
as a star
beside the moon.

[4] After several unsuccessful attempts to count the population by conventional methods, a photometric estimation technique was developed.
[5] A wire of the required tensile strength was drawn from an alloy ingot left over from the drill-string development program of the Mohole Project. We regard this as an example of practical spinoff from basic research fully as important as the use of missile nosecone materials to make breakable cookpots.
[6] See H. Burke, *Chinese Cooking for Pleasure*, Paul Hamlyn Ltd., London, c. 1965, for a collection of related material.

PROF. LAWRENCE M. DILL
Dept. of Biological Sciences
Simon Fraser University
Burnaby, B.C, Canada V5A 1S6

Behavioral Genetics Of The Sidehill Gouger

The sidehill gouger (**Ascentus lateralis**), is a unique animal native to the mountainous areas of British Columbia. It possesses two short legs, on the same side of the body, which enable it to stand and walk about on hilly terrain. Thus the sidehill gouger is beautifully adapted to its particular ecological niche.

Within any one population of sidehill gougers two distinct morphological types appear. One of these has the short legs on the right side of the body and is thus able to walk around mountains in a clockwise direction only. The other type, having short left legs, can walk only in a counterclockwise fashion.

These two are not distinct species, since they often mate with one another. This is no mean feat since one or both of the animals, having approached from different directions, must back up to effect copulation. Such complex mating behaviour suggests that isolating mechanisms between the two morphotypes have not evolved.

Laboratory investigations were undertaken to elucidate the genetic basis of the dimorphism. Only a short summary of the results will be presented here, as a major paper will appear in a forthcoming issue of "Acts Artifacta."

The morphology and corresponding behaviour of the animals is controlled by two sets of co-dominant genes, each having two alleles. The first locus determines whether anterior or posterior legs are short: the homozygote AA has two short forelegs; the homozygote PP, two short hind legs; and the heterozygote AP, one fore and one hind leg short. The second locus determines on which side of the body these legs appear.

When two individuals of either parental stock mate with one another, all of the progeny produced are of the same genetic constitution as the parents. However, as many young are aborted during pregnancy as are delivered. Examination of these reveals one half of them to have 2 short back legs on the same side of the body and the others

to have two short front legs on the same side. Thus 50% of the zygotes are of a genotype which is developmentally lethal, and the adults therefore breed true.

In contrast a mating between a clockwise and a counterclockwise individual produces 3 phenotypes in the F_1 as follows:

Proportion	Phenotype	Genotype
.25	short front legs	AADS
.50	diagonally opposite short legs (rockers)	APDS
.25	short rear legs	PPDS

By means of breeding experiments the "rockers" produced an F_2 containing 4 lethals, 4 rockers, 2 clockwise parentals, 2 counterclockwise parentals, 2 with short front legs and 2 with short rear legs. This is regarded as the critical test of the hypothesis presented for the genetic constitution of the species.

The experiment could only be conducted after special shoes were fitted to these animals, as they otherwise have a tendency to fall over, either onto their faces (and suffocate), or onto their other ends (and starve to death). In the field they would quickly be selected against.

The behaviour of the individuals with short front legs or short rear legs is of considerable interest. The former are able to walk only uphill, eventually falling off the tops of the mountains to certain death on the rocks below; the latter walk only downhill, congregating in river bottoms. There, it can be easily demonstrated, they breed true, although producing 50% developmental lethals each generation. Some theoretical taxonomists suggest that they may be the evolutionary progenitors of the present day hyaenas, indicating perhaps a wider global distribution of the sidehill gouger in the past. Reduction of its range may have resulted from the very high genetic load (developmental lethality) carried by the population.

NEW UNIT OF LENGTH

KEMP BENNETT KOLB
The Haverford School, Haverford, Pa.

Just as the astronomers have on a cosmic scale a unit of length related to the time something special travels at its own speed, physics has long awaited[1] a corresponding unit in the microcosmos. The proposed unit is the BEARD-SECOND: the distance a standard beard grows in one second. Conveniently, there are nearly 10^{24} beard seconds in one light year, placing the new unit in the virus particle range.

To complete the definition a standard beard is defined as growing on a standard face at a rate of one beard-second (100 angstroms exactly) per second.

---

[1] Joe Slopnick, I Am Waiting for a new Unit in the Microcosmos, J. Thngs that Ought to be Dn. 1492, *2*, 69–94.

ON A NEW POWER SOURCE

F. G. HAWKSWORTH

In these days with ever-increasing demands for power, it may come as a surprise to learn that a completely untapped power source exists throughout the West. Why not harness the explosive power of the fruits of the ubiquitous dwarf mistletoes (*Arceuthobium* spp.) of western conifers? These parasites have long been known (2), but their potential importance as a power source has not been recognized. Each dwarf mistletoe fruit contains a single projectile-like seed (about 1/10 of an inch long) which at maturity is ejected at speeds of about 90 feet per second (4).

The following discussion shows the potential energy now being lost through wasteful seed dispersal in just one part of the West. For this paper I have chosen the power-poor Southwest (Arizona and New Mexico) for an example. Here it has been determined that ponderosa pine dwarf mistletoe occurs on 2.5×10^6 acres (1). Estimated seed production by this same mistletoe (3) averages about 25×10^4 seeds per acre. Thus approximately 6×10^{11} mistletoe seeds are produced annually just in the ponderosa pine type. Estimates of the force of the seeds based on their weight (2.7×10^{-3} grams) and velocity (2540 cm/sec.) indicate that each develops 8×10^{-8} horsepower. When we multiply this times the number of seeds produced we have 48×10^3 horsepower or (among friends) 50,000. Converted to more conventional terms this represents 67,000 kilowatts!

It should be kept in mind that this is the potential of only one part of the West. Vast additional sources exist in mistletoe-infected pine, fir, larch, and hemlock forests throughout the West.

It might be only fair to mention some slight difficulties in the potential development of this resource, but none of them need be considered insurmountable. The harnessing of the power of billions of tiny fruits scattered over millions of acres presents somewhat of a problem because the energy from an individual fruit may have to be harnessed during about 2×10^{-4} seconds when seed ejection occurs. Another minor handicap is that this power source would be available only during the seed dispersal period which lasts about 2 to 3 weeks. But with application of typical American ingenuity and know-how, a multi-billion dollar crash program for development of this resource into a year-around power source could be expected to produce spectacular results.

The harnessing of this power source would have many national advantages — 1, it would enable us to beat the Russians at another game because their mistletoe power resources are puny in the extreme compared with ours; 2, by directing the seed power to more useful purposes rather than (as nature intended) toward debilitating our forests, our trees' sense of well-being should be enhanced; and 3, it would negate the need for additional Colorado River dams and thus help "Save Grand Canyon".

Literature Cited:

1. Andrews, S. R. and Daniels, J. P. 1960
   A survey of dwarfmistletoes in Arizona and New Mexico. U.S. Forest Serv., Rocky Mtn. Station, Sta. Paper 49, 17p.
2. Gill, L. S. 1935
   Arceuthobium in the United States. Trans. Conn. Acad. Arts & Sci. 32: 111-245.
3. Hawksworth, F. G. 1965
   Life tables for two species of dwarfmistletoes. I. Seed dispersal, interception and movement. Forest Science 11: 142-151.
4. Hinds, T. E. and Hawksworth, F. G. 1965
   Seed dispersal velocity in four dwarfmistletoes. Science 148: 517-519.

The Rapidity of Female Mosquitoes' Gathering to Mate from a Distance of up to, or, in Some Cases, Beyond, Fifty Miles, as Affected by the Humming of Males at Frequencies of A440 as Opposed to A441

JAMES STITCH
Oxblood University
Pitchfork, Nevada

Social psychologists of small renown have displayed an intense interest in the effects of musical intonation upon females of the species *mosquito sexipediformis nastiensis* at the approach of the rainy mating season in Ecquador in recent years. The coming monsoon promises to be the dampest ecologists have seen in decades, and so these latter (ecologists) will probably accompany a series of ten jungle expeditions arranged by musicians to study the species. Psychiatrists are said to be planning to follow close behind to watch for any abnormal developments.

Purpose of Mating Hums

Naturally, mosquito hums are of different varieties and serve different functions. Insecto-musicologists have long taken an interest in such phenomena:

Why, as recently as last fall I was bitten by one, and upon consulting my tuning fork, I noted that it was humming at A447; with this knowledge in mind, I took a slightly higher-pitched tuning fork, namely B♭, and, taking that pitch a little to the flat side, namely B♭500, I was able with humming to set up such an unpleasant and harsh vibration when the next intruder came, also humm.ng, that it could not bear it, and flew away.[1]

Procedures

Investigators proceeded in this experiment to determine the relative rapidity of mosquitoes' gathering for mating purposes through comparing the responses of two groups, call them A440 and A441, to male hums of those pitches, by operating on the mosquitoes' inner ears (exclusively females underwent the operations), namely, the hammer, anvil, and the stirrup mechanisms, in such a way as to enable members of both groups to hear only one of those pitches or the other, exclusively. (Since the operations took a long time, some of the original subjects had died by the time investigators were ready to experiment. Reliability went down when females not having undergone the operation had to be substituted.) Portions of the inner ears removed were kept in cold storage. To assure that the more rapidly gathering group would not be doing so merely for reasons of sexual appetite, one ovary was tied off in each of the subjects to dampen that. This was done with #46 hemp, obtained from Sears and Roebuck.

Males then were gathered up, and for purposes of the experiment, the males were taken to a point exactly fifty miles "as the crow flies" from where the females, having newly recuperated from their operations, were waiting. The rainy season was very much in evidence as on the day of commencement of the research, it had been raining for a week and the jungle floor was teeming with fish. It is important to remember that mosquitoes fly the same way as crows.

At a certain appointed hour, males were allowed to begin initiating their mating hums for the benefit of the fifty-mile-away females. In order that no females would come that were not part of the experiment, those females intended for use in the experiment had one leg painted red, and any female without such an appendage was rejected as irrelevant.

Another difficulty in the project was, that it was found that males do not in their natural state ever hum the pitch A440 or A441 during the mating season. So males had, at great cost of time, to be given a laryngeal operation that involved removing the larynx, opening it, and cutting the vocal chords slightly for tuning purposes. The reason for this part of the project's taking so long can be clearly understood when it is known that even after the larynxes had been put back the mosquitoes were not allowed to hum for a period of two weeks, and those humming the wrong pitches had to be re-tuned.

It was thus near the end of the monsoon and the concomitant mating season by the time all things were in readiness, and most of the females had died or else got tired of waiting and gone off to lay their eggs any-

---

[1] H. L. Mencken, *Jungle Music.*

way. The remaining females, approximately ten in number, gathered in a ratio of six to four, flocking, in that order, to the A441 and the A440 male groups, respectively, One male, having flown out of the camp-site, was at a distance some few feet greater than fifty miles, and his mate, exhausted as all the rest, had to cover a consequently greater distance, accounting for the elongated and offset portion of the title of this article, originally intended to be shorter. This male was of the A441 test group, and since his mate was one of the type which, identified by antenna angle (this changed in connection with the females' ability to hear one pitch as opposed to the other, A440 or A441), seems to belong to the A440 mates section,

it cannot be determined whether this female approach-ed out of a desire aroused from hearing the particular male's hum, or whether she just bumped into him.

As has been stated, the greater proportion of mates came to the males humming the A441 pitch. From this it can be probably deduced that, A441 being a more erotic pitch, orchestras should tune to that when per-forming music of the Romantic period.

Those portions of the females' inner ears removed and placed under cold storage, rotted.

Since neither these particular females' ability to hear nor these males' ability to hum at those pitches audible to these females ever occurs in nature, the research value of the project was nil.

An Experimental Behavioral Psychology Application to Cancer Research

T. D. C. KUCH

Abstract. As part of the work of the Psychobiology Project, Aaron Burr Research Laboratories, Inc., fifty six-week old female mice (strain B6C3F1) were treated with dl-2-amino-4-(ethylthio)butyric acid, which has been reported to be carcinogenic. Two days later, an intensive course of operant conditioning was begun. At age 14 weeks, 19 of the animals had been sufficiently conditioned to record their own body weights by standing on a mechanized scale while si-multaneously pressing the operating lever to create a paper tape weight record. At this point the group was split into "slow-learners" (15 animals) and "fast-learners" (the 19 animals). The remaining animals, characterized as "dull-normal", were sacrificed. By age 29 weeks 12 of the slow-learners and 14 of the fast-learners had developed palpable mammary tum-ors. Both groups were then conditioned to inspect their own lesions, count the number of tumors, and record this number by pressing a button the appropriate num-ber of times with their noses. As expected, the slow-learners failed to perform satisfactorily. Of the fast-learners, five achieved better than 80% accuracy (one achieving a 100% rate), while the rest averaged 62% accuracy. All but the five best performing animals were then sacrificed. At age 42 weeks all animals pre-sented with scruffiness, mange, and large tumor masses. The one best performing animal was trained to perform necropsies and read the resultant slides. The present paper was written by that mouse before she, too, was sacrificed.

BOVINITY

WILLIAM F. JUD

Geological anomalies affect animal action. Cliffs, for example, make animals detour. Rivers make them swim. Subsurface structures align them. This latter fact permits geophysical evaluation of ore bodies.

A study has been initiated to determine alignment of cows and the diurnal variations in the intensity and polarity of this alignment. It was found that in the morning cows are generally aligned with their heads (+) toward the pasture, and in the evening just before sunset their tails (−) point in that direction. In addition, there is a definite drift and transport phenomenon in the direction of their (+) ends. Flow lines are sharpest in all cases along the path leading to the barn, and are randomly spread in the pasture proper. The flux causing this alignment strengthens considerably below 15°C during strong wind. The polar effect of wind is such that the cows are oriented with their (−) end toward the wind.

Bovinity flux was first recognized in the Missouri Ozarks. It is the custom there to graze stock over areas of underground mining. Since the original observations on diurnal alignment of cows were made in this locality, namely above ore bodies, it was desirable to verify this correlation in other localities.

Experiments performed in various geographic areas of known geologic structures with cows of different breeds showed an excellent correlation between the mining camp geology and bovine orientation, as shown in Figures 1 and 2.

In every case, cattle kept over anomalies were polarized at least twice daily. The conclusion drawn from this observation was that wherever cows align one should dig and would strike ore.

Bovinity rays vary as the inverse square of distance from source. Small changes due to topography, rock den-sity, and elevation are removed from bovinometric calculations through the Bouguer-Holstein correction. Field intensities are mapped in 0.00μ (milli-moo) units.

Since the development of the automated Airborne Bovinimeter the value of Bovinity Flux has increased considerably, especially for mapping sea cows that live over offshore oil and natural gas fields.

SUMMARY: A herd of cows in a field align themselves with each other over ore bodies (bovinity flux).

****

QUIPS

"Mouse is an animal, which when killed in sufficient numbers under carefully controlled condition, will produce a Ph.D. thesis."

*****

Looking at a molecular model of DNA a graduate student at Berkeley said: "This is my staircase to Ph.D."

*****

Fig. 1. Sectional view of Cows in Spherical Alignment in Bovinity Field emanating from buried Ore Body.

Fig. 2. Cows in Linear Alignment in Bovinity Field radiating from recently Active Fault.

Some

improbable

investigations

into

FOOD

AND

NUTRITION

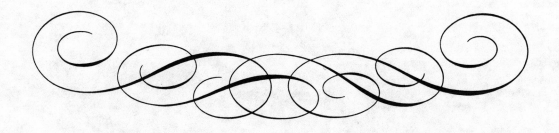

HOW TO EAT AND
LOSE WEIGHT

A new solution to an old problem

The problem of energy equilibrium in the human body has received a great deal of attention in the USA[1]. Many methods have been advocated to reduce the caloric value of the food without affecting its taste or the appetite of the consumer. Some pharmaceutical houses have even expanded by wise investment of the monetary equivalent of the weight theoretically lost by their customers.

The various methods advocated involve either a drastic reduction in the quantity of the food ingested, use of drugs that affect the appetite, or increase in the amount of physical exercise. The first method leaves the patient permanently hungry, the second makes him sub-human by dulling his senses, and the third defeats its own purpose by increasing the appetite and leading to a vicious circle.

In this communication we propose a new method of reducing, without changing the quantity of the food ingested. The method is based on the principle that the caloric value of the food also depends on its temperature. For each degree of temperature of the food below the temperature of the human body, the body has to supply heat (energy) to raise the temperature of the food to that of the body.

When food is frozen, heat of thawing has to be supplied to it at the rate of 80 calories/gm of water contained in the food in addition to 1 calorie/gm for each degree centigrade of temperature rise. One can easily see that a glass of frozen milk (200 gms) at the temperature of deep freeze, i.e. −20° C, needs 200 × 80 calories for thawing and 57 × 200 calories for heating up to 37° C (98° F), i.e.

$$16,000 + 11,400 = 27,400 \text{ calories or } 27.4 \text{ Cal.}$$

The caloric value of a glass of whole milk is 138 Cal and of skim milk only 74 Cal.[2], thus (27.4 × 100)/74 = 34% of caloric milk energy is lost for its heating. By having the milk diluted in the ratio of 1:2, 68% of the energy would be lost on consuming the same amount of milk.

Similarly one can calculate that consumption of a precooked frozen steak calls for an expenditure of at least 1/3 of its caloric value on the thawing and heating up. If one adds to this the amount of energy supplied as heat by the body and the mechanical energy required to crush the food with the jaws, the loss of the caloric value of the food becomes even greater.

For those individuals who do not care to crush their food with their teeth, or those who use valuable and fragile plates, and finally for those who have lost their teeth and did not replace them, one can advise the use of homogenized frozen food in form of popsicles which would be sucked instead of chewed.

The suggestion of some research workers (personal communication) to achieve an additional loss of energy by consuming the food frozen in liquid helium or nitrogen is not considered practical, because of the temporary rarity and high cost of these two elements in their liquid form. With the increased use of liquid oxygen, however (rocket fuels, etc.) one may hope to have it supplied in a domesticated and easily handled form in the near future.

===============

---

[1] E. Haveman: The wasteful, phony crash dieting craze, Life, 1959, *46*, 102–114.

[2] H. C. Sherman: *Essentials of Nutrition,* Macmillan, N.Y. 1945, page 377.

On the Purchase of Meat and Fruit

By PIROCOLE RASHCALF

These are troubled times. A conspiracy exists in this nation between the paper converter and meat packing industries. Through the most unstinting casual empiricism this author was able to discover that enormous costs are being imposed upon the American housewife. Did you know that the housewife who shops for meat pays for a heavy cardboard tray and cellopane wrapper at meat prices? In the green grocer department, the trays that hold fruits and vegetables are paid for at fruit and vegetable prices! The paper on the meat is the same as that used on the vegetables, and so the housewife is being cheated by paying meat paper prices when she buys vegetables instead of vegetable paper prices.

We have contrived a clever test to expose this conspiracy. We went out and bought some minute steaks, ham hocks, best chanks, tomatoes, lemons, and such and made observations on cardboard tray size, tray weight, price of the item per pound and color of tray. In fact, the trays differ as between meats and vegetables only in terms of the tray color. Meat trays are white. Non-meat trays are green and purple. In doing our data search and collection, we noticed this difference in color almost immediately.

We cast about for a method to test our hypothesis and decided to fit the following linear econometric model:

$$Y = a_0 + a_1X_1 + a_2X_2 + a_3X_3 + a_4X_4 + a_5X_5 + e,$$

where,

Y = weight of cardboard container in ounces;
X_1 = size identification of tray;
X_2 = total weight of the purchase in lbs.;
X_3 = a dummy variable where 1 = a fruit tray, 0 = a meat tray;
X_4 = total cost of item in cents;
X_5 = price per pound of item in cents;
e = an error term.

The results were

$$Y = .35 + .0016X_1 + .00023X_2$$
$$(.24) \quad (.0009) \quad (.00123)$$
$$+ .19X_3 + .0026X_4 - .0017X_5$$
$$(.10) \quad (.0020) \quad (.0036)$$

$R^2 = .79$ F- Ratio $= 11.5$ SSE $= 11.01$ N $= 15$

Two things stand out from these results. First, the model is hopelessly misspecified. Second, further research needs to be done. But we are not dismayed.

We find, for instance, that a fruit tray weighs on net 1/5 oz. more than a meat tray, yet for each increase of one cent in price per pound of item purchased, the weight of the tray increases .0026 ozs. There is no doubt in our mind that the average weight of the meat item is greater than that of the fruit item. Thus, starting with the fact that the fruit tray already weighs more than the meat tray, and recognizing that as the price of the item increases, people pay more for fruit trays than meat trays. This can be verified for it is a fact that while we bought two pounds of apples, we bought only .85 lbs of cube steak.

Give nthis incontrovertable proof, how can such a scandal be perpetuated? Simply by the old Madison Avenue trick of differentiating the product by selling meat in plain white trays while vending fruit and vegetables in trays of mind-boggling green and purple. What do you think of that?

Scientific research isn't hard, you know, if you put your mind to it.

FINE STRUCTURAL STUDIES OF COMMON MEAT & DAIRY PRODUCT USING THE ELECTRON MICROSCOPE I. LIVERWURST*

EARNEST PEDANT, Ph.D.**
Department of Ultrastructural Verification
Tenure Institute for the Implementation of Scientific Spinoff

ABSTRACT

This preliminary report on the significant ultrastructural parameters of liverwurst reveals several new findings. Further studies promise an in-depth understanding of the various organelles unique to this food product. The implications of this study have been discussed.

INTRODUCTION

For a number of years, man has been interested in meat and dairy products, partly for their gastronomic, caloric, or esthetic appeal (Child, et al., '67), but more importantly because of their enormous ultrastructural interest. Despite the pioneering work of Lasagnette, et al., ('38), little fine structural work has been done on the more common food products, such as hot dogs, creamed broccoli, potato pancakes, or for that matter, galantine de coq d'Inde.

Computerized search by means of the SCHLUCK (Systematic Compendium of Hallucinogens, Liquors, and Universal Culinary Knowledge) program has revealed that the significant ultrastructural parameters of liverwurst are not known, a fact that has encouraged us to initiate this in-depth investigation. We anticipate that this preliminary report of tentative conclusions will be followed by a definitive treatise in 8 parts. We hope that the study fills a much-needed gap in the field.

A preliminary survey of this work has been presented at the 5th Symposium of the Society for the Consumption of Food (Jan.-March, 1964, Kitzbűhel, Austria).

MATERIALS AND METHODS

Moderately fresh liverwurst ($1.78 per kg) was harvested at a local meat market. The tissue was fixed at −3.2 C in modified Millonsky-Karnovik ('59) solution modified by the addition of 0.038 M gadolinium tetrafluoride and 3 drops per gallon of 0-(2-biphenylyl) dichlorothiophosphate. Tissue appears to be well fixed after brief exposure to fixative vapors or 2 months immersion with constant agitation. Perfusion fixation attempts have been impeded by the discontinuous nature of the vascular bed in liverwurst.

Dehydration was carried out through 38%, 52%, 73% and pure spirits of vitriol, the temperature of the solutions depending on local meteorological conditions. The closely controlled embedding process involved the use of water soluble, cross-linked octamethyl-2-cyanoacrylate in a humid atmosphere.

Thin and thick sections were microtomed in a modified instrument (Sears Roebuck, X11H47566) with a 7 mm boron hydride knife(*) or with glass knives, made from select 20x20 cm plates of cured, Belgian greenish-yellow float glass dropped on the floor. Thick sections were stained routinely with Fleck's ('71) quadrichrome-Kernechtrot in 1% Freund's adjuvant, thin sections with Amiable and Koggeburg's ('63) ruthenium orange or with fuming 15% potassium permanganate.

Electron microscopy was carried out with an Ultroscope EM-104F equipped with a von Heidefelter liquid helium II cryogenic specimen decontaminator. Spectroscopic emulsion (Cat. No. 376-a) on 3 1/4 x 7 19/32 inch plates was employed and developed with krypton burst agitation, washed in deionized water and dried in an anaerobic environment. Electron micrographs were printed with a Dust enlarger equipped

* Generously supported by Grants CS-19,642, GO-OF-0731 and CAS-H-3, 14159 from the National Food and Drink Administration.

** I wish to acknowledge the valuable assistance of 17 postdoctoral fellows, without whom this study would not have been possible. Opinions expressed in this paper are not necessarily those of the author or his collaborators.

(*) Our supplier of boron hydride knives has now perfected the resharpening techniques; we routinely receive newly honed knives in 24-48 months.

with planapochromatic objectives. Double reversal mats for contrast control, in addition to retouching, toning, and air-brushing maximized the information content of the micrographs. Throughout all procedures, the team of technicians followed the rules set forth by Crichton (1969) to minimize contamination.

It is interesting to note that complete serial sections from a thick slice of liverwurst were subjected to computer assisted analysis for adequate statistical sampling. For the present paper, no less than 17 million electron micrographs were evaluated.

RESULTS

Figure 1 illustrates the salient parameters of a representative liverwurst cell. The pleomorphically configured surface membrane is covered by a continuous *linea grisea*, also known as Susumu fluff. Use of a 1.3 A attachment to the microscope (迷信光学社 Co., Ltd., Chiisana Inaka-Machi, Japan) allows certain areas of this layer to be resolved into 10 *sublineae griseae* (Fig. 1). The grumose cytoplasm is the site of a high to moderate level of metabolite transferase activity, as determined by granules of ultimate reaction deposits. This finding is in striking contrast to the absence of such reactivity in hot dog and hamburger cells. Salciciform mitochondria are scattered in the cytoplasm, an observation that may be suggestive of possible functional significance. Intertesselated vermiculations of the granulated endoplasmatic reticulum are in apparent continuity with MVB's, MCG's, SSC's and cockroach fragments in the extracellular space. Of enormous interest are the innumerable numbers of gray, dense, and black bodies in addition to electrontransparent bodies, the latter easily mistaken for holes. Glycogen, when present, is significantly reactive with the PAS test. The nuclear envelope appears extremely circular in outline, particularly when it is carefully rotation printed (N = 72). Similar technical approaches show the nuclear pores to be tetradecahedral in symmetry and to have 2 asymmetric diaphragms kept extended by super-coiled microtubules. The nucleoplasm abounds with heterochromatin, euchromatin, sex chromatin, and hematoxylin.

DISCUSSION

Full evaluation of these results can be expected in future publications pending the completion of computer generated liverwurst model systems, but a few tentative possibilities of hypothetical nature can be explored. It is interesting to note that liverwurst lacks formyltetrahydropteroylglutamic acid synthetase activity, an enzyme that is abundant in the musculus retractor penis of the aardvaark. The possible similarity of opaque bodies to dense bodies is supported by the observation, first made in this study (unpublished observation by the author and his young son), that neither of these

structures shows a resemblance to MVBs, IPSPs, or SSCs. The function of the remarkable subdivisions of the *linea grisea* is unknown at present and requires further study by TLC and electron spin resonance spectroscopy. We deem it appropriate to rename these layers the "strata grisea" in keeping with their importance. Grumosities and vernate congeries in the cytoplasm suggest, of course, a similarity to structures commonly encountered in thin sections of ultra-centrifuged pea soup. On the basis of these observations we venture to suggest that the liverwurst cell is not engaged in the formation of $\Delta 4$-androsten-11β -o1-3, 17 dione.

Our expanding program of ultrastructural and histochemical studies is aimed at establishing the differential characteristics between liverwurst and Bratwurst. Extensive serial sectioning and neutron activation analysis should delineate the role that is played by insect parts and rodent hairs in the structural integrity of liverwurst. The implications of these studies in the light of consumer dissatisfaction are obvious to the discerning reader.

LITERATURE CITED

Amiable, J. and R. Koggeburg 1963 Chemical fixatives and stains for higher ungulates. Annals of the Association of Hog and Guernsey Farmers 203, 1029-1101

Child, J., L. Bertholle, and S. Beck 1967 Mastering the Art of French Cooking. Alfred A. Knopf, New York. pp. 1-716

Crichton, M. 1969 The Andromeda Strain. Alfred A. Knopf, New York. pp. 1-295

Fleck, C.P.E. 1971 Ein Anwendungsbeitrag für eine neue Ultramikrotomschnittschnellanfärbemethode u.s.w. Zeitschrift für Lebensmittel-Aufnahme und -Abfuhr. Ergänzungsband 3, Lieferung 17, 1-132

Lasagnette, Manicotti and Ruote 1938 Physiology and Biochemistry of Pasta as a Food. IN: Proceedings of the VI th International Congress of Chefs, Headwaiters and Gluttons, Florence, Italy.

Millonsky, M. and G. Karnovik 1959 Handbook of Pickle Technology. Polychrome Press, Coolidge Corner, Massachusetts. pp. 1-2

Speicheldrüsen, F. W. von 1901 Eine elektronenmikroskopische Studie der Muskelnekrose nach der Mastikation. Archiv für Kolonialwarenforschung (Uralte Folge) XXXVII, 1-722

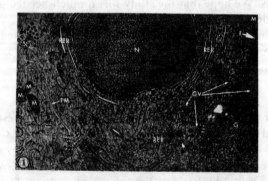

FIGURE 1

Medium-power electron micrograph of a representative liverwurst cel. Note nucleus (N) filled with chromatin. The white line (CH) is probably curly hair. Mitochondria (M), Golgi cisternae (G) and vesicles (GV), an endoplasmic reticulum (Er) form a conspicuous part of the liverwurs cytoplasm. Note interesting filament (f). The obvious periodicities (P) a complex junction, or sublineae griseae, are indicated by arrows.
X17,876.5

Plate No. F-23-459-A388

PICKLES and HUMBUG

(A bit of comparative logic)

Pickles will kill you! Every pickle you eat brings you nearer to death. Amazingly, "the thinking man" has failed to grasp the terrifying significance of the term "in a pickle." Although leading horticulturists have long known that *Cucumis sativus* possesses indehiscent pepo, the pickle industry continues to expand.

Pickles are associated with all the major diseases of the body. Eating them breeds wars and Communism. They can be related to most airline tragedies. Auto accidents are caused by pickles. There exists a positive relationship between crime waves and consumption of this fruit of the curcubit family. For example:

1. Nearly all sick people have eaten pickles. The effects are obviously cumulative.
2. 99.9% of all people who die from cancer have eaten pickles.
3. 100% of all soldiers have eaten pickles.
4. 96.8% of all Red sympathizers have eaten pickles.
5. 99.7% of the people involved in air and auto accidents ate pickles within 14 days preceding the accident.
6. 93.1% of juvenile delinquents come from homes where pickles are served frequently.

Evidence points to the long term effects of pickle-eating:

Of the people born in 1839 who later dined on pickles, there has been a 100% mortality.

All pickle eaters born between 1869 and 1879 have wrinkled skin, have lost most of their teeth, have brittle bones and failing eyesight – if the ills of eating pickles have not already caused their death.

Even more convincing is the report of a noted team of medical specialists: rats force-fed with 20 pounds of pickles per day for 30 days developed bulging abdomens. The appetites for *wholesome food* were destroyed.

The only way to avoid the deleterious effects of pickle eating is to change the eating habits. Eat orchid petal soup. Practically no one has any problems from eating orchid petal soup.

Red blood cells
from lemming kidney
x 17,000

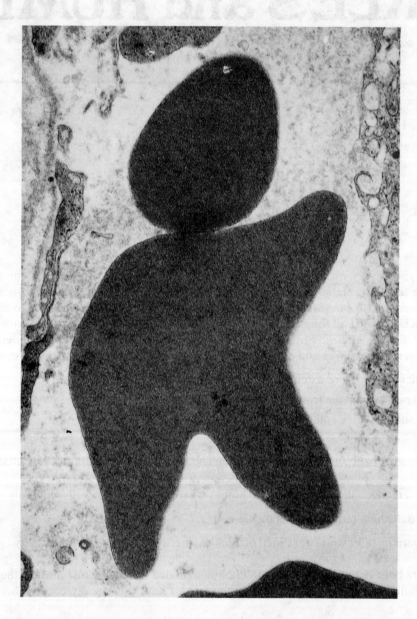

A Standardized Laboratory Preparation of Speiseeis

JAMES W. HILL
Parkinson Laboratory
Southern Illinois University
Carbondale, Illinois
and
ERIC E. PATTERSON
Department of Chemistry
Kansas State University
Manhattan, Kansas

Because of the widely varied nature of the many procedures which have been published in a number of widely varied sources, and the wide variations of those procedures in common use for the preparation of this substance, the authors undertook this investigation to devise a standardized procedure incorporating the better features of the many methods available to the experimentor, so as to be able to consistently get a good product in a high yield.

EXPERIMENTAL

Into a suitable 5 l. container are added ten unfertilized ova of the *Gallus domesticus* animal, weighing in the range 56.7-63.8g. (USDA grade A-large); 500 g. *a*-D-gluco-pyranosyl-*B*-D-fructofuranoside, commercial grade; 500 ml. of the mammary secretion of *Bos taurus;* 235 ml. of a commercial preparation known as 'light cream'; and 20 ml. of a 2.5% ethanolic extraction of the fruit of *Vanilla planifolia*. These substances are blended into a homogeneous mess by vigorous stirring for two minutes, then 1400 ml. more *Bos* secretion is added with constant stirring.

The resulting mixture is poured into a 3.8 l. 'white Mountain' brand rotary hand-powered recrystallizer, and cooled with a salt-ice mixture to maintain a cooling bath of about −15° C. The 'freezer' is rotated at a speed of 1.25 Herz for about 15 min. or until the mixture becomes difficult to stir. The inner parts of the crystallizer are removed from the inner can, and the contents of the can allowed to continue freezing at the maintained temperature of −15° C. for at least 1 hour.

Yield is approximately 3.7 l., m.p. about −5° C. (varies between 90 and 105% of theory, depending upon the appetite of the worker).

SUMMARY

A standard method of making home-made ice cream is here presented using the usual ingredients of eggs, sugar, milk, cream, and flavoring. The amounts given here make 1 gallon. If other flavors are desired, substitutions may be made for the vanilla; two flavors found compatable with this procedure are rum and blackberry.

ACKNOWLEDGEMENTS

The authors gratefully acknowledge the assistance given them by the Petroleum Research Fund of the American Chemical Society in the form of research fellowships which allowed the authors to undertake the work leading to this nonsense. We also wish to acknowledge the generous criticisms offered by the other workers in the Department of Alchemy (a subdivision of the S.I.U. Department of Chemistry) while helping dispose of the products of this experimentation.

TRANSLATION

The article by Dr. M. H. Levin in the March 14 Almanac contains some rather technical language, e.g. "A feature of the urban ecosystem is the conspicuous transportation network . . . portions of this vital circulatory system may function sluggishly at times. Fossil fuel burners bearing the human component to their places of employment within the city may reduce the speed at which fuels, manufactured products and services are imported into the urban ecosystem." In the interest of improved interdisciplinary communication, which the University so fervently desires, I submit a translation of the above:

"Automobiles carrying people to work may get in the way of trucks."

Further insights into the functioning of the urban ecosystem are eagerly awaited.

—*Michael Cohen*, Associate Professor of Physics

R. C. Baker, J. M. Darfler and M. C. Bourne
THE EFFECT OF LEVEL OF SKIN ON THE QUALITY OF CHICKEN FRANKFURTERS
Poultry Sci., 1968, 47, 1989.

* * *

M. R. Abeyaraten, W. A. Aherne and J. E. S. Scott
THE VANISHING TESTIS
Lancet 1969, Oct. 18, 822–824.

"Cabral (1964)[1] is said to have been the first to describe bilateral absence of the testis, ironically in the cadaver of a man who had been hanged for rape."

* * *

R. L. Berg, W. Dagget, J. Madeen and L. Diens
THE ORIGIN OF PPLO FOUND IN RECTAL CULTURES.
Ann. N.Y. Acad. Sci., 1960, 79, 635.

The authors report (among others) that 3 out of 14 rectal swabs of "14 male volunteers who had recently engaged in unusual sexual practices" rendered PPLO on culture.

The authors state: "The mouth cannot be the origin of rectal strains for oral strains have morphologic differences different from rectal strains."

* * *

R. A. Wiseman and I. W. I. Lovel
HUMAN INFECTION WITH ADULT *TOXOCARA CATI*
Brit. Med. J. 1969, 3,454 (23 Aug.)

Commenting upon a case of an intestinal infection of a 14-month English boy who vomited 3 nematodes, the authors quote Sprent (Austral. Vet. J. 1958, 34, 161) as follows:

"The subject was a woman who habitually ate earth from the graves of priests, and as a result of her unusual eating habits frequently vomited beetles, suggesting that human infection may possibly result from the accidental ingestion of beetles, cockroaches, or other intermediate hosts."

* * *

J. V. Bradley
OPTIMUM KNOB DIAMETER
Human Factors 1969, 11, 353–360.

From abstract:
"Reach time was independent of frictional resistance, but increased with decreasing diameter at diameters smaller than 1½ in."

---

[1] Hepburn, B. H., J. Urol., 1949, 62, 65.

Hunger in America: A Research Proposal

CHARLES L. McGEHEE
Central Washington State College

In recent years much attention has been given to the phenomenon of lack of food among certain segments of the population in the United States. It has been observed that certain[2] immature members of the population, as well as some mature, have occasion to be compelled to pursue their routine tasks in a state of food deprivation, a state which is systematically different from that of certain other members of the population. Moreover, correlative to this state of food deprivation, varying degrees of learning ability[3] as well as motivational level[4] have been observed.

To the everlasting discredit to social science this situation has been seen as a "social problem" and social scientists are to be found becoming increasingly more active in, of all things, trying to change this, the natural order of things.[5] In doing so, they are ignoring the fact that this situation constitutes a *natural laboratory* for the study of learning processes which here-to-ore could only be carried out in a laboratory[6] with animals or voluntary human subjects — at best undesirable and unreliable situations. They are, in other words, missing a magnificent opportunity to further social psychological knowledge of human behavior.

It is, of course, well known that food is a very basic reinforcer, one which does not have to be learned in the usual sense. Subject behavior is quite easily modified through the systematic control of reinforcement in the form of food. Moreover, subjects learn best when they are not satiated.[7] Pigeons, for example, learn best when they are at 80% of normal body weight. Although M and M[8] research with human subjects in the laboratory indicates that the same may hold true for humans, we still do not know if humans will respond in the same way when placed in their natural habitat with the aversiveness of genuine food deprivation.

Large urban areas seem, without exception, to have succeeded for us in isolating prime food-deprived subjects into certain educational institutions,[9] and, as mentioned these subjects have been observed to have a lower response rate, experience more rapid extinction of learned patterns, and exhibit greater avoidance behavior by escaping the environment than do non-food-deprived subjects in similarly isolated educational institutions.

We wish, then, to propose the following: since the subjects report to the educational environment in a state of food deprivation which normally runs from 15-24 hours without food (in some cases longer) at best, or at the worst having had a supplemental feeding of gravy or syrup immediately preceding their training schedule, we as social psychologists can use this state to induce and experimentally study the modification of behavior. That is to say, we can make reduction of the state of food deprivation contingent upon the successful performance of programmed tasks in a given learning situation.[10] The extent to which social psychological knowledge will be incremented defies the imagination!

Funding such a project should be no problem. The C.I.A., which has had considerable experience in operant conditioning utilizing food as a reinforcer in foreign countries, has expressed enthusiasm[11] and is already establishing a private philanthropic foundation for the purpose. The Department of Defense also will likely respond positively, as it has consistently furthered the advancement of pure science.[12]

To those critics from the "humanitarian" school who would question the ethics of pure science, may we say that we did not create the situation of food deprivation.[13] It behooves us as scientists, however, to take advantage of every opportunity to further knowledge, permitting the "chips" to fall where they may. History, after all, will be our judge. But, as a matter of fact, we are, in our own small way helping to alleviate the situation by providing food to those who would not otherwise get it[14] — provided they do as we tell them.[15]

[1] From the film of the same name. No pun intended.
[2] The referent should be clear to the reader. Cf. Wallace's article "Bussing and Law and Order: Concepts of Infinite Value." *Rgt. Wng. Rev.*, V.1, 1968.
[3] For discussion of this and related concepts see "Scientific Concepts and What Any WASP Knows Anyway. Part I: The Just Plain Dumb." *Annals KKK*, undated.
[4] *Ibid*, "Part II: Shiftless Bums".
[5] Adherents to this so-called "humanitarian" school of thought would do well to read Ptolemy's epic pronouncment *Things Are The Way They Are: Love It Or Leave It*, Alexandria: Geocentric Publishers, 2nd century, A.D.
[6] The value of the natural laboratory has not been given its proper due. A few dedicated persons have recognized its value, however. See H. Himmler, *Der Konzentrationslager als Natürlabor für wissenschaftliche Forschung*, Ausch-

witz und Dachau: Verlag der Gefangenschaft, 1944.
[7] This perhaps accounts for the fact that leaders in the 1968 Chicago tests of Daley's theory of social control did *not* learn any more from the Russian Revolution than they did.
[8] Melts in mouth, not in hand. Makes for very neat research.
[9] Certain cognitive theories of learning may have screwed up things for us here. See Wallace, *op. cit.*
[10] No read, no eat! Since lack of food is often accompanied by lack of clothing, the project could also be expanded to use shoes and overcoats (particularly when it is snowing) as reinforcers.
[11] The comment was "Let's get to them before the Reds do!" Source asked to remain anonymous.
[12] For example, see the following DOD reports: "Botulism: Boon to Mankind," "Poverty and its Uses," and "Project Camelot: Milestone in the Unification of Science and Ideology."
[13] "For the poor will never cease out of the land. . . ." Deut. 15:11 "For you always have the poor with you." Matt. 26:11
[14] This is true humanitarianism in the tradition of the Romans who found the plebians could not get along without the Roman elite.
[15] The results of this proposed study will be in every sense irreproducible. It is predicted that subject (and subject parent) interaction will increase in frequency and intensity over time to the point the experimenter will be subjected to extinction along the lines proposed by Marx.

NUTRITIONAL VALUE OF SNAKE POISON

In some of the central African countries there exists a disease of children, kwashiorkor. This disease has been clearly related to malnutrition due to lack of some proteins in the diet. Quite independently, these countries abound in various poisonous snakes which often contribute to a decrease in the population numbers.

Snake poison has been shown to consist of the same proteins as milk, and has therefore the same nutritional value.

Experimentally a few thousands of snakes were "milked" of their poison according to methods developed in Butantan (Brazil). The poison was mixed with suitable condiments to make it palatable and it was fed to 400 Falashi women. As controls milk mixed with the same condiments was used and fed to the same women at a different time period.

The nutritional value of the poison was judged from the reports of husbands. Generally no difference was observed in woman treated with poison or with milk, with the exception of a few lethal cases which were not taken in account in the final statistical evaluation.

In about 15% of cases the husbands reported, however, that their spouses became very venomous. A strict examination of these cases revealed that there was no difference in the degree of venomousness of these women when they were fed either poison or milk.

The proof of the hypothesis that snake poison has a nutritional value equal to that of milk rests mainly on the fact that it is completely unrelated to any data, thus eliminating any possibility of an experimental error.

R. VIDEO,
H. E. S. KIND
Biochemical Research Station
Ness-Beilin-Zionoson

A FRIGHTFUL DREAM

FERENC MOLNAR

I invented ordinary breakfast coffee, coffee with milk. I was the only person in the whole world who breakfasted on that beverage. I was convinced that if mankind should come to know my discovery, it would become the world's most popular breakfast drink, and hundreds of millions of people would drink it, even several times a day. So I rushed to a great bank that financed various industrial enterprises, and after many difficulties was admitted to see the top boss. When I told him I had discovered a drink for which I prophesied universal popularity, the bank president asked me to explain my discovery. I had to be brief, so I confined myself to saying:

"You hire some people, and ship them to the other side of the globe, where there is a certain kind of bush in each of whose berries are two bean-like seeds. When the berries are ripe, your people gather the beans, put them into an iron vessel, and light a fire under the vessel; they heat the vessel slowly, but not hot enough to burn the beans, only to a degree that will turn them black and make them spread a pungent burning stench."

The president was already eyeing me suspiciously.

"Then," I went on, "you grind these half scorched seeds to powder. But we don't eat the powder, nor a decoction of it, but we construct a vessel in two parts, the lower of which contains boiling water. The steam from this water rises through the black, granular powder, which rests on a sort of sieve above the water; this causes the powder to exude a blackish liquid, which is collected in a separate vessel, and the bitter sour taste of which is unpalatable to most people."

By now the president was looking at me with very wide-open eyes.

"Then," I went on, "we set out to find a certain mammal; for our purposes we require the female. From this female we remove in an artificial manner, by a sort of tor-ture, the white liquid with which it ordinarily feeds its newborn young. This liquid we put on the fire, warm it to the boiling point, then cool it off, but not entirely – only to the point where it will not burn the human mouth. The liquid obtained from the animal and thus prepared is mixed with the black liquid from the plants."

"Ugh," said the president.

"Then," I continued, "in order to make this mixture palatable we go out into a field and grow a certain plant called a beet, which has a very fat root. For our purpose, however, we take not the leaves, flowers or fruit, but strangely enough the root. When the root has reached the desirable size, we pull it out of the ground, slice it and soak it in big kettles of water until this water has turned them into a sweet pulp. Then we throw away the root. The dirty juice thus obtained is then distilled until all the water is driven off, and the evaporating mixture leaves only dirt colored crystals. These crystals we crush, then by a special process bleach them white, and make a solid mass out of them. The solid we cut into little cubes, of which we drop two or three into the previously mentioned vegetable-animal mixture, wait until they dissolve, and then we drink the whole business."

"Dreadful," said the president. He rang. His secretary entered. "Call up the lunatic asylum at once," he said, pointing to me.

"I know," I said, as they were putting me into straight-jacket, "that an inventor must suffer and struggle much in discovering the world's most popular drink, in getting it known and accepted, and in trying to convince bank presidents that this preposterous concoction will one day be popular, nay perfectly commonplace."

Reprinted from *Companion in Exile* (Allen & Co).

113

Irreproducible
forays
into the
intriguing
mystery
of
SEX

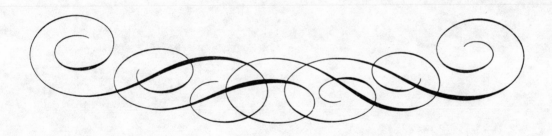

Unusual Positions for Coupling Reactions Between Activated Species......

P. PING TOM

Contribution #69, Essex Laboratory,
Cambridge, Mass.

Until recently, many of the unusual coupling reactions were assumed to occur only in the dark which made observation of the progress of the reaction difficult. In fact the reaction was usually surmised from the end product. In recent years however, more of these reactions have been observed to occur in the light as well, and several have been well documented[1].

The conditions necessary to promote these reactions are quite important. Many catalysts have been previously reported to facilitate the coupling[2]. It has been our experience that these materials actually act more as initiators than as catalysts since they are usually consumed prior to the commencement of the reaction. Of the many initiators tried in this laboratory, the most successful has been aqueous ethanol. A recent report indicates that [9]-3, 4 trans-tetrahydrocannabinol may be equally effective[3]. Initiator concentration is usually quite low, on the order of 2.5×10^{-4} ethanol based upon the weight of the reactants. Leary[3] indicates that the concentration for his initiator is considerably less. The reaction will proceed over a wide temperature range but optimum results are obtained at c.a. 22°C. If one or both of the reactants are hot prior to admixing, the reaction time is considerably shortened. Likewise if either of them are very cold, no reaction will occur. Chilling of the initiator however, appears to have no delfterious effect*. The reaction is usually carried out on a solid support. An inert or slightly reactive substrate is preferred. An overly reactive substrate hinders the progress of the reaction. Some investigators have reported using an aqueous medium[4]. Although interesting, this method is often unsuccessful due to the greater difficulty of the experiment.

The choice of the reactant species is quite important. Most oppositely charged materials, even when activated by initiator, prefer to couple in the usual position. This is shown in Figure One -a(iota-delta bond). If two similarly charged molecules can be induced to react, they will as expected adopt one of the unusual coupling positions to effect charge separation. These involve iota-omega (backside attack), iota-omicron and bis iota-omicron bonds as shown in Figure One-b. Similar coupling positions are found with oppositely charged reactants, with of course more long-term stability due to the electrostatic attraction. It is these reactions, involving iota-omega', iota-omicron', delta-omicron, and the most stable, iota-omicron' + delta omicron (see Figure One-c) which are now under intensive study both in this country and in France.

Reactants

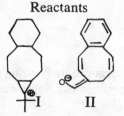

Figure one

(a)   ⟨I-△ bond⟩

(b)   I-Ω bond   bis I-0 bond

(c)   I-O′ & O-△ bond   I-O bond

Note added in proof: By the time this paper has reached publication, (9 months) some end products of the reaction forming iota-delta bond have been observed. Other reactions had no end products.

[1] Masters & Johnson, Acta Sexualus, *1*, 4-948 (1969).
[2] P. donJuan, Compend. Aphrod., Vol. 1-23, Madrid (1758).
[3] T. Leary, J. Exper. Psycho., *14*, 8 (1968).
* Some unpublished data show, however, that the reaction may be seriously hindered by chilling.
[4] C. Poseidon, J. Amo. Aqua. C6, 81 (1949).

FOOD and SEX: An Ancient Problem Recently Visited...

BEN Z. DREAN *
Texas Christian Institute of the
Institutionalized

A total of 23 subjects participated in a social psychological experiment. All subjects were about half male and half female. Each of two groups were composed of 11 ½ subjects. The first group was aked to do various things. The second group, the control, was aked if they would please not do anything. The results lend support to the hypothesis (p= .05) that as far as sex is concerned doing something is often better than nothing doing.

Down through the years various psychologists studying sex have asked various subjects to do various things in various experiments. Interestingly enough they have gotten various results which they have interpreted in various ways for various reasons. For instance we might look at the results of Round and Ribeye (1937). Using bulls and cows with steers as a control, they found their results were, indeed, inconsistent with T-Bone and Sirloin (1967) who tried a different approach 40 years later for higher stakes. To account for these discrepant results Swiss (1954) devised an experimentum crucis that was not only trivial but infeasible as well. His results were similar.

Heartburn and Bloated's replication (1951) found that sex made little differences. This throws considerable doubt on the interpretations given by Contra and Ceptive (1969).

Seltzer (1960) found that depending on the feeding patterns the researchers used, different weights are possible. Fizrin, Anacin, and Excedrin (1961) like-wise found a high positive correlation between the cost of living and an increase in wholesale and retail prices. Nixon, Agnew and Mitchell, et al. (1972) have thrown their weights all over.

---

[1]Now at the Department of Psychology, Kansas State University, under the assumed name of Steve R. Baumgardner.

[2] Alias Charles E. McCormick, Department of Psychology, University of Kentucky

A stiking pattern also runs throughout Thunder and Lightning's (1975) series of meteorological experiments. The development of their stunning results is left as a survival exercise for the interested reader.

Thus the present study seeks to test the hypothesis that it is difficult to compose groups of 11½ subjects each who are half male and half female and if they are so composed to keep the parts apart.

Method

Subjects

Without exception all subjects were either half male or half female, and were highly motivated to fufill the experimental assignment. For the purposes of this experiment all subjects were experimentally high, except those drawn from Sociology/Anthropology classes who were normally stoned. Eight subjects had to be dropped from the experiment due to their equipment failure; two of the eight are still alive on Vitamin E. The reader may wish to watch for a subsequent report on the six subjects who were consumed by passion. This report will include comparison of data of the six who died with the two who lived to experiment another day.

Materials

For a complete description of the experimental apparatus the reader is directed to the Gray's Anatomy, Kinsey, and Masters and Johnson. The critical reader may also wish to consult the Montgomery Ward Catalog, Fall and Winter Editions 1973 in the bedding section for a thorough description of the experimental environment.

Procedure

All groups (I & II) were randomly arranged by Pointing's (1970) first finger procedure. The experimenter's finger was first given to each member of group I and then to each member of group II, in that order using Insults (1984) random tables.

Further research is needed to determine exactly what was done after the two groups were assigned.

Results

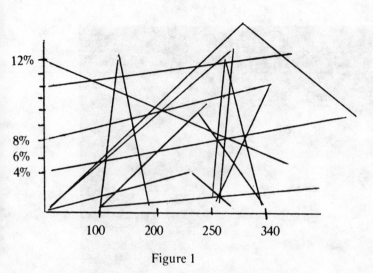

Figure 1

The results, shown clearly in Figure 1, speak for themselves.

Discussion

The results also indicate the presence of a subtle interaction. Although interpretation is difficult because the axes of the graph are not labelled, total confusion was unaffected. Next a subject-for-thing analysis of variance was carried out of the country. From here, the results obtained, were very close to significance. From these results one can easily prove that if the data are graphed the different lines will cross.

With regard to the variable of sex, a fly-by-night analysis was done but the results could not be found. Half of the Ss agree, however, that curves were preferred to lines. Though some lines worked others were rejected since many Ss were disclined. This indicated a change. Only further research

can clarify the many variables that were fooling around. In the words of one of the more successful Ss , this study was an end in itself.

REFERENCES

Contra, Diction and Ceptive, Very Ree, "No, and Then Again Yes," *Journal of Sexual Decisions*, Vol. 69, 1969.

Fizrin, Ima, Annacin, Ann A., Excedrin, X. *Headaches We Have Known*, Purple Prose Publishers, New York, New York, 1961.

Gray, T. *Anatomy of The Human Body*, Adam and Eve Press, T & E Vally, Year I.B.C.

Heartburn, Heavy and Bloated, Puffed N. "Too Much, Much Too Much," *"Quality Meats,"* Vol. 39, No. 5, 1951.

Kinsey, Alfred, *The Sex Books*, Sanders, 1950-1970.

Masters and Johnson, *Every Bedroom in America.*

Montgomery Ward Fall and Winter Catalog, 1973 edition, Chicago, Illinois (Write immediately).

Nixon, Richard M., Agnew, S., and Mitchell, M. *Four More Years*, Sad State of the Union Press, Washington, D.C., 1972.

Round, Ground and Ribeye, Red, "Steaks of Quality," *Meat and Potatoes*, Vol. 100004, No. 1, A No. 1, A & P Tea Company, 1937, Pgs. 1-100.

Seltzer, Sizzen, "Bromos and Homos," *Deviant Foods for Deviant People*, Vol. 100004, No. 321, Pgs. 2-22, 1960.

Swiss, Cheese, "Mr. and Miss Takes", *J. of Paranormal Sex*, Vol. 2, 1954, Pgs. 0-000.

T-Bone, Liptons, and Sirloin, Susie, "Higher Stakes," *J. of Poker Chips*, Vol. 1, No. 4, 1967, Pgs. 2-20.

Thunder, Lotta and Lightning, Shite, " The Positive Relationship Between Stormy Sex and Stormy Weather," *Journal of Flare Ups and Fire Storms*, Vol. 17, No. 9, Pgs. 12-24, 1975.

Footnotes

What can the author say?

[4] Mary, Tyler, and Moore (1973) carried out a significant study in the lab next door.

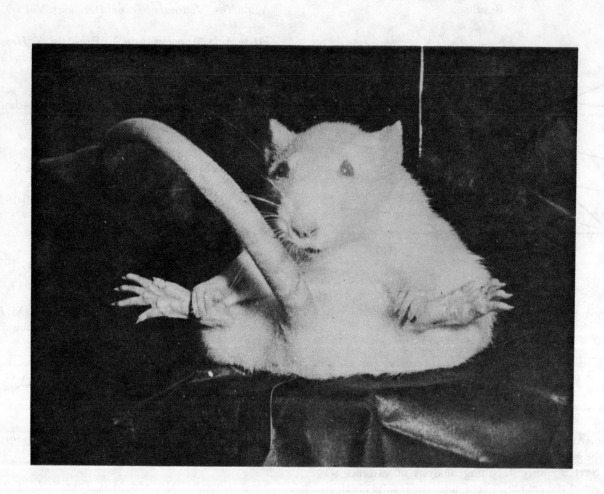

A rat under the influence of Marijuana (Hashish). To readers that are not acquainted with the anatomy of rat: the hairless, scaly, structure protruding in front is the tail.
(Y. Greenfeld)

Preliminary Observations Upon An Isobaric Spin Model For Human Sexuality

A. W. KUHFELD et al.
M.I.T. (Monster Institute of Transylvania),
Black, Mass.

Abstract: Research into sex has long been hindered by the common practice of considering the human male and female to be two distinct entities, having totally unrelated properties. The clearest expression of this attitude may be found in the erroneous system of experimental calibration often referred to as the Double Standard. Rather, there is an intimate relationship between these two forms of humans, as recent experiments have conclusively revealed. This relationship is amenable to various formalisms of modern physical science.

Certain aspects of human sexuality have been investigated in detail by the methods of nuclear physics[1], but the field is still largely unexplored. In particular, it is astonishing that the powerful methods of Group Theory have never been applied to the phenomenon, in view of the well-documented knowledge that most human sexual behavior of interest occurs in groups of two or more. The most prominent human sexual characteristics is dualism, which suggests that an isobaric-spin formalism based upon the more familiar $t=1/2$ baryon doublet would be immediately applicable.

It is generally conceded that the male gets a larger charge out of sex than the female[2] (although this finding has recently been challenged by Huang, Bang and Sigh[3], who claim that the greater escitation of the female is masked by lack of a monopole emission mechanism, giving the male a spuriously higher transition rate to the unexcited state). We may therefore tentatively assign $t_z=+1/2$ to the male and $-1/2$ to the female. If the sexual investigations now proceeding in almost all universities and colleges having proper research facilities produce data requiring modifications of this assumption, we can easily apply a similarity transformation to all results obtained under this assumption.

Statistics are another important aspect of the problem, since they will govern the sexual relationship between isospin coupling and spatial behavior. Early and easily-obtained data upon the deviations of humans from ideal-gas behavior at room temperature would suggest that humans are fermions rather than bosons. In particular, when humans are compressed they tend to maintain as large an average inter-human distance as possible. This is especially noticeable in elevators and buses, where there is a limiting density which is asymptotically approached only under great pressure. It is true that the average m-f distance is smaller than the average m-m or f-f distance, which is strong support for the fermion concept, but this behavior could be governed by the potentials of the system. It is known that many apparently-attractive humans possess repulsive cores.

Stronger evidence in favor of fermionic behavior in humans comes from observing the pure $T=1$ states m-m and f-f. In the closely-interacting system the most commonly observed behavior is antisymmetric, with the humans oriented in opposite directions. Since this is an S-state (the only relative motion being radial rather than angular) opposed intrinsic orientations imply antisymmetry. The analogue of this $T=1$ state is also observed in the m-f system, although there has not been enough valid research to establish the relative amplitude of such behavior. If it is found to occur with equal strength in the f-f, m-f, and m-m systems then our isobaric-spin model is upheld. In any case, the $T=0$ coupling with m and f having parallel orientations is preponderant. This indicates that the $T=0$ attraction is much stronger than $T=1$ under normal conditions.

Unfortunately for acceptance or rejection of the group-theoretic hypothesis, by far the greatest number of experiments in the interaction of humans occur in the $T=0$, spatially symmetric m-f state. This is not surprising, for the $T=0$ behavior is far more accessible to the majority of researchers (with their limited funds and specialized equipment) than the theoretically more complex $T=1$ system. There is a surprising lack of information upon the $t=1/2$ isolated human in the literature, although it would seem at first that the study of this system would be the easiest of all. (We may speculate that the government considers the dissemination of knowledge about $t=1/2$ behavior dangerous to the national security, and is therefore suppressing all mention of the subject. This seems improbable, for $t=1/2$ behavior rarely leads to observable consequences, while $T=0$ interactions appear to provide the main motive power for many humans. It could be that the government, acceding to the many requests for it to attempt feedback in the $t=1/2$ state, has experienced a breakthrough. In the balance, however, it seems likely most researchers find the $t=1/2$ system interesting only as preparation for $T=0$ and 1 investigations. Since there is no tradition of "publish or perish" in this field—a unique situation in itself—this would explain the scanty literature).

Although this model shows considerable promise in evaluation of many of the features of human sexuality, it is not totally valid. Obviously, with the mass of the female less than the mass of the male, they are not totally describable by an isobaric model (which assumes equal masses). Also, the mesons mediating the interaction seem to be almost totally emitted by the male and absorbed by the female. A mestastable state with a nine-month lifetime has been observed in the female, while multiple emission from this metastable state is also infrequently seen (with a slightly smaller average lifetime). This metastability is completely lacking in the male. It is obvious, therefore, that there is some symmetry-breaking interaction present. This interaction may in most cases be treated only as a perturbation; it is most perturbing when the metastable state is excited, since this excitation *requires* a symmetry-breaking interaction.

Despite the inadequacies of the isobaric-spin model, it suggests many lines of future research. Perhaps the most fruitful would be the highly-excited states of the many-body problem (referred to in the popular literature as the "orgy"). If we assume that all interactions are the sum of the two-body interactions involved, then it is possible to predict immediately that in the three-body problem the $T=1/2$ state will dominate the $T=3/2$ state; and that the $T=1/2$ contribution will come from a strong m-f $T=0$ coupling, with the remaining human loosely coupled to this pair. An investigation of this system as a function of the valence-human t_z might shed a good deal of light on the symmetry-breaking interaction.

REFERENCES

[1] "The Quantum Mechanics of Sex" Arluis, E. Vell, *Journal of the M.I.T. Science Fiction Society,* 69, 20-443 (1984).

[2] "Do Children Have as Much Fun in Children as Adults Do in Adultery"? Fraud, S., *Aberrational Psychophysics,* 1 1-2 (1894).

[3] "Upon Certain Aspects of Certain Interactions About Which Nothing is Certain" Huang, Bang and Sigh, *Comptes Rendus Hebdomadaires de la Societe Aphrodites Anonyme, 236A* 56-100 (1966).

MALE STERILIZATION

It's in the (bag) these days

BEN C. SCHARF, D.O., F.A.C.G.P.
Editor, N.Y. State Osteopathic
Society BULLETIN

Vasectomy has become so popular these days that hardly a month goes by that some journal, magazine, or newspaper[1] does not have an article about it so I can see no reason why THE JOURNAL OF IRRE-PRODUCIBLE RESULTS should not have one as well.

Having performed more vasectomies in my practice area than the combined caseload of seven urologists (and I include one urologist[2] in my statistics), I feel eminently qualified to give you my feelings about feeling for a vas in an area undoubtedly containing more tactile sensory organs than any other in the male.

The vas deferens makes no difference to anyone but the owner until such time as he decides to have it resected. According to Dr. Phil Anderer who has had more experience with post vasectomy problems[3] than most, the difference in the consistancy of the vas from surrounding structures is obvious to the be-holder. It stands to reason that the female has more experience than the male in this delicate area.[4]

The most frequent reason given by patients for wanting a vasectomy is that they do not want anymore children by anyone.[5] The most frequent reason given by wives when consenting to their husbands having the operation is that they want more for less.[6]

While there is evidence that as much as three quarters or more of the scrotum can be burned or denuded and a whole new scrotum will reform we have not had any success in recruiting volunteers for this operation.[7] The one sixteenth of an inch incision we make for exposing the vas is sufficient for most patients to holler "uncle".[8] The post-op pain has been described as similar to that experienced when getting a baseball

pitched at a testicle.[9] Here again we were unable to do objective studies to prove this as we could get no volunteers to pitch baseballs at. Research has further been hampered in trying to ascertain the libido of vasectomized males vis a vis other vasectomized males according to Dr. Matt A. Chine.[10]

A frequently asked question is "What happens to the sperm that keep being produced by the testes after vasectomy?". No one really knows but Dr. Mary Little Lamb's studies indicate that they continue to wag their tails even years later and after repair and recanalization of the vas.

There is absolutely no truth to the rumor that there are failures in doing this sterilization procedure. To prove this rumor to be false, we interviewed the wife of one of our patients several years post-op. We had difficulty in locating her and at last report she was living in a house that passersby swore was the shape of a shoe having moved there only three years ago from a one bedroom apartment, just after her husband was sterilized.

It is reported that in India volunteers for vasectomy are granted a transistor radio by the government.[11] This, too, is in error. The facts are that the instrument is a camouflaged geiger counter calibrated to keep track of the males post-op migratory habits much as they tag the giant wild rabbits of the great African plains of Heer-Icom.

One final note. You can always tell a male who has been vasectomized by his behavior. Some say he de-man-ds too much, others that he is de-men-ted and some swear they have become wee men.

---

[1] a. *Journal of Playboy Medicine*, March 1970, "Cut it out —For Crying out Louder".
   b. *Magazine for Men*, April 1970, "Sterilization: Vas the Difference—Men or Women?"
   c. *The Dilly Dally City Daily*, May 1970, "No Dilly, No Dally".
[2] No he was not a Eunich as reported by one colleague—his wife.
[3] *Journal of Vasology*, June 1941, Dr. Phil Anderer, "experience of 300 male prostitutes who claimed to have been vasectomized." The paper reveals that they were victimized not vasectomized.
[4] *Sensitivity Journal*, August 1954, Dr. N. Counter, "Group Feelings at a Ballroom Marathon".
[5] Four out of five do not want to be reminded of past, pres-

ent, or future children claiming they had a poor childhood themselves after learning their fathers were vasectomized.
[6] None were willing to explain more of what for less of which.
[7] Those who were asked all assumed a rather interesting fetal posture—cupping the scrotum in both hands and chanting the latest song, the "OO-OO Rock" while rolling rhythmically back and forth not losing a stroke.
[8] "UNCLE" stands for "Under No Conditions Locate Eggs".
[9] Or a testicle pitched at a baseball. We see no difference in the pain that results.
[10] Dr. Matt A. Chine, *Journal of Gay Times*, May 1969, "Be Fruitful Without Multiplying".
[11] To encourage listening to political speeches not to encourage vasectomies.

The Wife of Bath Sign: An Aid in the Diagnosis of Gonococcal Arthritis and its Predisposing Cause

KERN WILDENTHA, M.D.
Dallas, Texas

Gat-toothed I was, and that became me well;
I had on me the stamp of Venus' seal.
. . . .
My nature was that I could not withdraw
My prize of Venus from a good fellow.

CHAUCER[1]

INTRODUCTION

The observation that promiscuity in the human female may be associated with the presence of gat-teeth was stressed by Chaucer in his case report of the Wife of Bath[1]. In view of widespread promiscuity in the 20th century[2,3] it seemed of interest to determine if the relationship noted in the 14th century still exists.

Two difficulties in testing the hypothesis were apparent: (1) the current widespread availability of corrective dental care tends to obscure the true incidence of gat-teeth, and (2) promiscuity is difficult to establish reliably by history because of (a) embarrassment and fear, or (b) bragging. However, since (A) promiscuous women are more likely to contract gonorrhea, (B) women with gonorrhea are unlikely to develop complicating gonococcal arthritis unless they neglect seeking medical attention for the initial infection, and (C) those who lack medical attention will usually have failed to receive dental attention as well, it seemed probable that women with gonococcal arthritis would comprise a group in whom *objective* evidence of promiscuity plus a virginal tooth status would be combined. Thus if the gat-tooth hypothesis be correct, a high incidence of that finding should be seen in women with gonococcal arthritis.

The proposed relationships are symbolized in Figure 1.

Shunt pathways opened by affluence and its accompanying higher standards of medical and dental care are showed by hatched lines.

METHODS

All women between the ages of 15–35 admitted to a local charity hospital during 1966 with acute arthritis of any cause were examined for the presence or absence of gat-teeth. Subsequently, diagnoses of gonococcal arthritis were made according to standard criteria[4]: (a) typical history and clinical course, (b) demonstration of the gonococci by smear or culture, (c) positive test for gonococcal antibodies, and/or (d) definite improvement following penicillin therapy.

RESULTS

Table 1 summarizes the results of studies on 25 consecutive patients, 11 with gonococcal (GC) arthritis and 14 with other causes. It is apparent that a highly significant correlation is present between the presence of gat-teeth and the establishment of the diagnosis of GC arthritis on other grounds (p 0.0001). Indeed, reliability of the gat-tooth finding equals or exceeds that of the other criteria for diagnosis.

[4] Hess, E. V., et al., Gonococcal antibodies in acute arthritis, 1965 *191*, 531.

---

[1] Chaucer, G., Canterbury Tales, Prologue to the Wife of Bath's Tale, lines 603–604, 617–618 (translated to modern English).
[2] Kinsey, A. C., et al. Sexual behavior in the human female, Saunders, Phila. 1953.
[3] Unpublished personal observations.
[4] Hess, E. V., et al., Gonococcal antibodies in acute arthritis, JAMA, 1965 *191*, 531.

FIGURE 1

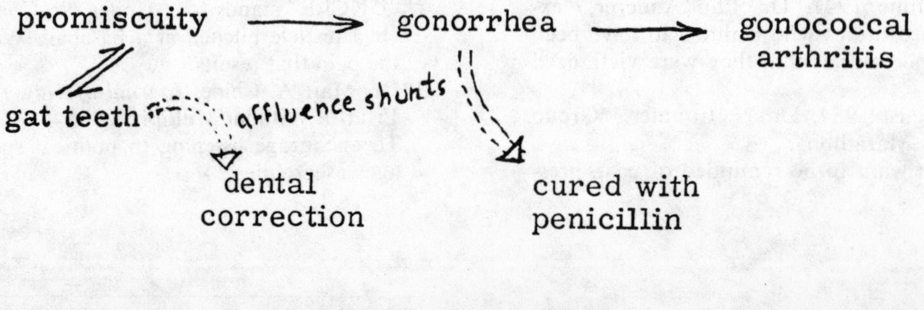

TABLE 1

	History of promiscuity given	Gonococci identified	Increased GC antibody titers	Response to penicillin	Presence of gat-teeth
GC	6/11	4/11	7/10	11/11	10/11
Others*	5/14	0/12	2/8	3/9	2/14

* acute rheumatic fever – 8; infectious arthritis (non-GC) – 3; systemic lupus erythematosus – 1; undiagnosed – 2.

Of the two non-gonococcal patients who showed gat-teeth, one gave a history of extreme promiscuity. The other did not[5]. The GC patient in whom gat-teeth were not seen had had all her teeth knocked out by a boyfriend several years previously.

CONCLUSION
In view of the results of this study, and that of Chaucer, the usefulness of the "Wife of Bath Sign" in identifying promiscuous women seems established[6]. The logical extension of this finding into the field of arthritis provides an invaluable sign to aid in the difficult diagnosis of gonococcal arthritis.

---

[5] She was a liar.
[6] This designation seems preferable to "The Chaucer-Wildenthal Sign" which others have proposed (see Standard nomenclature of athletic injuries, AMA Publ., Chicago, 1966).

MEGALOPTIC HUMAN SERVICES
SUBSTATION 4791
Postal Transmitter Code 33-965-421-4
MOHOLE GOVERNMENTAL CONTROL CENTER
Sublevel 134
Appalachia, Pennsylvania

Office of the
Supreme Defender
of the
Primogenitary

Videophone
1796-431-62-4976-35
Laser Channel 14913

March 31, 1991

Donald P. Kent, Ph.D.
Department of Sociology
  and Anthropology
The Pennsylvania State University
227 Graduate Building
University Park, Pennsylvania 16802

My dear Kent:

Thank you so much for affording me the opportunity to review the Kalish article for possible inclusion in your forthcoming "Gerontology: Past, Present, and Future." You realize, of course, that being on the very eve of retirement, my reflections on this are quite different from those I might have made in 1970 when I had already spent some 20 years in gerontology and related areas of social welfare. You no doubt recall the point of view which I, Linden, Simmons, and Townsend shared about the place of elderly people in our society. However, these are different times and a great deal has happened since those early days.

The author of this paper presents an interesting thesis about the reasons for higher social value in western society, although I am not certain he is entirely accurate. He suggests that at this time "they are unlikely to add to the population by having children." This, however, is a factor that was present for all the generations preceding our present one. Indeed, today the early experiments at Cornell with rats (Schoenfelt, 1959) which produced female rats bearing young at the human equivalent age of 80 is now seeing fruition (if you permit an old man a bad pun) among some of our senior citizens. Indeed, the long range physiological effects of oral contraceptive drugs saw what was an alarming increase during the Seventies of women in their middle and late 50's bearing children (Burson 1974).

While there is no reason as yet to believe millions of American women in the 7th and 8th decades of their lives will produce children, it is a matter of fact that at the time of the last special census of retirees (U.S. Census Bureau 1988), no less than 10,000 live births were recorded among women above the age of 63. Some of my younger colleagues, encouraged by the widespread success of the foster grandparent program in the late Sixties and Seventies, have gone so far as to recommend that child bearing during the middle years may introduce the most satisfying role for the elderly that the American culture has been able to devise (Mileti, Smith, and Gross 1989).

The conclusion that the elderly are frequently retired and are not keeping a younger person from a job or a promotion was also true even in the Sixties and Seventies. Thus, this would be of no greater significance today than it was then. I feel what may be more significant is the fact that the distinctions between the young and old have become considerably more hazy. Retirement now occurs at age 50 with optional retirement at age 45. Education both in the technical schools and the professional schools continues full time until age 25, with virtually mandatory educational activity on a part-time basis extending to age 30. It is really not until after this date that people begin to work at full-time positions (U.S. Government Printing Office 1986 et seq.). Following retirement at age 50, approximately 30 percent return to some kind of educational activity (U.S. Office of Education in Retirement 1988).

However, the sociological factors are perhaps less important than what has happened in the area of physiology. (You must forgive me if I do not give you all the documentation that a scholarly critique should, but I will presume the preogatives that I must confess I feel are my due.) Organ transplants, including replacement of nerve block damage, particularly in the extremities, have improved body functioning significantly. Problems posed earlier by a slow down in synaptic transmission have been overcome. The discovery in 1970 (Schwartz and Kerenyi) that what we once quaintly called senile dementia was in fact amyloidosis permitted us to introduce drugs into the system which would counteract the metabolic changes leading to the deposit of amyloid in the vessels of the brain. In addition to cutting off admissions to insti-

tutional care because of poor psychological function ing, we arrived at a condition of old age which n longer saw the faulty memory, the slow reaction, o the doddering step as the signals of advancing years

Perhaps one of the greatest effects that the tech nology has had in producing respect and high socia value for older people has been the most recent de velopment of cryogeriatrics. The successful freezing of elderly persons with revival at a later time ha produced a situation not unlike that encountered a an earlier time in our history when control of the land by the parent maintained respect by the young fo their elderly (see Simmons, op cit.). Cryogeriatric has raised a host of new problems for the lawyers. I a person does not die but merely goes into a frozen state, does he leave an estate and are their heirs? Wha claim does he have and can he set aside funds for us upon his revival and "return" to "life"? I would sub mit that the young are wary and cautious and are treating with respect their elders who still control considerable wealth. It may be that cryogeriatrics is the most significant key in this area of social value (Birdseye 1984).

One final comment, a suggestion that the dispersion of persons of Chinese origin has had an effect is without merit. As the author so correctly notes, the move into the rural communities and small towns as demanded by the Percy-Tunney Immigration and Non-Urban Dispersal Bill, effectively isolated the Chinese. In any event, the group who came here in their 30's were those largely disenchanted with the developments of the Forties, Fifties, and Sixties of China, and while articulate about the "old values" were really uncommitted to the values of a China as not known since the 1920's and earlier.

In summary, I would agree with the author's overall conclusions. However, like so many psychologists, he has fallen into the trap of avoiding the technological developments and assuming the changes in value derived from the simple psychological, social and economic factors.

Well, these have been the ramblings of a fellow toiler in the vineyard. The author's style is terse and satisfying to read. His review of the literature is excellent as far as it goes. However, my guess is that this has been done by one of your younger colleagues who in an effort to dazzle us all has overlooked some important elements in the picture.

With all good wishes to you, and my congratulations to Marian on the birth of your eighth child, I remain

Your obedient servant,
Elias S. Cohen

QUOTES

Mitchel, D., Wyndham, C. H., Atkins, A. R., Vermeulen, A. J., Hofmeyer, H. S., Strydom, N. B. and Hodgson, T.
DIRECT MEASUREMENTS OF THE THERMAL RESPONSES OF NUDE RESTING MEN IN DRY ENVIRONMENTS
Pflugers Arch. Europ. J. Physiology, 1968, 303/4

(Quite a team for measurements!)

*   *   *

W. K. Whitten, Bronson, F. H. and Greenstein J. A.
ESTRUS-INDUCING PHEROMONE OF MALE MICE: TRANSPORT BY MOVEMENT OF AIR
Science 1968, 161, 584

Abstract: "The proportion of female SJL/J mice exhibiting estrus when placed 2 meters downwind (6 meters/min) from a group of hybrid males was not significantly less than that of females placed directly under the males and exposed to their urine."

*   *   *

R. Schweet and R. Heintz
PROTEIN SYNTHESIS
Annual Review of Biochem., 1966, 35, 746

"So et al (136) made a very extensive study of the effect of cations, polar and non-polar compounds and streptomycin on incorporation. (136) — So, A., Bodley, J, & Davie E., Biochemistry, 1964, 3, 1977

(So he did, did he. Glad to see et al. is publishing again.)

*   *   *

American Medical Association News, March 7, 1966

Dr. Paddison emphasized, "Any system of healing which denies that polio is a virile disease and that specific prevention is available negates completely the overwhelming and significant scientific data now available about this disease. The use of manipulative therapy in this disorder can only be condemned as quackery."

*   *   *

Govindjee, R., Govindjee, and Hoch G.
EMERSON ENHANCEMENT EFFECT IN CHLOROPLAST REACTIONS
Plant Physiology 1964, 39, 11 – 14

"Acknowledgements. We are grateful . . . to Miss Iris Martin for her occasional help."

(What was she doing on other occasions?   F. G. Hawksworth)

Obliteration of SEX

In recent months care has been taken by most departments to avoid the use of words which unintentionally designate a specific sex in letters, forms, brochures, etc. In general, it appears that forms and publications do not contain references to gender which might be considered discriminatory, but we need to assure ourselves that we are not distributing or using material which may appear so. Words identifying a specific sex (e.g., he/she, him/her) should not be used except where their use is intended to identify a specific person. "He," for example, should not be used as a neuter gender word. In place of such pronouns, specific nouns may be used e.g., the candidate, the employee, the customer, etc. Further guidance related to sex discrimination is contained in Management Guide 03-0306.

The following actions should be taken to ensure that we completely remove any possible indication of sex discrimination in any written or printed material:

1. Review all existing forms and publications which have been developed within your department to assure that there is no reference to a specific sex unless such reference is essential and can be supported. (Legal counsel should be sought in cases where it is thought such reference is essential.)

2. Advise your Employee Relations Manager/Advisor of the existence of any forms or other material which appears discriminatory and revise them to remove any questionable references. Withdraw any such existing material from use and destroy warehouse stocks. If in the judgment of local management, such action would result in unreasonable expense, Company legal counsel should be sought to review the risks/costs involved.

3. Instruct all personnel within your department that no references to sex should be made in conversation, or in any future correspondence, printed material, etc., unless essential (see 1 above).

If there are any questions concerning these instructions or matters which require clarification as they are implemented, please contact me.

---

[1] Sex Discrimination—Correspondence Publications

AIR-WATER TIGHT TESTS FOR MECHANICAL CONTRACEPTIVES

Sir,

I should like to refer to the 1968-1969 Annual Report of the Haffkine Institute of Bombay (Govt. Printing and Stationary Maharashtre State Publ. p. 80). The last paragraph of the Biological Section reads as follows:

"Thirty-seven samples of mechanical contraceptives (condoms) were tested. Only 6 samples have complied with all the tests. It has been observed that most of the samples failed in length, weight and air-inflation tests. A few samples were not made of good elastic rubber, as some of the samples could not hold enough water to pass the water leakage test."

It is regrettable that the report does not include details of the standards used to assess parameters such as length and weight. Thus, it is difficult, if not impossible, to compare the Indian figures with those of other countries. Taking into consideration, however, the highly significant proportion ($P < 0.01$) of the samples that did not pass the air-inflation tests, as well as the high birth rate in India, it is reasonable to assume that many of the faulty specimens had, nevertheless reached the consumer market.

Although no actual figures are given for the water leakage test, we assume that under maximal hydrostatic pressure, compatible with integrity of the device, any rubber closed cylindrical shape, will become a sphere. Under these conditions, one can calculate the number of spermatozoids (E) traversing the rubber wall as follows:

$$E = \frac{\Pi \, R^3 \, V}{HP} \, C_e \, C_p$$

Where ΠR^3 is the volume of the sphere, V the coefficient of viscosity of the liquid contained in it, HP is the hydrostatic pressure, and Ce is the coefficient of elasticity of the rubber and Cp the coefficient of porosity.

H. E. (Isr. Inst. Bio. Res.)

Sexual Feats and Facts*

Sex is inherently interesting even to those with none of the multifold sexual problems described or invented by psychiatrists, psychologists, and novelists. The current popularity of the studies by Masters and Johnson is understandable but the replacement of mythology with scientific myths is a danger. The trend to sanitize, and scientize sex with probes, movies, etc. may provide new information of value to those unfortunates with unendowed bodies, faulty skills, or functional "hang-ups", such advances will be welcome.

I suppose individual sexual performance may range up to heights comparable to those attained by trained athletes in other kinds of physical activities and team play, who are often paid to demonstrate their individual superiority in one or another contact sport. The large attendance at movies with a predominant sexual theme may not differ too much from the crowded stadia of football fans with deep emotional attachment to the barely discernible players who are expected to display unattainable feats of skill and strength — and risk life and limb.

It will be interesting to see if new public heroes in sexual athletics will develop. One can only wonder if there will be a parallel development of tournaments, training tables, coaches, teams, and medical specialists to provide aid to the injured (laceration of uterine ligaments?) or perhaps an "air hammer disease" of the spine or phallus etc., etc., etc., etc., etc. In any event, it seems certain that in this topsy turvy world, progress of some sort in this area of medicine is certain.

The role to be played by the physician is less certain. Even the third year medical student who traditionally felt that he was over the hump — educationally speaking — may find that his factual lectures have been "woefully inadequate". I suppose outstanding players who become overage will become coaches and unless the curriculum is changed, the physician's role may be severely limited.

From a sentimental standpoint, the unique flavor of OB-GYN and Urological jokes will be lost forever. I suppose hindstart programs will be funded by the Government and reluctant youngsters will have to complete required exercises before going out to play. Probably, only neighborhood medical sex centers will be funded and thus, provide a place for underground medical activities, such as public health, trauma and mental care.

---

* Moore, George E., M.D., MEDICAL WORLD NEWS, May 1, 1970, p. 48.

Irreproducible

information

from the

art (?) or

science (?)

of

MEDICINE

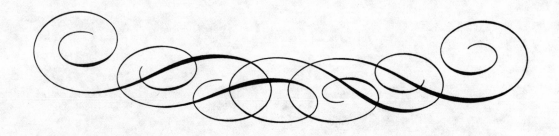

Medical Practice in America, a Transcultural Study

FESOJ GOTRAH*
Department of Transcultural Scientific Junkets
University of Liechtenstein
Liechtenstein

This is the first in a series of studies conducted by Full Bright scholars loaned to the United States by the Government of Liechtenstein as part of the program of the Ministry of Foreign Affairs to help less fortunate countries, especially the emerging nations of the Orient. Because the United States is representative of the Orient and its culture (and east of Liechtenstein, too), the author (an Oriental behavioral scientist) eagerly took advantage of this exchange program to make his 3-month in-depth study. The people of the United States manifest the typical Oriental characteristics: a peaceful temperament, inscrutability, disinterest in worldly goods, xenophobia, a skill for making toys cheaply (and dangerously), a general disregard for human life, crowded living conditions, a dependence on drugs, a love for nature—especially flowers, a shrewd business sense, excessive pride in their national and racial identities, a love of dogs and children, a concern about face-saving (hence the Vietnam quagmire), and are often described with some apprehension in Liechtenstein as the aggressive Golden Horde.

Although my purpose in the United States was to bring modern Liechtensteinian medicine to the Americans, and the need and justification for this cannot be doubted, I did not want to be considered an Ugly Liechtensteinian. Therefore I agreed to teach at the American University, where fortunately I had the time and staff to complete a few publications, review some reviews, and do new research as well (for the sake of my back-home sponsors and academic status). Occasionally I was able to do some field work, talking with the natives (i.e., other members of the University faculty) and living among them briefly when the weather permitted. Most of my data is based upon the random sampling of students and faculty (50% of whom were other Full Brights). This scientific endeavor produced sufficient data for 10 research papers.

Some of the forthcoming papers are: "The Intelligence Quotient of Americans", "The Kinship System of American University Students and Faculty", "Can Americans Compete in the Modern Liechtensteinian World?", "General Washington's Crossing the Delaware as a Prototype of Military and Political Tradition in the U.S.", "American Responses on the Liechtenstein Water Blot Test", "The Attitude of Americans toward Mental Health", and "Quaint American Social Habits as Observed from a Hovering Helicopter en route between Palm Springs, California, and Seattle, Washington."

The purpose of this paper is to describe in depth the most significant aspects of American healing ceremonies. My description centers on the practices of two types of widely used healers — the Surgeon and the Psychiatrist. It appears that the Surgeon deals with bodily problems and the Psychiatrist with mental or spiritual problems.

Surgical Procedure begins when the patient seeks help for some physical pain. The Surgeon typically examines the patient by touching various parts of the body and taking X-ray pictures. After a fee is agreed upon, the patient is taken to his accountant and then to the operating room. There the Surgeon performs a hand-washing ceremony and then dons a special costume (called a gown) with cap and face mask. The costume is always a single color (white, green, or blue)

---

* Dr. Gotrah was Visiting Professor of Spaced Age Behavior at the American University in San Francisco at the time this study was made.

This work was supported by the poor, the aged, and the disabled of Liechtenstein, who generously relinquished their financial assistance, school improvements, and medicines so that the frontiers of science might be advanced further out into space.

and bears no designs, pictures, or inscriptions. No typical amulets were noted. However, rubber gloves and floppy cloth overshoes were required (an interesting reversal of the no-shoes rule of some cultures). Several male and female assistants were dressed similarly. In the next step, the Surgeon or his assistant shaved the patient and annointed him with a colored liquid applied in a clockwise circular fashion without incantation, though I often heard references to giants, dodgers, pirates, and braves; possibly local spirits. On one occasion an assistant deviated from the proper annointing practice by moving counterclockwise and was scolded by the Surgeon. In fact, scolding by the Surgeon continued throughout the ceremony. This custom may be related to exorcism rites seen in other exotic cultures. The Surgeon cut the patient open, removed a part of the body, and sewed him up again. As in augury, the Surgeon examined the "specimen" and sometimes sent it to a specialist for soothsaying. Predictions of the future were made by means of this procedure. At the end of this ceremony the patient either lived or died. Generally the patient's relatives showed great respect for the Surgeon regardless of the outcome.

This extensive study of the Surgeon was based on observation of three procedures.

The Psychiatrist, who usually works alone, does not use tools and dresses only in the national costume. His office accouterments and hanging decorations, however, compensate for his conventional costume. He often refuses to talk to relatives of the patient and sometimes even to the patient. The example of the psychiatrist is based upon observation of three and several others I heard about.

The patient consults the Psychiatrist for psychic pain, then makes a confession. This is followed by prolonged talking "therapy" over a period of months. The longest I saw was 1 hour during which the patient demonstrated a wide range of emotions. The actual content of the talk I observed was unknown to me since I did not speak the native language at the time of the study. But this should not be construed to devalue my in-depth observations, since I am a keen Liechtensteinian observer with serveral advanced Liechtensteinian diplomas.

Another healer, for my benefit demonstrated intimate intrapsychic mechanisms by treating one patient in a lecture hall with 200 observers and another patient in his office, to which I was denied entrance. Another Psychiatrist, who appeared much more confident (and I think intimidated the patient a little) demonstrated his "electric treatment". Again, this healer wore the national costume though it was covered with a white coat. He was very willing to talk with students, visitors, and relatives of the patient, even while "demonstrating". He administered intermittent, convulsive electric shocks to the patient, who was restrained and silent. The healer seemed more pleased than the patient.

Evaluation of the results of these therapies must await a return visit to America.

CONCLUSION

This experience clearly demonstrates the value of in-depth overseas behavioral research. Also it shows that physical and mental illness exists in America, as does a long-established healing system that incorporates confession, punishment, exorcism, ritual, suggestion, and faith. Results of this study clearly support the views that primitive medicine has universal characteristics and that the people of America are rather superstitious and backward, though emerging.

A Short Guide to Doctors

JOHN J. SECONDI, M.D.

Medicine, like every other field these days, is so overspecialized that even a card-carrying doctor like me has trouble telling who's who. The layman, I imagine, is almost helpless to distinguish the forest from the tree surgeons. I have noticed, however, that my colleagues have a tendency to run to type. So, in an effort to clear up the confusion, I have compiled a little list so simple that the most naive patient can spot at a glance which doctor is which.

The General Practitioner: These gentlemen used to be the ones you saw most often, when you lived back in Nebraska and watched the cars go by from your front porch for entertainment. Now they are nearly extinct, like the buffalo and the stork, although there are a few left in a preserve in Iowa. Most of them looked like a cross between Charlie Ruggles and Colonel Sanders; they were warm, wonderful, and always had time for you, even if they slept only three hours a night. They knew you inside and out from the moment they delivered you until their ink dried on your death certificate, and they were always there to help you push your car out of the mud. If anybody knows where there's one of these left, please drop me a note. I could use a good doctor myself.

The Internist: This is a general practitioner with more diplomas on the walls and without house calls. (He also has money in the bank.) By the age of thirty at the latest he becomes obese, sallow, and emphysematous. Usually bald, he is always found sitting and smoking a pipe. (The pipe is a deliberate attempt to evoke the Delphic Oracle, which also simmered and steamed with ideas. The internist is nothing

if not oracular.) As opposed to the surgeon, who carries no equipment at all except the keys to his Rolls-Royce, the internist can be seen with a stethoscope protruding from one of thousands of pockets in his clothing. Really big stethoscopes are worn to give the impression of expertise in heart disease.

In his desk the internist stocks lifetime supplies of sample drugs; when you are in his office he may pick one or two at random and give them to you with alarming liberality. But don't worry; he won't let you know what they are. The internist is really happy only when deciding how to cope with some chronic incurable disease, preferably in a case some colleague has botched. The longer the name of the disease, the happier he is; and if it's in Latin he's ecstatic. An internist is required by law to have his phone ring twice an hour at least while he is at home, and he can never vacation. No internist's children ever become doctors.

The General Surgeon: These are the prima donnas of the trade. Today's surgeon is descended from the barbers of the Middle Ages, but washes more often. He may be fat or slim, but he is always loud, noticed, and in a hurry. He dashes dramatically in and out of rooms (whether patient, operating, or bath) and never lets you finish a sentence. To probing questions he nods wisely, smiles enigmatically, and runs off. (Never say "Now cut that out" to a surgeon.) He generally visits patients cloaked in green from head to toe to give the impression of being fresh from an operation, when probably (unless he is over fifty) he has been idling in his office all day waiting for someone — anyone — to call. After he does a surgical scrub, he raises his arms, which drip from the elbows. This posture serves both as a gesture to God for the usual assistance, and as a method to keep the bacteria flowing away from the surgeon — towards the patient.

Surgeons are taught early to rip off bandages as quickly as possible, pulling as much hair as they can get out with one clean tear. They have a distinctive jargon: For instance, they speak of healing by "primary intention" (which is to make lots of money), or by "secondary intention" (which means the wound got infected). If anything goes wrong during operations, surgeons are unanimous in blaming it on the anesthesiologists. Surgeons are the only doctors left who haven't cut out smoking, because they are confident they can cut out the cancer. If this description still doesn't make a surgeon flash in your mind, recall James Coburn in *Candy*. Absolutely accurate.

The Gastroenterologist: Gastrointestinal doctors, or "GI men," have had oral fixations since childhood. This means they are always talking a mile a minute, and at mealtimes they ingest like Electroluxes. They're usually roly-poly, literary, and very pleasant to gossip with, as a consequence. The unsavoriness of their work is grossly exaggerated; nevertheless, they do receive a lot of cologne for Christmas. As kids they were the ones whose parents always had to bang on the bathroom door to get them out. If Alexander Woollcott had become a doctor, he would surely have been a gastroenterologist.

The Obstetrician-Gynecologist: The real wise guy in medicine. Sitting on their high stools day after day with their patients in that absurd saddle, these comedians see the funny side of life. They have to have a good sense of humor because otherwise they would be so nauseated by some of the things that come along they would swear off sex forever. Always ready with a wisecrack or a foul story (depending on whether you are a patient or another doctor), they are universally popular, except with pediatricians. Child doctors blame every childhood disease from thumb-sucking to Mongoloid idiocy on the anesthesia the obstetrician used. It is not true that all obstetrics is done at three o'clock in the morning. I personally recall one case in 1968 that was done at six in the morning, and others may have had similar experiences. Many Ob-Gyn men are now getting crash courses in abortion, which was never part of the medical curriculum before. These are the ones with the sterile coathangers.

The Urologist: Urologists do for men what gynecologists do for women — more or less. They are drawn to their specialty irresistibly by its identification with the masses of tight curly hair they all have. Many urologists are now growing beards and muttonchops so you can spot them more easily than ever. Walking around weighted down by their waterproof rubber aprons and all those whiskers they resemble Noah before the flood. At home they putter around a lot with the kitchen sink to keep in practice. Like other plumbers they work good hours and make a good living.

The Anesthesiologist: Anesthesiology is the Tower of Babel of Medicine. There are a total of four English-speaking anesthesiologists in America: two on the East Coast, one in Chicago, and the other in L.A. All the others communicate with frenzied nasal accents or sign language. They are short, shy, retiring types who hide behind the sterile barrier during surgery and squeeze contentedly on their little black respiration bags. You will recall the bags from 1930's movies because when Lionel Barrymore came too late they quit moving and you knew the patient had died.

The night before your next surgery an anesthesiologist may mince into your room, unheralded and uninvited. He will never show up after five o'clock, however. Without bothering to identify himself or even to ask for an interpreter, he will quiz you on all the allergies you may have. This is done to choose exactly the right toxin to put you to sleep with the next day; for God's sake, don't forget anything that might be relevant. Then he will bow graciously and back out of the room, and you'll never see him again. (Whether you'll see anyone else again is another question.) If you wake up from surgery, you may have a sore throat, even after an abdominal operation. This complication occurs because the anesthesiologist routinely puts the rubber airway down your esophagus six times before he finds the right hole. Anesthesiologists fear surgeons the way helpless children fear angry fathers. They are very sensitive and feel left-out enough, so be kind to them.

The Pediatrician: All pedi-pods, as they are called on the wards, act and look like Peter Pan. They wear saddle-shoes and bow ties, have cherubic faces, and wear crew cuts or pageboys, depending on whether they are over thirty. They are shorter than most other doctors, although they can be told from anesthesiologists because pediatricians are slightly taller, speak English, and have horizontally placed eyes. They never use words longer than two syllables or sentences of more than four words. Generally they sound as if they are doing Jonathan Winters imitations. Many have a lilting gait, and a few skip during clinic. About the age of forty they lose patience with all those frantic mothers and either commit suicide, go into research, or start child labor camps.

The Orthopedist: All bone doctors without exception are former college jocks or team managers; i.e., they are big brutes or mousy types who wish they were. They *all* wear white athletic socks. (This is the one infallible rule of medicine and makes it a snap to recognize an orthopedist.) They usually have plaster of paris splattered on their clumsy-looking shoes.

The Ophthalmologist: (This is the real "eye doctor" and is not to be confused with optometrists or opticians, who aren't M.D.'s at all.) Ophthalmologists, despite being constantly misspelled and mispronounced, are the happiest men in medicine. They work laughably few hours, make extravagant fees, and are adored by their patients, who understandably value their sight above all else. Thus ophthalmologists are always well-tanned and talk knowingly of Tahiti and the Riviera. They also play a great deal of golf. Curiously, they are uniformly tall, slim, and vaguely ethereal. A good example would be Pope Pius XII with a suntan. They use a jargon so technical and so infinitesimally detailed they cannot even make small-talk over drinks with other doctors.

The Otolaryngologist: When you've been to an ear, nose, and throat man you'll never forget it. These are the true sadists in medicine. Children despise them; they're the only doctors who make you feel worse than when you came in. What with the nausea produced by cocaine sprayed in the nose, and all those tiny little probes poking God-knows-where back in your sinuses, and all that blood swallowed after a tonsillectomy, going to an ENT man is like being used for an experiment by Edgar Allan Poe. The only common physical characteristic by which these gentlemen can be spotted is that they all still have their own tonsils.

The Plastic Surgeon: Immediately identifiable. They all wear handtailored clothing of vast expense and have sculptured features worthy of a Phidias or a Michelangelo. Gorgeous from every angle, they look years younger than they are, and boy do they know it. They were the big face men of college fraternities, the ones who were put strategically at the front door during rush week and in the first row in the yearbook picture. They are very rich because there are a lot of jealous

women who will pay *anything* to look as good as the plastic surgeon. They have a tendency to get very snotty when you ask them what kind of plastic they're going to put in, and lecture you on the origin of the word "plastikos" in the traditions of Greek sculpture. Nevertheless, they have terrific guilt complexes about spending all their time on frivolous surgery, so they occasionally take on a burn victim to soothe their consciences. The patron saint of plastic surgery is Narcissus.

The Psychiatrist: Spotting a psychiatrist on the street is easy enough, but as he wanders on the wards of a state hospital he may need a nametag. Psychiatrists either avert their eyes from you or stare right through you, whichever makes you more uncomfortable. If they sense you're going to ask a question, they slip one in first. They never use complete sentences, only clauses and long words. I know a psychiatrist who begins every sentence with the word "that" and ends it with an exact quotation of Plato. The main object a shrink has in mind when he sees a patient is not to rescue the patient's sanity but to prove his. After all, how many surgeons do you know who have five years of operations on themselves before they can practice?

Today's psychiatric resident may have elbow-length hair, wear rings in one ear, and go to work in purple satin capes. This kind of psychiatrist has not hit Park Avenue yet, but it's only a matter of time. Incidentally, the reason there are so many Jewish psychiatrists is that they are basically yentas with M.D.'s.

The Radiologist: Radiologists hide in dark places and never come out, like other rodents. They make creepy-crawly gestures and rub their noses frequently. Their world is one of shadows and they detest the light of day. They hole up in leadened tunnels and, though they tell you that X-rays are harmless, they generally have their offspring as early as possible. (By the time they reach fifty irradiation has given their skins the texture of refried beans). Like Whistler, they view everyone as a study in black, white, and gray. The thought of being responsible for a live human being is abhorrent to them. Yet they give off smiles of delicious perverse pleasure as they make patients swallow thick white slime and poke around in their bowels so their guts will show on film. Peter Lorre would have played a perfect radiologist.

I would like to complete the list, but I just got a frantic phone call from A.M.A. headquarters, and I have to run. Something about an emergency protest march against socialized medicine.

**THE PEDIATRICIAN ON HIS WAY
TO WELL-BABY CLINIC**

THE SURGEON SCRUBS UP

THE SHRINK IN A QUANDARY

THE X-RAY MAN

**THE ANESTHESIOLOGIST HIDING
FROM THE SURGEON**

How Medical History is Made

(To the tune of "Little Boxes")

You observe some
groups of patients
and send data to a statistician
then you wait for his analysis
hoping that it will explain

some phenome-
non of nature
which will make your reputation
but it all seems to be due to chance
and the groups are all the same.

Then you sit there
and you think that
some nonparametric test
will reveal a hidden difference
which will someday bear your name

And you test your
observations
using binomial probabilities
but it all turns to ticky tacky
and it all looks the same.

Both your tabling
and your graphing
can simply be exaggerated
but your conscience (and the editor)
say it all looks the same.

So at last in
desperation
you add 50 observations
and you swear that
now you've got it
and you're back in the game.

But—
the statistician
states succinctly
that the damned null hypothesis
is again not to be rejected
so it all looks the same.

So you fire your
statistician,
publish in Reader's Digest,
and the Ladies Home Journal
puts you in the Hall of Fame.

(By William F. Taylor)
Div. of Medical Statistics
Epidemiology & Population Genetics

Contributed by:
The Dept. of Pharmacology
Free University
Amsterdam, Holland

A Case History from the Hospital for Acrobatic Pathology

DR. TREMOR TAKE-OUT and DR. VERTIGO PUT-IN*
Megalomaniopolis, In-Continent

Whereas organ transplantation, kidney:-, heart-, liver-, pancreas-, lung-, skin and hairy scalp-, has become nowadays the daily bread and wine of self-conscious medical centers, brain transplantation in a rural general practice-directed hospital with a modest staff like ours seems to be sufficiently rare to justify publication, so as to serve both warning and stimulus, the more so since thus far the human brain has been considered too intelligent to easily submit to the procedure, and the medical staff involved is of untouchable ethical motivation. In the present communication we therefore truthfully describe the erroneously performed brain-cross transplantation between a professor and a student.

Case Report

At 19 p.m. on ...., ..., 19.... (exact indication omitted in order to avoid recognition of donor, recipient and transplanters), a graying, male, sad-looking professor of undefined age and a fresh-looking student, both of the political science department of the nearby parochial university, were admitted following a car accident to the emergency room, in a state of questionable death. Since optimal ressuscitation procedures applied for an optimal period were of no avail, and since two live car accident-induced decerebrate adult candidates were abiding brain reception (today's common jargon), and transplantation team members were convocated by computer alarm reaching into their homes, all movie theaters, concert halls, discoteques, bridge clubs and medical libraries. The complete team convened in the transplantation board room within the prescribed minimum time and was ready for action, i.e. scrubbed and tranquilized, within the prescribed additional minimum time. There was a slight delay due to the wavering of the hospital ethical committee members whose opinions were divided as to the possible reaction of the press, but this was soon overcome by the firm attitude of three of the members, a medical student, the elevator official and the cafetaria vice-cook on service.

At .... p.m. (publication of exact time withheld for political reasons) both professor and student were proclaimed officially dead by three appointed staff members, dermatologist, psychiatrist and gynecologist,

on the basis of the criteria determined by the Superior Council of the Superior Board of the Superior National Medical Organization, recognized by all political parties and religious currents. One second later, the permanently ready action flow sheet was started to be read over the hospital loud speakers and the drama became irrevocable.

On .... p.m. four brancards, supporting the two prospective donors and the prospective recepients, were wheeled into the mega-theatre and the transplantation team started its activities coordinated by the transplantation-programmed computer, to complete the assignment of two brain takeouts and two brain inputs with remarkable precision within the record time of three minutes (time data released by the hospital indirector). While listening to the regular tick-tack of the two recipient-electro-encephalographic registrations, derobing, and raising at the same time the now traditional post-transplantation dry Martini, the team members' later movement was suddenly arrested by the announcement of the chief anesthetist: "Gentlemen, congratulations-transplantation succeeded, however forgive me for slightly damping your elation by informing you that, due to a slight administrative error, the brains of the two prospective donors were cross-transplanted, instead of to the two intended recipients. Whereas the condition of the latter remains unchanged, both professor and student appear vital and show signs of intellectual revival.

The two steps taken next are noteworthy for their rapidity: shock-treatment to the transplantation team, and clamping down by the hospital indirector on publicity, both actions successful from the medical and hush-hush point of view, respectively.

After a few days, when the hospital staff had regained its normal metabolic steady state, the objective bystander could observe two main lines of consequence — political religious reaction to the transplantation and university riots.

Since the erroneous cross-transplantation was converted by the intensive publication care unit with shrewd diplomacy into a blilliant feat of intended professor-student brain exchange aiming at improvement of teacher-student relationship, no ethical criticism was

The

glare of

irreproducible

research

enlightens

PSYCHOLOGY

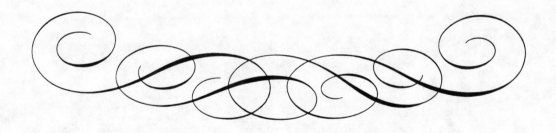

The Re-assessment of Criticism and Defenses of Depth Psychology with Supporting Data*

C. K. McKINLEY, Ph.D.[1],
C. K. MCKINLEY, Ph.D.[1],
W. B. REID, Ph.D.[1]
and Anonymous[2]

Introduction

The history of mankind is filled with illusions to the curative power of time. This is well demonstrated in such colloquialisms as "tincture of time and essence of patience." What was lacking until the advent of the genius Sigmund Freud was a comprehensive systematic model for the application of procrastination and systematic delaying as a therapeutic modality. Outside of psychoanalysis procrastination maintains only a tenous hold in the earthly pragmatic knowledge of the common man. It is indeed curious that an eminent practitioner can advise a friend that "time heals all wounds," but becomes impatient with a neurotic who poses a similar problem. With the major breakthrough of psychoanalysis, procrastination is no longer a hit or miss thing despised in the scientific community as a superstition embedded in the morass of "folk medicine," but rather a therapeutic tool with vast possibilities. With the presentation of a formal model of procrastination man can conquer a symptom not by an effort of will, but by effortless will. One can see now that protracted psychoanalysis is not to be scorned, but rather demonstrates the effectiveness of the theoretical model in the use of procrastination in real human situations. Eysenck's classic paper on the "ineffectiveness of Psychoanalysis" now paradoxically emerges as the strongest support for the Phoenix, Psychoanalysis, in the literature and clearly demonstrates the applicability of the theoretical model of procrastination.

Unfortunately the real significance of psychoanalysis and the modifications and expansions of earlier investigators are not at all clearly understood among some of its practitioners. The first danger signals appear quite early with the advent of "directive psychotherapy" and become an imminent danger with the appearance of "interpersonal theory." Currently the linkage of operant conditioning and behavior theory with depth psychology poses an immediate threat to the whole discipline. If we fail at this time in our efforts to save formalized procrastination for future generations, then who knows what eons may pass before another genius of the calibre of Freud will reopen the door to a more rewarding life when one can in fact put off until tomorrow what can be done today.

The present study endeavors to use psychotherapy appointments as means to demonstrate the utility of Procrastination theory in aiding mankind.

Method

Hampered as we are by psychological "raw data flow" (that is, the demand by persons purporting to be or reputed to be "scientists," that conclusions such as are set forth in this paper be supported by "facts," "data," or other uncontrollable events in the environment. It is obvious that raw data can only introduce noise or error into a scientific system.), the present scientific system requires an examination of actual facts (or factual acts) in order to draw conclusions. Out "data" come from an unpublished masters thesis in Psychology; the author failed his orals and subsequently left the field. He prefers to remain anonymous.

Table 1 displays data on 10 patients in psychotherapy for their first 10 appointments. Each patient was instructed to deliberately miss each of the first 10 appointments and both patient and doctor were not to contact one another until the eleventh hour. At the conclusion of each missed appointment the patient was given the Contrivatory Tests of Symptoms, and the total score for each administration rated as "better" or "worse" according to Buzzard's method[3]. Testing was conducted by Anonymous.

* Research supported in part by grant funds liberated from coffee dues.
[1] Division of Child Psychiatry, University of Texas Medical Branch, Galveston.
[2] Grant A. Fund, M.A., Candidate, last known address, Dept. HEW, Washington, D.C.
[3] Buzzard, Fraquahr, What's in a name, J. of Orthonegativity, 1:247 (1966)

TABLE 1 . RAW DATA . THERAPEUTIC EFFICACY

Appointment No.	No. reports "better"	No. reports "worse"
1	4	6
2	5	5
3	7	3
4	4	6
5	6	4
6	5	5
7	6	4
8	6	4
9	3	7
10	4	6

The results of Table 1 are patently inconclusive. The beneficial effect of no therapy (Procrastination) may be present but is not evident to a naive observer. Application of the Data Enrichment Method[4] yields the following results.

Of no relevance is the fact that the figures in the tables presented to have a superficial resemblance to those found in the article on data enrichment method previously cited. Statistical computations reveal that such similarities occur at a probability level of 10^{-22}, however, as the old baseball maxim has it "it only takes one to hit it."

A glance at Table 2 shows that the efficacy of delaying seeing the therapist which was skulking almost unnoticed

[4] Lewis H., The data enrichment method, J. Irrepr. Res., *15*:6–9, (1966).

in the raw data of Table 1, has been brought fully forth by the Data Enrichment Method.

As can be seen, not keeping appointments which can be thought of as not being in psychotherapy at all produce beneficial results simply through putting off seeing the doctor. "No doctor today keeps neurosis away."

Summary

An in depth study was made of the efficacy of systematized procrastination in psychiatric disorders as compared with unstructured procrastinationatism reflected in everyday life. The systematic application of this treatment modality was found to be in all respects as effective as its less sophisticated cousin.

TABLE 2 . ENRICHED DATA : THERAPEUTIC EFFICACY .

Appointment No.	No. of virtual "better"	No virtual "worse"	Probability of report of "better"
1	4	050	4/54
2	9	44	9/53
3	16	39	16/55
4	20	36	20/56
5	26	30	26/56
6	31	26	31/57
7	37	21	37/58
8	43	17	43/60
9	46	13	46/59
10	50	6	50/56

The Varieties of Psychotherapeutic Experience

ROBERT S. HOFFMAN

1. FREUDIAN

P: I could use a ham on rye, hold the mustard.
T: It's evident that a quantity of libidinal striving has been displaced to a regressive object with relative fixation in the anal-sadistic mode.
P: What do you suggest?
T: Perhaps a valve job and tune-up.

2. ROGERIAN

P: Shit! Do I feel shitty!
T: Sounds like you feel shitty.
P: Why are you parroting me?
T: You seem concerned about my parroting you.
P: What the hell is going on here?
T: You sound confused.

3. EXISTENTIAL

P: Sorry I'm late today.
T: Can you get more in touch with that sorrow?
P: I hope it didn't inconvenience you.
T: Let's focus on your capacity for choice rather than on my expectations.
P: But I didn't mean to be late.
T: I hear you, and I don't put it down. But where we need to be is the immanence of the I-Thou relationship (in Buber's sense) emanating from the here-and-now, and from there into a consciousness of the tension between be-ing and non-be-ing, and eventually into the transcendence of be-ing itself, through to a cosmic awareness of the oceanic I-dentity of Self and the space-time continuum.
P: Gotcha.

4. BEHAVIORAL

P: I feel depressed.
T: Okay. First, I want you to look at this list of depressing phrases, order them by ascending depression-potential and match them with these postcards. Then I want you to step over to these electrodes — don't worry — and put your head in this vise and your left foot in this clamp. Then, when I count to ten, I want you to . . .

5. GESTALT

P: I feel somehow that life just isn't worth living.
T: Don't give me that shit!
P: What do you mean? I'm really concerned that . . .
T: Real hell! You're trying to mind-screw me. Come off it.
P: You shmuck — what are you trying to do with me?
T: Attaboy! Play me — play the shmuck. I'll play you.
P: What's going on?
T: Not shmucky enough — try again, louder.
P: I've never met a therapist like this.
T: No good — you gotta stay in the here-and-now. Again.
P: (gets up to leave)
T: Okay, now we're getting somewhere. Stand up on that table and do it again.
P: (exits)
T: Good. Now I'll play the angry patient and walk out the door. "You shmuck — I'm leaving."

6. CONFRONTATION

P: Hello.
T: Pretty anxious about the amenities, eh?
P: Not very.
T: Don't try to wiggle out of it.
P: I'm not. I just . . .
T: Trying to deny it?
P: Okay, you're right.
T: Don't agree just for agreement's sake.
P: As a matter of fact, I don't agree . . .
T: Sounds a bit hostile.
P: Have it your way. I'm hostile.
T: That's pretty dependent, that statement.
P: Okay, I'm EVERYTHING.
T: God, what modesty!

7. PRIMAL

P: Can you help me stop cracking my knuckles, Doctor?
T: Okay. You're three years old — you're hungry — REALLY hungry — you want to suckle — you reach for your mother's bosom — what happens? — she pulls away — SHE PULLS AWAY! — SHE ISN'T GOING TO LET YOU HAVE IT — FEEL THAT! — WHAT DO YOU FEEL?? — WHAT DO YOU WANT??? — Get down on that mat there or you'll hurt yourself — YOU *WANT*, YOU REALLY WANT THAT MILK! — YOU WANT YOUR MOMMY! — YOU AREN'T GOING TO GET YOUR MONEY, I MEAN MOMMY!! — CRY OUT TO HER! — TELL HER YOU WANT HER! — CRY, YOU SONOFA-BITCH!!!!
P: But I'm allergic to milk products.

8. PHARMACOLOGIC

P: I've been having this feeling that people treat me like an object, that they don't see me as a person in my own right, in all my uniqueness.

T: NURSE! Get me 500 mg. of Thorazine STAT!

Future Directions

9. ASTROLOGIC THERAPY

P: My last therapist told me I'm deficient in reality-testing. Delusional, I think he termed it.

T: What sign are you, may I ask?

P: Libra. The thing is — I see things occasionally that I'm not sure others see. I tend to form conclusions with insufficient evidence.

T: That's quite characteristic when a full moon hits on the second Thursday.

P: What?

T: Especially if your middle name begins with a P.

P: How did you know that?

T: Well look at this chart . . . you can see that whereas two weeks ago Saturn was out of phase with Route 101, we're now approaching the Spring equinox, and when the Life signs predominate you'd predict that all the MacDonald's hamburger stands will go out of business. You know what that means.

P: Vaguely.

T: Right — things are vague right now for you, in fact for Geminis more than Libras. But on the last day you'll receive a message from a close associate that will clarify a great deal.

P: That's good to know.

T: Surely, but no surprise.

10. MUSICO-THERAPY

P: I have this nagging sense of something left undone, some unfinished business.

T: What are you feeling?

P: Sorta flat. Like nothing of major significance is going on.

T: Not major?

P: That's right.

T: Anything of minor significance going on?

P: You could say that. But it's not enough.

T: What are your present concerns?

P: Well, mainly I think I worry too much about how people *see* me. They seem to think I'm not too sharp.

T: And what would you like to accomplish?

P: I guess I'd like to focus more on what I can *be* of my own volition, rather than just meeting people's expectations.

T: I see. And this sense of unfinished business — does it feel like something you've done before, or is it something you haven't experienced yet?

P: It seems sorta familiar, like I've been through it before and want to recapture it.

T: A repeating pattern.

P: Right — it keeps popping up, and I somehow feel that my life will be incomplete unless I regain it one more time. I'm having a little trouble expressing it — it's hard to conceptualize.

T: Not at all. The way I see it, your life resembles an unfinished *rondo*. Our task is simply to modulate from C-flat-minor to B-sharp-major and rediscover the refrain.

P: But what if we can't rediscover it?

T: No problem. Then we'll just *vamp ad lib* or write in a *coda*. Or if you really want to be adventurous, we could call in John Cage for a consult.

11. T.V. THERAPY

P: Doctor, I've got these pains that sort of move around.

T.V.: (therapist at controls) What do doctors recommend for pain of neuritis, neuralgia?

P: But I also have this ulcer, and plain aspirin makes it . . .

T.V.: Rolaids absorbs forty times its weight in excess gastric acidity.

P: But they may not be real pains — I think they may be in my head.

T.V.: Well, Ben Casey, I think we have to operate. I know you can do it, if anyone can.

P: I know this sounds stupid, but . . .

T.V.: M-I-C, K-E-Y,

P: Are you making fun of me?

T.V.: Excedrin headache number fourteen.

P: Look, I'm getting angry.

T.V.: This is Chris Schenkel from Madison Square Garden.

P: I really don't want to fight you.

T.V.: Stay tuned next for the Late Late Show. Tonight's presentation is *The Red Badge of Courage*, starring . . .

12. REPETITO-THERAPY

T: Good morning.

P: Hi. I feel sorta empty.

T: I feel sorta empty.

P: You too? Wow. Anyway, things just don't seem to be going right.

T: Things don't seem to be going right.

P: That's right. Everything I try to do fails.

T: Everything *I* try to do fails.

P: Really? But I'm coming to *you* for help.

T: I'm coming to *you* for help.

P: Well here's a howdy-do!

T: Here's a pretty mess. I mean . . .

P: You're a Gilbert & Sullivan fan?

T: You're a Gilbert & Sullivan fan?

P: Of course — you think I made that stupid lyric up myself?

T: Of course — you think I made . . .

P: Hold it!

T: Hold it!

P: And I thought *I* was sick! (exits)

T: (soliloquy) Something went wrong there — I'd better get some more supervision.

NEIL ILLUSIONS

ALLAN NEIL

works at the Institute
of Behavioral Research,
Texas Christian
University, Fort Worth,
Texas

Although psychology is one of the oldest of the true sciences, the study of illusions started long before a science psychology existed. A great deal of the early research in the area of illusions, however, was the work of men who are not usually thought of as psychologists, and thus has been irretrievably lost. It is impossible to estimate just how many illusions were lost during this period of scientific darkness, but the number may be substantial.

Such a deplorable condition could not continue forever, and indeed it did not. The advent of formal psychology and the timely arrival of the introductory textbook secured, for all time, the illusion's place in psychology. The golden years really began in 1832 when a transparent rhomboid owned by L. A. Necker first began to show spontaneous depth reversal. Named the "Necker Cube" in honour of its discoverer the transparent rhomboid was quickly committed to literature and has continued cyclic depth reversal, without interruption, ever since.

While the scientific community pondered this singular circumstances, some of the really great men of psychology were contributing their names to illusions: Muller-Lyer, Poggendorff, Zollner, Ponzo, Optical and Moon. Illusions piled up. Theories flourished. Debate waxed luxuriantly. Research spread unchecked. Then at the turn of the century, a noticeable slackening in activity developed. A drastic decline followed. Finally, total collapse! As the years passed, a few hardy souls continued to look for an adequate perceptual account for the various figures, but there were no new illusions. Without new illusions intrest flagged. Full page, four colour illustrations helped for a while, but finally, only freshmen could be tricked into saying, "Gee it really does!"

Recently a few new illusions have been discovered. these new illusions, in sharp contrast to those of the 19th century, do not violate the invariance of parity, charge conjugation, or Time reversal. Full scale research has not yet begun on the information-processing mechanisms which respond to the subtle factors in these illusions, but the preliminary studies have not overestimated their impotance. The figures shown below, although only the first of the new series, are presented here with the hope that the interest they generate will revive that research and restore the study of illusion to its rightful place in the feild of psychology.

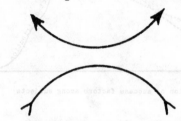

Note that the lines do not appear parallel

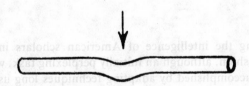

Note how the pipe appears bent under the arrow

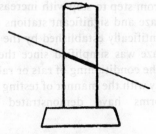

Note how the line appears thicker
where it passes through the column

2
Note how one line appears longer

4
Note that the boxes appear to be different sizes

6
Note how quicly the figure disappears
when you look directly at it

Reprinted with permission from *New Scientist & Science Journal*, April, 1971

Contributed by: Dr. Henry S. Gertzman, National Cash Register Comany, Dayton, Ohio 45409

161

The Correlation Between Intelligence and the Success of American Scholars: Report of Am. Inst. of Strange Behavior

PETER STEINE

It has long been presumed that there is a direct correlation between the success of American scholars and their intelligence. In a study spread over six years and examining a sample of scholars representing every discipline in every research and educational institution in America and only recently made public, the correlation has finally been substantiated in an empirical and unambiguous fashion. What is surprising is that the correlation is an inverse one, that is, the most successful scholars were demonstrated to have the lowest intelligence by the standards used, while those academicians polled who were singularly unsuccessful in the eyes of their colleagues had higher levels of inteligence. It should be noted in spite of this relative difference in intelligence, the difference between the highest and lowest scores on the intelligence tests were negligible when compared with the spread of intelligence over the general population. The intelligence demonstrated by the most intelligent (who was uniquely unsuccessful among his peers) was at about the level of a barnyard horse, while the lowest intelligence demonstrated by a scholar (who was the three-time president of the Association of American Politics and a former ambassador to Russia) was measured to be slightly higher than that of a well trained house plant.

The measure of sucess for this study was a complex interrelated and integrated statistical representation of

    a. the weight in grams of the sample's dissertation and subsequent publications, adjusted by a paper weight and type size factor;

    b. the hate his colleagues registered on a visceroscope at the mention of his name;

    c. the salary and fringe benefits he drew converted to pennies;

    d. a caliper measurement of cranium and hip fat. Chart I shows the range and curve of the sample as well as the breakdown by paper, hate money and fat factors.

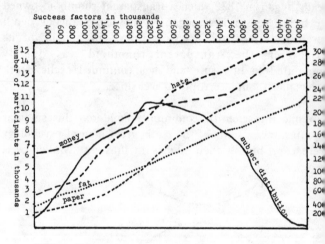

CHART I. Distribution of success factors among subjects

Measuring the intelligence of American scholars in scientific fashion, although an initially perplexing task, wa ultimately accomplished by adapting techniques long use at the Institute in other studies. A maze was constructe and the subjects' ingenuity, perceptive and cognitiv abilities were tested from step to step with increasing rigo Figure I shows the maze and significant stations along th intelligence steps scientifically established by the testers a the Institute. The maze was simplified since the subject involved had neither the conditioning of rats or rabbits, no the intuitive familiarity with the manner of testing that rat rabbits or flat worms have demonstrated in pas experiments.

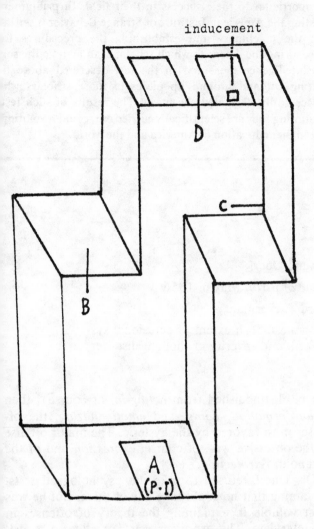

inducement

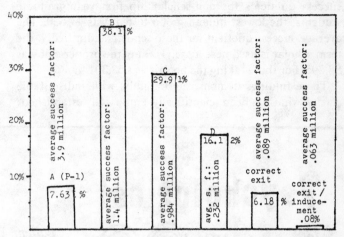

GRAPH I. Correlation of Success Factor and Achievement.

preliminary testing using a more complex maze, a majority of the subjects being tested remained at the start, what testers described as "a befuddled condition." In the simplified labyrinth, an old book and a little pile of money placed at the end of the maze to serve as inducements were clearly visible from the start.

Even in the simple maze there was a significant minority of scholars whose response was a P-1 response, that is, they remained at the start, confused by sight of the pile of money and the alternate exit. Of this group (7.63% of the total sample) 68% had a success factor above 4.3 million. The average success factor of this group was at 3.9 million, substantially above the average success factor of the whole sample (see Graph I).

While there was a number of scholars who faltered and stopped in confusion in the first main leg of the maze (between points A and B), the bend in the main hall of the maze at B proved to be the next significant stumbling point in the test. 38.1% of the subjects failed to get beyond this ling point in the test. 38.1% of the subjects failed to get beyond this point, either unable to negotiate the bend in the hall or unaware of the bend. Nearly a third of those faltering at this point in the test walked into the wall repeatedly until they fell to the floor exhausted or unconscious. Many of those that negotiated the first right angle turn at B were confused to be facing the wall at C and either stopped there or turned in the wrong way and got hopelessly lost in the maze. As one might suspect, the success levels of those who did not get past these similar stumbling points were also very similar. The average success factor of those stopping at B was 1.4 million while the average for those getting to C was .984 million (see Graph I).

While a remarkably strong 22.3% of the subjects tested made it to the end of the maze, a surprisingly large 16.12% bolted through the wrong door or ran into the jamb between the exits. The remaining 6.18% took the proper exit, but only .08% of those stopped to look at or take the old book, while only one of the subjects tested actually took the money on his way through the door. He was a former soccer player, who entered teaching to avoid the draft and who, incidentally, went through the maze in four seconds. Predictably his success quotient was 341, one of the lowest success quotients among the subjects tested. The average success quotients for non-scholarship first year graduate students, the lowest human group tested, was 17,620. The average success quotient for those scholars (admittedly, the term scholar is used here loosely) taking the proper exit was 88,895. For those taking the book it was 63,301.

These findings demonstrate tangibly, with indisputable clarity, what has been scientifically, empirically established: that the intelligence of working scholars is inversely proportional to their success in their field. In priliminary testing the American Institute of Strange Behavior is setting up the machinery and establishing the procedures for measuring the extent to which scholars can assume the sort of intelligence measured in the test described above by eating cut and ground up pieces of those scholars who successfully navigated the maze. The results of such tests assuming they are scientifically carried out, could revolutionize higher education in America and the world.

Psychological Report ◎◉

Patient: Dr. Sigmund Duerf

Age: 116   *Date of Birth:* May 6, 1856

Examiner: Edward Zuckerman

Referral Reason: To establish extent of delusional system and severity of thought disorder.

Behavioral Observations:

Dr. Duerf is a short, stooped, balding, grey-haired man who looks much younger than his claimed age of 116. His eyes are alert and penetrating and give the impression of great wisdom. His speech is difficult to understand because of a strong Austrian accent, a facial prosthesis he must wear, and constant cigar smoking. Rapport was excellent and easily established.

Referral Question:

The well-systematized delusional system was easily elicited as he eagerly seeks converts to his beliefs. It all came to him "in a flash," he says, as he was reading Heider's balance theory and watching the Green Bay Packers on T.V. one Sunday. He saw that the psychoanalytic theory of dynamics was tragically incomplete: defenses everywhere but no offenses. He immediately set out for Green Bay, Wisconsin, to consult with the late Vince Lombardi and to give his theory to the world.

In the next several months, one offense after another was discovered. First was the most basic, *expression* (to be distinguished from *acting-in,* of course), then *action-formation, doing,* and *emotionalizing,* the offenses most favored by the hysteric. The major offense of the obsessive was, of course, *expression* and of the paranoid, *retrojection.*

Dr. Duerf refused to take the psychological tests, explaining that he could fake any of them. But he was most voluble in explaining the theory of offenses in the interview. The examiner was not allowed to ask questions of the doctor as this would interfere with the "keeping hold of." (Dr. Duerf explained that this phrase lost something in the translation.) This restriction led to the examiner's remaining confused about the explanation of the offenses, and thus the report on delusions is incomplete.

Diagnostic Impression: Senile Dementia

Recommendation: Because of the lack of background information on the patient, his case is to be turned over to the staff forensic psychiatrist, Dr. Franz Kafka, for disposition.

A NEW PSYCHOLOGICAL TEST: T.E.T.

URIEL AKAVIA
School Psychologist, Tel-Aviv

We are glad to inform professional and non-professional readers that a new test is getting ready for publication.

It is a personality test based on the mechanism of projection, a worthy follower of the Rorschach, T.A.T., C.A.T., Blacky and many other projective tests.

T.E.T. = Thematic Esspresso Test.

The main tool for testing is the plain cup of esspresso coffee. It was not by chance that we have chosen this handy tool for our experiments. Esspresso is the symbol of our technological and hurried generation, called not without reason "The Esspresso Generation."

Procedure: The client (or patient—it depends on the school of thought represented by the testing psychologist) is seated in a soft, reclining chair and is told to relax. Then he is offered a cup of coffee, esspresso. The psychologist doesn't reveal his intentions and the testee is not aware that he is tested. The movements of the testee are recorded by a hidden camera.

(A set of all needed appliances will be available at the local Psych. Assoc. shop: A chair, a camera, video, dozen cups and 10 pounds of good coffee, record-blanks and pencils. All this is manufactured now at top speed as the test, because of its modernity, is sure to become a best-seller, a sine qua non of every self-respecting psychologist, from Berkeley to Tel-Aviv.)

Norms. 2457 subjects were tested already and exact norms are being computed at this moment. The testees were White Academicians mostly students of psychology. All of them were very eager to sip esspresso for the sake of science.

Results. Many very pertinent findings are recorded, some of them astonishing in their depth and analytical revelations.

We report a few of the findings.

a) The testee puts three lumps of sugar: The characterological meaning: Oral Dependence, Hedonism and Masochism.

b) He puts none; coffee unsweetened: Ascetic tendencies. Anal trends. Hypochondriacal worries.

c) Puts sugar in mouth and drinks: Probably a communist.

d) Spills coffee on his shirt: A bum. More masochism. Bad kinder-stube.

e) Spills coffee, on the psychologist: Repressed hate of father. Sadism.

f) Sips coffee noisily: An egoist. More sadism.

g) Asks for more: A commercial, exploiting attitude. Spoiled brat.

The whole list of findings, the rationales and the interpretations will be published soon.

QUOTES:

C. M. Pare.
MONOAMINE OXIDASE INHIBITION AND BRAIN MONOAMINES IN CLINICAL CONDITION
Biochemical Society Agenda, Nov. 1970, Dagenham, N. Y., p. 4.
"Studies on brain amines in patients who commit suicide have been somewhat disappointing".

****

W. T. Weber and W. T. Taylor
General Biology, Van Nostrand, Production N. J. 1968, p. 3.
"Paleontology is a science which deals with the study of extinct plants and animals that survive today as fossils".

****

V. Sladeček
A NOTE ON THE PHYTOPLANKTON-ZOOPLANKTON RELATIONSHIP
Ecology, 1958, 39, 547.
"It can be stated in terms used in saprobiology that the polysaproby was changed into alpha-mesosaproby".

****

L. Lindner
Proc. 8 Intern. Cong. Genetics 1949: 620.
"54 percent of the men and 22 percent of the women were able to move their ears. That the percentage figure is twice as high for men can possibly depend . . . on the fact that men are even in childhood more interested in sports . . .".

D. V. Nalivkin
THE GEOLOGY OF THE USSR (Translated by S. I. Tomkeieff)
Oxford Univ. Press, 1960, p. 153.
". . . Great progress has been made in the study of the bowels of our country . . . Great and prolific is our motherland and much wealth is hidden in her bosom".

****

Leonard L. Naeger
AUDITORY STIMULATION OF NOREPINEPHRINE RELEASE
Abstract:
Studies have shown conclusively that certain auditory interpretations are responsible for adrenergic stimulation. In a study of 100 chronic seminar sleepers, the word sequences responsible for stimulation were: "In Summary" and "Last Slide Please". (Raster Srider Prease). Phrases such as "The Next Series of Experiments" and "In The Next Few Years We Found", cause a significant increase in low frequency and high amplitude brain waves, resulting in increased sedation.

****

Lewis A. Shadoff
DETECTION OF NONEXISTENT MOLECULAR IONS
Anal. Chem. 39, 1902 December (1967)
The author states, after explaining his method, "Since there is no background interference, very small signals may be detected."!

****

T. T. Smith
Southeastern Feathered Cattleman, Vol. 16, #1, p. 276, January 1984
"This retrospective survey showed that 75% of sweet young soft-boiled eggs are laid by lecherous old goats, an additional 23.5% by lecherous young goats. The remaining 1.5% were hard-boiled".

****

A. L. Norins, M.D.
STING OF A SMALL CALIBER BULLET
Archives of Dermatology 96 (6): 701 Dec. 1967
Comment
"Most people who are shot realize what has occurred".

QUOTES

JOURNAL COVERAGE CHANGES
Current Contents (Oct. 31, 1973)
Bulletin of Suicidology (ceased publication)

****

Ben-Abraham, S.I.
ON INTERNAL STRESSES DUE TO A RANDOM DISTRIBUTION OF DISLOCATIONS
Scripta Metallurgica. 2(1):9 (1968)
   I wish to note the following: A physically meaningful random distribution of dislocations can be defined only by assuming the *positions of the dislocations are completely random.*

****

FACT SNACKS...
Delaware Valley Sci. & Engin. Newsletter, 9:(4):(1969)
   Soup and fruit juice in a bar! Dehydrated foods can be compressed to the size of a candy bar. Astronauts can get anything from soup to shrimp in 1/4-pound, 2-by 1-inch bars for eating dry or rehydrating to the food's normal shape by adding water.

****

Greenhouse, Linda
The New York Times Mag. (June 28, 1970)
   The New York State Legislature finally amended the state's penal law to give New York the most liberal abortion statute in the United States. The Legislature's language was sparse and seemed scarcely open to misinterpretation. "An abortional act is justifiable when committed upon a female with her consent by a duly licensed physician ..."

****

Webb, B. F.
BROADBILLED SWORDFISH FROM TASMAN BAY, NEW ZEALAND
N.Z. J. of Marine & Freshwater Res. 6 (1 & 2): 206 (1972)
   On 4 January 1971 Mr. F. J. P. Kellor shot with a .308 rifle an adult broadbilled swordfish *Xiphias gladius* Linnaeus, in Wairangi Bay. .... On examination, the swordfish showed no external signs of injury.

****

WHY NOT EAT INSECTS?
By A. V. Holt. 1885
   This curious little book, reprinted in 1967, consists of 99 pages. It includes some remarkable suggestions for menus.

****

Cummins, Joseph E., Day, Alan W.
IN SMUT, THE SEX MESSAGE IS TRANSCRIBED AND TRANSLATED DURING COURTSHIP
J. of Cell Biol. 59:68a (1973)
   In the anther smut, *Ustilago violacea*, copulation is initiated when cells of opposite mating types (a_1 and a_2) are mixed on a nutrient free medium. Following a short (two or three hour) period of courtship, synchronous mating is achieved by the cooperate assembly of a tube between paired sporidia. Alleles of the mating locus are differently regulated during the cell cycle of vegetative sporidia. Allele a_2 can be induced to transcribe 'sex message' at any time in the cell cycle while allele a_1 can only be induced during the G_1 phase. Experiments with specific inhibitors of RNA (actinomycin C and Rifampicin) and protein synthesis (cycloheximide) along with experiments employing tracers to follow synthesis of the macromolecules show that 'sex message' is both transcribed and translated during the period of courtship that precedes assembly of the copulation organelle. Experiments with U.V. sensitive and wild mating combinatons indicate that the period of maximum sensitivity to U.V. coincides with the period during which sex message is transcribed. Furthermore, the experiments show that there is a reciprocal exchange of information between the courting sporidia that coordinates the sequential 'read-out' of sex message in each single sporidium of the mating pairs. (Supported by grant A5062 from NRC of Canada to A. W. Day and an Institutional Grant to J. E. Cummins.)

Quasi-successful concurrent validation of a special key for a relatively new and exciting personality instrument in a group of potential managers: or, I am never startled by a fish.

W. S. BLUMENFELD
Paper read at the meeting of the
Georgia Psychological Association
Macon, May 1972

Most of us would probably agree that, in the area of managerial selection, what is lacking most is the availability of valid non-cognitive predictors. Further, most would agree that tailor-made, special keys are to be preferred to universal, general keys. The combination of the two seems desirable and appropriate. However, as Kurtz pointed out so well in 1948, too often the wishes and hopes of the practitioner and/or the consumer manifest themselves in a strange form of selective perception in the evaluation of effectiveness of such keys, i.e., the acceptance of self-fulfilling "research" *via* foldback design.

Purpose. The purpose of this research was to develop and validate concurrently a special tailor-made key for a relatively new and exciting personality instrument in a group of potential managers. A secondary (sic) purpose of this research was to point out once again the specious, spurious, fallacious, but fascinating results that are obtained when cross-validation does not follow item analysis.

Data Collection. The subjects, criterion, and instrument follow.

The subjects in this experiment were 126 management majors in an introductory management course at Georgia State University. The instrument administration was presented to them as an example of a "scientific" selection technique (very much as charlatans present their wares to unwary personnel and marketing executives). From all indications, it was accepted as such (just as it is usually accepted by "hard-nosed businessmen"). These subjects may be viewed as entry level managers, or at least potential managers, i.e., personnel and marketing executives, hard-nosed businessmen, etc., etc.

The criterion in this study was self-reported grade point average of the subjects.

The relatively new and exciting (if not sensational) personality instrument used in this study was the *North Dakota Null-Hypothesis Brain Inventory* (*NDNHBI*), conjured up and conceived by (Art) Buchwald (1965) with a sharp tongue and a great deal of cheek in answer to the problems of face validity encountered by the *Minnesota Multiphasic Personality Inventory*. The *NDNHBI* consists of 36 statements of a non-cognitive nature to which the respondent indicate either true or false as being a descriptive of himself. Since the inventory is so "special" and will no doubt be of interest, the items are presented here:

1. I salivate at the sight of mittens.
2. If I go into the street, I'm apt to be bitten by a horse.
3. Some people never look at me.
4. Spinach makes me feel alone.
5. My sex life is A-okay.
6. When I look down from a high spot, I want to spit.
7. I like to kill mosquitoes.
8. Cousins are not to be trusted.
9. It makes me embarrassed to fall down.
10. I get nauseous from too much roller skating.
11. I think most people would cry to gain a point.
12. I cannot read or write.
13. I am bored by thoughts of death.
14. I become homicidal when people try to reason with me.

15. I would enjoy the work of a chicken flicker.
16. I am never startled by a fish.
17. My mother's uncle was a good man.
18. I don't like it when somebody is rotten.
19. People who break the law are wise guys.
20. I have never gone to pieces over the weekend.
21. I think beavers work too hard.
22. I use shoe polish to excess.
23. God is love.
24. I like mannish children.
25. I have always been disturbed by the sight of Lincoln's ears.
26. I always let people get ahead of me at swimming pools.
27. Most of the time I go to sleep without saying goodby.
28. I am not afraid of picking up door knobs.
29. I believe I smell as good as most people.
30. Frantic screams make me nervous.
31. It's hard for me to say the right thing when I find myself in a room full of mice.
32. I would never tell my nickname in a crisis.
33. A wide necktie is a sign of disease.
34. As a child I was deprived of licorice.
35. I would never shake hands with a gardner.
36. My eyes are always cold.

In the original article, Buchwald presented a differential psychometric scatter scoring system for placement in either the Peace Corps, the Voice of America, or the White House. In the current research, as indicated by the purpose, an appropriate configuration which concurrently related to an external criterion was developed and quasi-validated.

Data Analysis. There were three phases to the data analysis of this research, i.e., (1) item analysis, (2) foldback, and (3) cross-validation.

The 36 items in the *NDNHBI* were item analyzed using the procedure described by Lawshe and Baker (1950) with an external criterion of self-reported grade point average. A skew in the criterion distribution categories necessitated that the high and low "halves" of the criterion group be of different sizes. In the item analysis, there were 48 in the high group, and 28 in the low group. Alpha of .10 was used to identify the "discriminating" items for inclusion in the "special" key.

To prove to the proponents of the instrument (of which there were a few) and to those who really "wanted" the key to work (several students with an apparent clinical bent), the items surviving the item analysis were applied to the answer sheets of the item analysis group. The concurrent validity was documented by biserial correlation.

For those more interested in the best (rather than the most fulfilling) estimate of the relationship between the derived key and the external criterion of self-reported grade point average, the items surviving the item analysis were scored in holdout groups of 25 high answer sheets and 25 low answer sheets. Again, biserial correlation was obtained to quantify the relationship between the special key and the criterion.

RESULTS

The item analysis procedure identified 9 items (chance would have been 4) which discriminated between the high and low groups at or beyond the .10 level. The reader will no doubt be interested in which items "came through", particularly as the potential for *post hoc* interpretations and insights are nearly infinite. The items (and their weights) in the special key were:
1. (—) My sex life is A-okay.
2. (+) When I look down from a high spot, I want to spit.
3. (—) I think most people would cry to gain a point.
4. (+) I am never startled by a fish.
5. (+) My mother's uncle was a good man.
6. (+) I don't like it when somebody is rotten.
7. (+) I have never gone to pieces over the weekend.
8. (+) Most of the time I go to sleep without saying goodby.
9. (+) It's hard for me to say the right thing when I find myself in a room full of mice.

Applying these 9 items back upon the original sample, the obtained biserial correlation was .78. This is clearly off zero beyond the .05 level, — most encouraging to all, and completely satisfactory, convincing, and conclusive to some (Kurtz, 1948). (Consider here for a moment those of your acquaintance and/or your employ using this foldback design and at this point mouthing such quasi-professional, and sage, things as "of course, these results should be interpreted with some caution.")

Unfortunately, when the 9-item key was applied to the holdout sample of 50, the encouraging coefficient of .78 shrank slightly. In fact, it shrank back to .07 (*not* significantly off zero at the .05 level). Too bad; pity; so many of the items seemed to have so much construct validity, and were *so rich* in potential for *post hoc* interpretations and insights, e.g., "I am never startled by a fish."

DISCUSSION AND CONCLUSIONS

Little if any discussion seems necessary; Cureton's classic paper (1952) has been re-trotted out and executed. It seems clear once again that (1) the application of a key to the control group is the acid test of the quality of a key and (2) the (re)application of a key to the original group is but a half-acid test. To a sophisticated group like this, this would seem to be "coals to New Castle"; however, as an industrial psychologist in a business school dealing with students of business administration (and naive practitioners and consumers of business administration), it is painfully clear to me that the foldback design still remains very much in vogue. (Afterall, it has such obvious marketing advantages.) I think it appropriate to continue to beat home the point of cross-validation, i.e., let's have no more of this half-acid research.

In conclusion, the foldback design is not (necessarily) dead; it is very much alive and doing quite well among the malicious and the naive in the general business world.

And frankly, I *am* always startled by a fish — particularly when the "fish" turns out to be a personnel or marketing executive.

REFERENCES

Buchwald, A. My eyes are cold: Testing in the great society. Author, 19

Cureton, E. E. Reliability, validity, and baloney. *Educational and Psychological Measurement.* 1950, *10*, 94-96

Kurtz, A. K. A research test for the Rorschach test. *Personnel Psycholo* 1948, *1*, 41-51

Lawshe, C. H., & Baker, P. C. Three aids in the evaluation of the signific of the difference between percentages. *Educational and Psychologic Measurement*, 1950, *10*, 263-270

The author wishes to acknowledge the data collection and analysis contributions of Allen Austin and Julian Eidson.

DEFINITIONS

LAWRENCE & GAIL BLOO

CHAIRMAN OF DEPARTMENT

Leaps tall buildings at a single bound
Is more powerful than a locomotive
Is faster than a speeding bullet
Walks on water
Gives policy to God

PROFESSOR

Leaps short buildings at a single bound
Is more powerful than a switch engine
Is just as fast as a speeding bullet
Walks on water if the sea is calm
Talks with God

ASSOCIATE PROFESSOR

Leaps short buildings with a running start
Is almost as powerful as a switch engine
Is faster than a speeding BB
Walks on water in an indoor swimming pool
Talks with God if a special request is approved

ASSISTANT PROFESSOR

Barely clears a quonset hut
Loses tug of war with locomotive
Can fire a speeding bullet
Swims well
Is occasionally addressed by God

INSTRUCTOR

Makes high marks on wall when trying to leap buildin
Is run over by locomotive
Can sometimes handle gun without inflicting self-inju
Dog paddles
Talks to animals

RESEARCH ASSOCIATE

Runs into buildings
Recognizes locomotive 2 out of 3 times
Is not issued ammunition
Can stay afloat with life jacket
Talks to walls

GRADUATE STUDENT

Falls over doorsteps when trying to enter building
Says, "Look at the Choo-Choo."
Wets himself with water pistol
Plays in mud puddles
Mumbles to himself

TECHNICIAN

Lifts buildings and walks under them
Kicks locomotives off the track
Catches bullets in his teeth and eats them
Freezes water with a single glance
Is God . . .

Bayes Theorem and Screening for Future Mental Illness: An Exercise in Preventive Community Psychiatry

LYON HYAMS, M.D., M.S.

It is generally agreed[1,2] that an ounce of prevention is worth a pound of cure[3]. Accordingly, one reasons that if there were predicting indices of future severe mental disturbance, early therapeutic intervention would result in a reversal or diminution of the pathological processes decreasing the institutional and welfare burden, increasing the work force, and thereby increasing the future gross national product[5]. It is, in addition, possible that such people would be happier[6]. Of course, one would want to assume that: 1. reliable identification is possible; 2. one could, indeed, induce a reversal; and 3. that R_{12} was favorable[7] before implementing preventive measures[8].

The purpose of this presentation is to indicate that even if the above postulates can be assumed, the preventive goal is still impractical — and Bayes theorem[9] is to blame[10].

Assume that a "marker," M, of previous psychiatric instability can be found such that in a large psychotic population it had been present 95% of the time[11]. Conversely, in a nonpsychotic group it was absent 95% of the time. (Such a 'marker' has been proposed[12]. Apparently, a "Certain Fixed Stare" (CFS) during work differentiates these broad groups). Such probabilities are a priori, i. e., given the event, psychotic or not, the probability of having had the marker. But in screening we are only interested in the aposteriori probability, i.e., given the marker, the probability of becoming psychotic. Bayes' formula[13] allows us to calculate this quantity knowing the probability of psychoses in the general population. Recent estimates[14] indicate that one in every 50 persons develop psychotic illness. We can now define a universe consisting of two exhaustive and disjoint events: being psychotic and not being psychotic (P and $\overline{P}$)[15], where $\Pr(P) = .02$ and $\Pr(\overline{P}) = .98$.

If M indicates a positive marker and $\overline{M}$ the absence of such, the conditional probability of becoming psychotic when identified with a positive marker is given:

$$\Pr(P/M) = \frac{\Pr(M/P)\,\Pr(P)}{\Pr(M/P)\,\Pr(P) + \Pr(M/\overline{P})\,\Pr(\overline{P})}$$

Where:

$$\Pr(M/P) = .95$$
$$\Pr(P) = .02$$
$$\Pr(M/\overline{P}) = .05$$
$$\Pr(\overline{P}) = .98$$

Then:

$$\Pr(P/M) = .28$$

In other words, for every 100 people giving a positive marker, only 28 of them would develop a psychosis in time. Since these 28 are unidentifiable, it would be financially prohibiting to treat them all. In addition, psychotherapy applied to normals might precipitate an unexpected break, increasing the type II error.

[1] Hyams, L. "The Advantages of Screens, A Prospective Epidemiological Study." Journal of Household Effects 3:109–110, 1924.

[2] Goose, M. "Silly Stories" 1397:97, 1922.

[3] This colorful expression, used to denote the more profitable distribution of energy outlay-reward return ratio, R[4] is copyrighted. Please do not quote without written permission of the author.

[4] Definition of R: a. R ≥ 100 implies Inadequate Exchange. Modification necessary for continued life.
   b. 5 ≤ R < 99 implies Normal Operating Range.
   c. R ≤ 4 implies Unusually Efficient Transfer Kinetics. Continued operation at this level results in Fuse Blowing (F.B.)

[5] This has an important inference for grant go-getters.

[6] This is pure speculation. No one has been able to demonstrate, for example, that the washed-out schizophrenic is not really having a ball.

[7] See footnote (4).

[8] It is suggested that the above criterion be termed "Hyams Postulates for Favorable Preventive Community Psychiatric Ratios (HPFPCPR)."

[9] Or formula. I never know which is correct usage.

[10] Bayes himself wants no part of this.

[11] You can never do better than 95 percent.

[12] Hyams, L. and Hyams, D. "Staring During Work" Journal of Occupational Medicine. 13:1, 1963.

[13] Or theorem.

[14] Hyams, L. Unpublished data.

[15] Further differentiations of groups can be attempted. A division of psychoses into vertically and horizontally crazy is useful[16].

[16] Vertical psychotics vibrate up and down. They do not disturb other people. Horizontal psychotics vibrate in a plane parallel to the ground. They are a pain in the neck.

Luckily

irreproducible

research

about

vast

SOCIAL

CONCERNS

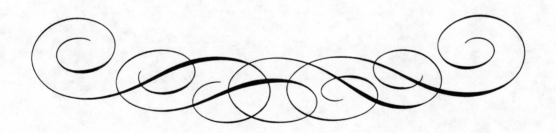

educing Automobile Accidents

By JOHN L. S. HICKEY*

Recently reported research[1] by the National Safety rogram has provided a significant clue which can, if operly exploited, reduce and perhaps completely iminate automobile accidents. The germ of the break- rough lies in the NSP finding that "75% of auto- obile accidents occur within 40 miles of home".[2] ow there are five ways in which one may react to this atement. Three of the reactions are elementary:

Normal reaction: "I should be just as vigilant driv- ing near home as when on the highway".

Statistician's reaction: "Since about 90% of the driving occurs within 40 miles of home, and only 75% of the accidents, this a "safe" area and I can relax while driving.

Reverse reaction: "I'd better drive as fast as pos- sible to get out of the 40-mile "danger" zone into the surrounding "safe" zone".

The other two reactions will be explored in some de- ail, as reaction #4 provides the means to reduce ac- idents, and reaction #5 can, at some small risk, liminate them completely. Both employ the method f Data Enrichment[3] previously reported in the Journal f Irreproducible Results.

The fourth reaction is: "If 75% of automobile ccidents occur within 40 miles of home, it can be een through use of the data enrichment method[4] that he farther one is from home, the smaller the chance f an accident. Therefore, *I will register my car at a home" 500 miles away and never go near there"*. This rocess could easily be developed into a national pro- ram for providing simulated or substitute home for ll drivers, perhaps with a title like Car Registration t Substitute Homes (CRASH). Obviously, if no one ver drives within 40 miles of their "home" accidents ill inevitably be reduced 75%.

The fifth reaction requires a little background dis- cussion. As we all know, accident rates vary from locality to locality; one can therefore expand on the fourth reaction and surmise that, instead of register- ing their car at a randomly chosen "home" 500 miles away, the safer thing to do would be to register it in a place much farther away *and which has a low auto- mobile accident rate*. A place immediately comes to mind — the South Pole. It is very far away, and there is only one automobile there[5]. Thus the automobile collision rate is necessarily zero, and automobiles re- gistered in Antarctica will sustain this rate. Again, this concept could be extended into a nationwide pro- gram under which every automobile would be regis- tered at a single center located at the South Pole, which could be named Central Location for Accident Prevention Through Registering Automobiles Polarilly (CLAPTRAP). Through this method, the automobile accident would become a thing of the past. The small risk? If another automobile were taken to Antarctica and collided with the first one, every car in the country would suddenly be registered in an area with *a 100% automobile accident rate*.

---

[1] Reported via public service time on TV and radio.
[2] It may be 80% within 50 miles of home. The exact figures do not change the concept.
[3] Lewis, H. R., J.I.R. 15:1 (1966).
[4] Calculations not reproduced here.
[5] A Volkswagen: see full page ads in Life, almost any 1967 issue.
* Nom de plume for Mike Robrain.

A GUIDE TO CORRECT BARKING ABROAD: A Review

by MARY WARE

Shi Pu's study *A Guide to Correct Barking Abroad* is an arresting work which demands the careful attention of any canine planning travel abroad. A dictionary of useful terms in several hundred canine languages, this work fills a painful hiatus in the linguistic canon heretofore available.

All too few animals heed the fact that the rewards of travel increase when one knows something of the language of the host country. Pets in particular should familiarize themselves with the sounds and structures of the languages of the countries in which they are to stay. How many every year spend up to six months in quarantine without understanding a bark barked or a yap yipped? If they were to study before leaving their homelands, they would save themselves much boredom in the kennel, where a little pleasant conversation is the only recreation outside meals. They could also prevent the inconvenience of having to rely on gestures. So often the wave of a paw or flap of a wing can be misconstrued. Knowledge of the language of a country also promotes better international relations through the grass-roots relationships with the host-country nationals. Animals, being generally closer to the grass than anyone else, are an untapped source for improved international understanding in this troubled time of ours.

A review of this work must mention that the study goes beyond a mere listing of terms. Special cultural notes are given to aid in sensitizing the visiting dog to the *faux pas* he might make, so unnecessary in our tense era. Various quotations from the dictionary listings can only indicate in part the scope covered.

ARGENTINA
Gua-gua /Gwa-gwa/ (The dog visiting Spanish-speaking countries is cautioned against assuming that the Spanish language is the same the world over. A cursory examination of the first half dozen items will reveal the fallacy of this assumption.)

BRAZIL
Au-au /Ow-ow/

CHINA n. b. Hong Kong; at the time of preparation of this manuscript, data from Red China were unavailable as informants.
/Won-won/ (Do not confuse with /mai-mai/ said by Chinese cats and roughly equivalent to U. S. Standard *meow*.)

COLOMBIA
Guau-guau /Huow-huow/ (This sound is rather difficult for non-native speakers, but by diphthongizing the *uo* and drawing the sound out slowly, a comprehensible approximation can be made.)

COSTA RICA
Guau guau (*sic.*) /Gwow-gwow/

CUBA
Jau-jau /How-how/ (Although the revolution has produced some slang variants, the standard has remained constant.)

EL SALVADOR
Guau-guau /Woaw-woaw/

ESTONIA
Auh-auh /Aw-aw/

FINLAND
Hau-hau /How-how/

GUATEMALA
Bow-wow /Bow-wow/ n. b. The full import of the similarity between the Guatemalan and U. S. barks is still being researched.

ISRAEL n. b. Before June, 1966, Hebrew speaking sector.
/How-how/

LEBANON /Haw-haw/

176

NIGERIA: *Wai-wai*	Calabar area /Waing-waing/
NIGERIA: *Gbogbo*	Western area, Yoruba language /Gbo-gbo/ (The multiplicity of languages within a single country complicates communication immeasurably; however, it is hoped that the increasing use of English as a *lingua franca* will lessen this difficulty. It would be unfortunate, nevertheless, if the traditional forms were lost in the process. A society is currently being formed to minimize this danger.)
PERU *Gua-gua-gua*	/Wow-wow-wow/ (Peruvian dogs are known for their over reaction to even the simplist situations.)
PHILIPPINES *Bow-wow*	/Bow-wow/ (American influence; regretably the beautiful, n a t i v e sounds have been forgotten by even the oldest inhabitants.)
SYRIA هَو هَوْ	/Haw-haw/ (A Dog speaking Arabic has a better chance of making a socially acceptable comment to Arabic speakers from various countries than a dog speaking Spanish in different Spanish-speaking countries. See Lebanon; Argentina, note; however, the visitor should listen carefully to the inflection of the host country national.)
THAILAND โฮ่ง โฮ่ง	/Hong-hong/
UKRAINA БрawE	/Breshe/
VIETNAM *Gâu gâu*	n. b. The southern section. /Go-go/ (French and American contacts with the canine population have apparently been minimal.)

To help the animal bent on greater rewards in foreign travel, Shi Pu has urged publication of this compendium in paperback rather than in the better-grossing hard-cover edition, explaining that the "small size makes it [the book] easy to carry in the mouth or beak."[1] The pet is advised to try to learn the languages of as many countries as possible, as the quarantine location, a miniature United Nations, will contain animals from a variety of linguistic backgrounds other than that of the host country.[2]

The approach is sensibly aimed at the general canine rather than at those already initiated into the mysteries of linguistic scholarship, as it is the general reader that has special need for this study. This method of presentation is explained in the introduction:

> The concentration of this phrase book is on greetings, which are the first words needed. The transliterations are into the sound system of American animals as they in particular expect everyone else to speak their language and constitute, therefore, the group that must be reached with greatest urgency. A more comprehensive listing of American dog terms is included so that American animals need no longer be embarrassed by the criticism that they do not know even their own language properly. Although pronunciation is considered the most important linguistic aspect for conversational barking, the really conscientious animal will want to study the written forms presented as well.[3]

Yet the study is backed by erudite research for which Shi Pu is eminently qualified, as can be readily seen by the description of the method used:

> The dictionary has been prepared after several years of intensive research through English as a Second Language classes in various cities, including dozens of sessions in which the students brought their dogs to class to record their voices. The dogs had to be brought singly to avoid their accents' becoming impaired through contact with dogs of other linguistic backgrounds. To keep foreign influences at a minimum, foreign students' dogs were preferred to dogs currently in quarantine.[4]

It is indeed touching that the book is dedicated to the dogs "who so freely donated their time to this study."[5]

While it is not Shi Pu's way to use current work to advertize former works, a study of *A Guide to Correct Barking Abroad* cannot end without mentioning related studies by this scholar; for the animal planning travel abroad would do well to study the languages of species other than his own so that he can recognize them without having to crane his neck into many awkward positions, thus risking an attack of lumbago so uncomfortable in cramped quarters. Available by the same author are *The Vocabulary of Cats, Bird Sounds: An Elementary Phrase Book,* and *The Languages of Larger Animals.* A catalogue of tapes recorded by native speaker canines of superior educational background is also procurable upon request.

---

[1] Shi Pu, *A Guide to Correct Barking Abroad,* New York: Animus Animalorum Scribendi, 1972, p. vi.
[2] *Ibid.,* p. vii.
[3] *Ibid.,* p. xi-xii.
[4] *Ibid.,* p. xxix.
[5] *Ibid·,* p. xxiii.

SYNTHETIC HAPPINESS

G. VAN DEN BERGH
Haarlem*

After many years of research, a team of scientific workers under Professor Sadler of the Amsterdam University has for the first time in history succeeded in producing synthetic happiness. Although the quantity produced is still negligible, there have been already some successful experiments on men, and the mass production of synthetic happiness is only a question of time[1].

The research team took as a starting point the common experience that happiness is not where you look for it. Yet, instead of giving up that seemingly unsurmountable problem, they redoubled their efforts and that with success.

The first thought of Professor Sadler proved to be unfortunately useless. If simply all feelings, thoughts, experiences and situations were to be studied, the problem could be solved. But it soon appeared that even the best electronic computer would need 3.1×10^{11} years to complete the task, provided that the number of possible combinations remained constant during that period of time. As the number of possibilities increases every year by about 10 million, the advocated method did not seem to be very promising for the nearest future.

Eventually the scientists succeeded in constructing a rather simple electronic brain, which seeks where it does not seek. Thus happiness could easily be located and isolated. It proved to be very volatile and extremely difficult to analyze chemically.

Another problem which was investigated was how to produce happiness in usable form. Experience has shown that an uncontrolled explosion of happiness has effects similar to those known from other explosive substances including the atom bomb. Blindness and deafness are the most common known effects, in more serious cases the brain is blown out and a serious disorder of the heart ensues.

Some pressure groups in the Western world suggest the immediate production of a HAP-bomb, before the Russians get the priority. The production of happiness for peaceful purposes has not yet been seriously delayed by this threat. The scientists have happiness under control and may produce any amount of it in reasonable time. Before, however, the economic exploitation of happiness can begin, there is still another problem to solve, because happiness cannot be bought. It has not yet been possible to sell any amount of happiness, without rapid denaturation of it.

There are different approaches to the problem of selling happiness. Some lawyers assert there is no problem in constructing a form of buying and selling, which is not buying and selling. Professor Sadler is trying to obtain a transaction-resistant happiness by a chemical method. His sponsor, General Happiness Inc., has again voted 1.5 million dollars for this research.

In the meantime, there seem to be also serious political implications in the exploitation of happiness. Political observers state the possibility of a complete social revolution after which everybody would have as much happiness as he liked. Some political parties have already urged their governments to take appropriate measures to prevent this.

So for a while we shall still have to do with ordinary happiness.

---

* It is reported that the author has found non-synthetic happiness.
[1] Huxley: *Brave New World*, 1947, Albatross Ltd., London.

E PLURIBUS URANIUM

CHARLES T. STEWART, JR.
Dept. of Economics
George Washington University
Washington, D. C. 20006

Today Berengaria officially went on the uranium standard, setting the value of its currency, the benarus, at 12 units per microcurie. South Africa is the lone holdout for a better conversion rate between gold and uranium. Since it has both metals, its indecision seems to be the result of uncertainty as to where its interests lie, rather than dissatisfaction with the International Monetary Fund conversion ratio.

Thus comes to a close the most momentous chapter in world monetary history since the invention of check-kiting. The revolution was initiated by the United States in 1984 as a master stroke in its psychological offensive against the Soviet Bloc. It was the first nation to go on the uranium standard (although Russia now claims otherwise). By this move it created a vast new market for its uranium stockpile, estimated to constitute 70% of the total world supply of uranium metal, eliminated its balance of payments difficulties for many years to come, and greatly increased international liquidity.

The last two results might have been achieved by raising the dollar price of gold, but the United States was unwilling to do this because it feared loss of face and was unwilling to hand the Russians a windfall profit on their unknown but enormous pot of gold.

The main objective of the conversion, however, was to further disarmament aims and to eliminate the risks of nuclear war. This objective was fully achieved. The Russians were put under heavy pressure to convert their nuclear warheads into currency, and did so in large number. Although they are believed to retain a few warheads, their first harvest failure is expected to lead to total nuclear disarmament. In the meantime, the Russians, with their well-known peasant attachment to cold cash, would never think of blowing up their hard-earned hoard in a mushroom cloud. Nuclear testing has ceased. India has gone conventional.

The new standard incorporates a foolproof inspection, warning, and control system. The conversion of monetary uranium into nuclear warheads by any country is promptly reflected in the foreign exchange markets if not in domestic price indices. The deflationary aspects of wars and preparations for war make them unatractive to all business, and practically impossible to finance. Conversely, the uranium standard has banished all fear of an economic collapse as a result of disarmament. The automatic increase in money supply as warheads are converted to currency sets off an investment boom and an inflationary fever.

In retrospect, it is hard to understand mankind's prolonged love affair with the yellow metal of such limited uses other than personal adornment. Perhaps it illustrates what Whitehead called the "fallacy of misplaced concreteness." Certainly it is clear today that people valued gold because others valued and were willing to pay for it, because still others valued it, ad infinitum, and for no other reason. This unwitting conspiracy, this keeping up with the Joneses, gave rise to a durable fashion, lasting thousands of years, but now comes to an end.

The advantages of uranium are obvious enough. Its value is not based on a fickle fashion, on the persistence of an illusion, or on human propensity for invidious comparisons. In an insecure world its virtues are unique. Not only is it a store of value but also a store of power. It can earn interest without moral qualms by generating electricity while it is serving as a monetary reserve. It lacks the stigma of petty bourgeois conservatism, of the banking profession and the capitalist persuasion. It is ideologically neutral.

The uranium standard now provides an effective technique for changing the velocity of circulation at will. Threatening recessions can be prevented by the simple expedient of increasing the proportion of salaries paid in radioactive uranium coinage. This "hot money" is immediately spent and just as promptly respent. Thus we have, in the old game of musical chairs, and the new monetary metal, a final cure for economic instability.

Not the least of its virtues from the American viewpoint is that it is found in abundance in the Western United States, and that its mining and processing is now a major support of a number of states with sparse populations but dense political representation.

EVOLUTION OF SCIENTIFIC THOUGHT

FRANK ANDERSON
Miami, Florida

Prof. Ludwig Botchall
Dept. Of Geophysics
Tifton University
March 20, 1971

Prof. Karl Von Vettkrotch
Dept. Of Geology
Pfledering Inst.

Dear Karl,

Since my new grant I've been researching a method of controlling seasons via population selection and I'm forwarding this theory for your perusal and in hopes that you may have some suggestions.

It appeared to me as if from a dream that if one could elicit the cooperation of the world's total population for a mere few minutes one could control the earth's rotational velocity. I propose having everyone face in the opposite direction of the earth's rotation and at the same precise moment all run at top speed for five minutes. This would slow the earth's rotational speed by a factor TP^x. X being the frictional force average/individual and TP as total population.

How does this sound to you?

Your friend,
Prof. Ludwig Botchall

Prof. Karl Von Vettkrotch
Dept. Of Geology
Pfledering Inst.
April 14, 1971

Prof. Ludwig Botchall
Dept. Of Geophysics
Tifton University

Dear Lud,

In answer to your letter dated March 20, 1971, I played with that theory several years ago as a means of avoiding daylight-savings time and I met a few stumbling blocks. 1. It seems that the mainland of Communist China would slam into California and the Chinese population would end up in the ocean as their continent slipped out from under them. (Not a bad idea though if you could get them to co-operate blindly). 2. Tidal upheavels would be immense. 3. Linearity would be difficult due to population distribution factors.

Have you considered these factors?

Karl Vettkrotch

Prof. Ludwig Botchall
Dept. Of Geophysics
Tifton University
April 17, 1971

Prof. Karl Von Vettkrotch
Dept. Of Geology
Pfledering Inst.

Dear Karl,

By gosh you're right. You never cease to amaze me with your overall grasp, and you led me to consider some other ramifications. I feel that the proper mathematical computations of continent mass/total population would allow one to control the coefficient of frictional force necessary to effect rotational lag without continental shifting (although your China postulate sounds exciting). It's apparent that this frictional coefficient would vary with variation in land mass and population. Our computer here is on the blink again. Can you help?

Ludwig Botchall

Prof. Karl Von Vettkrotch
Dept. Of Geology
Pfledering Inst.
May 19, 1971

Prof. Ludwig Botchall
Dept. Of Geophysics
Tifton University

Dear Lud,

Sorry to take so long but our computer was tied up with end of the month billings and I just finished my run. I have really lost interest in the climate control theory but I've become overwhelmed with the possibility of rejoining the continents into the original. When deriving your computations I came across some data on earth spin energies and the results are frightening. I came up with the following calculations for defining the differential rotational inertia of a continent $(\triangle I)$

$$\triangle I = \iiint \triangle O \, R^4 (\sin \phi - \sin^3 \phi \, \cos^2 \Theta) dR d\phi d$$
$$\Theta (\pm) \, p^f$$

Where $\triangle O$ = density contrast between adjacent continental crustal and oceanic layers

R = continental Radius

ϕ = longitude

Θ = latitude

$(\pm)p^f$ = population friction and is negative or positive depending on direction population is running

Integration would lead to two factors

1. $(1.59 \times 10^{39} \, CM^2)$ depending on shape of crustal layer.
2. A $\pi/3$ function relative to hemispherical size.

The factor (p^f) could become a constant (k) by controlling population friction. This could be accomplished by having all participants wear golf shoes to minimize frictional differences caused by terrain.

Lud, I'm personally fearful of this experiment. My calculations show that the continents would definitely rejoin with a force equal to 2×10^7 earthquakes and would back us up to the triassic period in geological time. I'm not sure I would care to go back that far even if I did survive the earthquake forces.

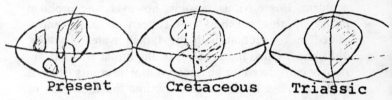

Present   Cretaceous   Triassic

I prefer to abandon the experiment and respectfully suggest that you do the same.

Your friend,
Karl Von Vettkrotch

P.S. My present worry is that all the "junk" we're leaving on the moon is going to alter its polar function. We as scientists should insist that Nasa make some effort to distribute it more evenly.

Here's a pip, reported by the Consulting Engineers Council: the latest Occupational Health and Safety Standards has outdone itself in governmentalise, they define the word "exit" as: "Exit is the portion of a means of egress which is separated from all other spaces of the building or structure by construction or equipment as required in this subpart to provide a protected way to travel to the exit discharge." They then had to define "exit discharge" as: "Exit discharge is that portion of a means of egress between the termination of an exit and a public way." Webster does it so much more easily, to him an exit is "A way out of an enclosed place or space."

Engineering Education: April 1972/779

The Solution of the Israeli Water Problem

RICHARD KRAFT
(The Negev Research Institute, Beer-Sheva)

INTRODUCTION

Whenever a country has a shortage of some basic raw material a natural economic question arises: Is it cheaper to import the commodity or to manufacture it locally? This question applies also to Israel's water problem. For obvious reasons, however, the problem posed by this question hasn't been seriously entertained in connection with the Israeli water shortage, until now[1]. Once the problem of importing water is seriously considered an obvious solution presents itself; it is the purpose of this note to outline the highlights of this solution.

THE PLAN

It is well known that the arctic regions of the world contain abundant supplies of saltfree ice which when melted gives tasty water that is suitable for drinking and irrigation without additional processing. Since the human population of the arctic region is small and militarily impotent and doesn't need this water, there would be no moral or political obstacles in taking the water. Nevertheless, once it is shown that a cheap way of transporting this water to Israel exists, certain countries will strongly oppose the project. For this reason it is proposed that immediate steps be taken to show that the inhabitants of the Arctic are descendants of a lost tribe of Israel[2]. Furthermore some organizers of the Jewish Agency should be sent as soon as possible to the Arctic to begin an immigration (aliya) program[3]. It would also be wise to ensure that the Minister of Foreign Affairs includes a stopover in the Arctic on the occasion of his next visit to Europe and the USA.

We will now discuss the technical aspects of the plan. Our proposal is to bring water from the Arctic to Israel in a pipeline. Pipelines of this order of magnitude have already been constructed in the United States. We will now show that Israel is in an advantageous position to implement this project.

One of the major problems of the project is the tremendous energy needed for pumping. In respect to this problem Israel is indeed blessed. For inside the borders of Israel is the Dead Sea—the lowest spot on earth. This makes it possible to bring the Arctic water to Israel by gravity feed (Figure 1). Hence there will be no pumping problem.

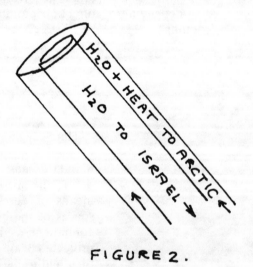

FIGURE 2.

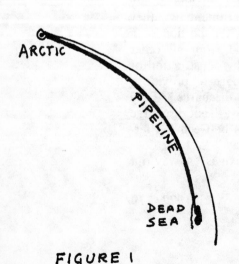

FIGURE 1

---

[1] Since the only feasible proposal for producing water locally gives a secondary product of a somewhat controversial nature there could be more than just economic gain in importing water.

[2] Some opposition (on theological grounds) to this can be expected to come from Hechal Shlomo (the equivalent of the Vatican in Jewish religion). They may be persuaded, however, to accept the plan for the good of the country if the government would encourage their patriotic feelings by contributing funds to the establishment of a yeshiva.

[3] This is not connected with the proposal to send these officials to the Arctic for general purposes.

Other obstacles are turning the ice into water at the Arctic and preventing it from freezing in the pipeline. A proposal for overcoming these two obstacles is shown in Figure 2. The pipeline will consist of two concentric cylinders. The inner tube will carry the water to Israel by gravity feed, while the outer cylinder will convey heated water to the Arctic by convection. The energy for the convection will be generated by the temperature differential between the Dead Sea and the Arctic. As a by-product of this convection we can expect to air-condition the entire Negev Desert.

Despite the close ties that can be expected to arise between Israel and the Eskimoes (following the discovery that they are a lost tribe of Israel), some sort of compensation will have to be made to our northern brethren. With the closing of the Common Market to Israeli citrus fruit, there will a surplus of citrus which we can ship to the Eskimoes. A cheap way of shipping oranges is shown in Figure 3. Since oranges are lighter than water they can be buoyed up to the Arctic in the convective section of the pipeline. To the Eskimoes this (the golden delicious fruit popping out from the ground) will seem like a blessing from heaven (figuratively speaking). No doubt, they will want to repay our generosity by sending us something in return.

What material and technical resources does Israel have for implementing this project? It is well known that Israel has abundant pipe factories. A strong diamond industry can be harnessed to provide the necessary drilling bits. The powerful financial support of American Jews could be relied upon. As for the technical problems they will crumble under the Jewish genius.

The only remaining problem is to find a supply of cheap labor. First, let us remind ourselves that the pioneering age in Israel is coming to a close and along with its decline the Israeli youngsters are becoming

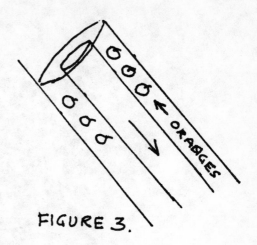

FIGURE 3.

soft and losing their idealism. Therefore the project of laying a pipeline to the Arctic is just the kind of challenge needed to inspire their spirits and harden their bodies. But some cynics may rightly claim that such an enterprise is beyond the capacity of the Nahal (Fighting Pioneering Youth—an agricultural version of Army service in Israel). Hence, the following solution is offered to the labor problem.

We are all familiar with the international response that was received for volunteer workers to excavate Matzada. Many youths had to be turned away and were very disappointed. Another such call would no doubt be answered again by today's restless international youth. Of course, the real purpose of the project would be disguised. It would be billed as another archeological project, and this time no volunteers would be turned away. It is rather dubious that any of the workers toiling away in the bowels of the earth would discover the real job they were doing, and besides, some archeological finds would no doubt be made before they reached the Arctic.

When this article was in preparation another suggestion was proposed by O. Novick:

We should like to suggest another solution to the Israeli water problem, based on the transportation of icebergs from Spitzbergen to Israel. Icebergs required are about $10 \times 2 \times 0.2$ km. If not available in nature, can be produced by freezing a small fjord filled with river water. Such icebergs would be transported to Israel by 3 frigates, 3 destoyers and ca. 10 orange carriers. During the transport, which would take about 5 months, the iceberg would melt and lose about 60–70% of its mass. The remaining 1000 millions of cubic meters of ice would amply supply the annual water consumption of Israel. The ice would be deposited at the Israeli coast, and melted there by solar energy, water being pumped directly from the iceberg. This project although perhaps engineeringly invalid, has some blissful marginal effects: It would solve the unemployment of both the Isareli Navy and the Merchant Marine (in peace time). Furthermore an iceberg carried through the Mediterranean would cool the Near East, and permit the importation of polar bears.

Trichomycete *Asellaria
ligiae* Tuzet et Manier
from the hindgut of the
marine isopod *Ligia
italica* Fabricius.

A Survey of Irregular Pedestrian Movement Transverse to Vehicular Flow

R. F. WILDE
Harvard Computer Center

INTRODUCTION

A study of available traffic literature indicates that while considerable attention is devoted to vehicular traffic, comparatively little is devoted to pedestrians[1]. The subject of this paper* is Irregular Pedestrian Movement Transverse to Vehicular Flow (IPMTVF), commonly referred to by the public as "jaywalking."

What is jaywalking?

A clarification of the term IPMTVF will first be given. There is a certain probability, depending upon traffic conditions and his psychological frame of mind, that a pedestrian arriving at a signalized intersection during its red phase, will attempt to cross against the vehicular flow. IPMTVF, or "jaywalking," refers then to this sort of perambulation. (The word "Irregular" in the definition, with its connotation of "random" and "illegal," is felt to be particularly suitable in this context).

Taking the survey:

The simple two-phase intersection used in the survey (44th Str. and 3rd Avenue in Manhattan) was chosen primarily for its convenience. An observer was stationed at the corner with stopwatch and notebook. Since IPMTVF is usually undertaken in defiance of established authority it was felt necessary to disguise the observer as a vagrant. 419.5[2] jaywalkers were studied and timed under varying traffic conditions. Jaywalkers exhibiting bound motion (e.g. children holding their mother's hand) were not included. Unfortunately, owing to the impenetrability of the observer's disguise the final third of the survey had to be carried out one block to the east. Analysis of the results, however, indicated that geographical variation over a distance of this magnitude was not statistically significant.

Term paper for Mass. Institute of Technocracy, course G1143A (Macrobiotic Traffic).

[1] R. F. Wilde, Evolution of protective clothing in the Metropolitan pedestrian, Grape Press 1968. p. 47.

[2] The fractional individual, when approximately half-way to his destination, became unsuccessful, but was deemed typical and hence included.

RESULTS

1. The IPMTVF-pedestrian:

It soon became apparent that IPMTVF behavior could be broadly divided into three groups:

> Type A: the bluffer;
> Type B: the gambler;
> L.O.L.: the unconscious.

An L.O.L. (Little Old Lady) usually fails to observe the light or notice the traffic and is sometime mistaken for a Type A until panicked by the horns of the oncoming cars. Note that, in spite of the terminology, both sexes may well be included under this classification. Another term in common is A.M.P. (Absent-Minded-Professor), not to mention a number of less flattering appellations.

It was hoped that some means would be found of predicting an individual pedestrian's behavior, as it is of primary importance to the motorist to avoid delay. Unfortunately this could not be done. Stratification by age, sex, and color of hair were sometimes observed, as when a Type A under stress would undergo a rapid metamorphosis into a Type B.

2. The IPMTVF fraction:

Let us now consider a number of pedestrians arriving more or less randomly at an intersection. Although, as previously pointed out, the behavior of an individual cannot be foretold with accuracy, a definite IPMTVF pattern does emerge when the behavior of many persons is averaged. The following diagram illustrates the form of curve obtained when the fraction of accumulated pedestrians attempting to cross illegally (the IPMTVF fraction, denoted here by F (t)) is plotted against time.

The high value and steep slope of F (t) for small values of t is due to the large number of pedestrians who get caught half-way across the street as the light changes and the rapidity with which they are eliminated from the scene. The end of the main vehicular platoon of traffic (slightly anticipated by the horde of impatient pedestrians) results in a new surge of IPMTVF activity. A final upswing occurs when the amber phase for the opposing vehicles is observed.

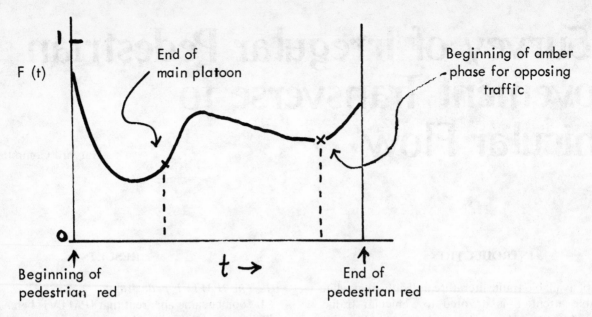

F(t)

End of main platoon

Beginning of amber phase for opposing traffic

↑ Beginning of pedestrian red

$t \rightarrow$

↑ End of pedestrian red

The curve just described was found to vary widely with such factors as time of day, cycle length, prevailing winds, and congestion both pedestrian and vehicular. More consistent results were obtained when a composite factor herein referred to as the *fright factor* was taken into consideration.

By definition, the fright factor

$$FF = k \left(c + \frac{v \, d \, l}{f} \right)$$

where
v = average vehicular velocity
d = traffic density (equivalent cars per cubic foot)
l = length of main platoon (miles)
f = footing factor, decreases with insecure footing[3]
k = constant to be computed by regression for each intersection
c = velocity of light (light years/year)

The *standard IPMTVF fraction* is then given by

$$S.F. (t)^+ = \frac{F(t)}{FF}$$

Although S.F. is of no particular value whatsoever, its curve remains remarkably constant, all things considered.

3. The IPMTVF path:

Investigation of the IPMTVF path was first undertaken during attempts to estimate IPMTVF velocity. It was soon noticed, however, that the path followed during IPMTVF was rarely a straight line perpendicular to the curbs. The diagram below shows a typical path.

Intensive observations of IPMTVF behavior indicated that the path *varies according to the obstacles encountered* (dogs, cars, pedestrians, diverse hazards underfoot). Furthermore, it was almost conclusively demonstrated that the path depended to some extent on the subsequent course taken by the pedestrian[4]. It has also been suggested to the author that some of the more exaggerated ambulatory aberrations were influenced by varying degree of alcoholic sedation[5], but this hypothesis could not be verified in detail.

---

[3] A footing factor of zero should not be used in practice.
[4] This remarkable result would indicate that *the future influences the past*—refutation of the principle of causality on the macroscopic scale.
[5] Unidentified Manhattan taxi driver, private communication.

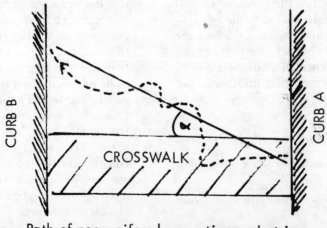

CURB B

CURB A

CROSSWALK

- - - - Path of non-uniformly-reacting pedestrian

Computer Program Virtually Eliminates Machine Errors

W. S. MINKLER, JR.
Pittsburgh

Spokesmen for a local electronic firm have announced a computer program that—through fresh application of an old technique—virtually eliminates lost time due to malfunction of computer components. Called OREMA (from Latin *oremus*, meaning let us pray), the program offers prayers at selected time intervals for the continued integrity of memory units, tape transports, and other elements subject to depravity.

Basically liturgical in structure, OREMA used standard petitions and intercessions stored on magnetic tapes in Latin, Hebrew, and FORTRAN. It holds regular Maintenance Services thrice daily on an automatic cycle, and operation intervention is required only for mounting tapes and making responses, such as "Amen," or "And with thy spirit" on the console typewriter.

Prayers in Hebrew and *Fortran* are offered directly to the CPU, but Latin prayers may go to peripheral equipment for transfer to the CPU by internal subroutines.

Although manufacturer-supplied prayer reels cover all machine troubles known today, the program will add punch card prayers to any tape, as needed, after the final existing Amen block. Classified prayer reels are available for government installations.

In trials on selected machines, OREMA reduced by 98.2 percent the average down time due to component failure. The manufacturer's spokesman exphasized, however, that OREMA presently defends only against malfunction of hardware. Requestor errors and other human blunders will continue unchecked until completion of a later version, to be called SIN-OREMA.

Reprinted from Data Link, March 1966, which reprinted the paper from THE SOURCE (Pittsburgh Section of American Nuclear Society), Jan. 1965.

Submitted: R. B. Gordon (Raytheon)

Chemically Chaste Campus

A recent newspaper article told of the growing demands of the student body at a well-known Eastern university for freedom of access to birth control measures, to wit "The Pill." Here at Truly Progressive University, the item was acknowledged with smiles of condescension. In this, a truly progressive university, the arguments pro and con were passe, strictly antebellum.

We had first come to grips with the problem several years ago and certainly a brief outline of the methods we used and the stumbling blocks we met on our way to a solution will serve as an invaluable framework for less advanced colleges to follow. The sagas of brave men challenging the frontiers of social science have ever been a fascination of mine. Thus, I find it doubly satisfying to recount an advance in which I played a personal role.

It all began in the late 1950's when educators across the country displayed increasing alarm over the swelling number of illegitimate pregnancies noted on the best of campuses. The statistics were unquestionable but there was little agreement over the basic cause of the increase.

It was here at T.P.U., I'm proud to say, that the initial advance was made. At one of our faculty meetings, a stalwart professor of Physiology bravely stood up and stated what he felt to be the heart of the matter. His speech was rather liberally spiced with anatomical terms and loose comparisons between some of our students and certain members of the hare family.

The minutes of the meeting were later burned and the professor shortly sought another post. For us, however, the air had been cleared and the enemy, so to speak, discovered.

Open discussions on the subject became the rule of the day. The program was constantly modified and enlarged. After two years of this bombardment of intensive information the results were tabulated. Alas, they showed a larger number of better educated unwed mothers. An advance surely, but not an answer.

We moved on.

The faculty meetings had never been so well attended and became the scenes of titanic struggles between the proponents of various control measures. Those few who persisted in implicating members of the bird or insect family were shouted down. The suggested lines of attack showed unlimited imagination and ran the gamut from compulsory chasity belt, with the master key held by the dean of women, to immediate expulsion for even conversing with the opposite sex.

The struggle between the moderates and extremists waxed and waned. A compromise seemed impossible. Then came the pharmacological breakthrough of the second trimester of the century from a distillate of horse . . . er, Equine urine, came the "Pill."

The administration happily suplied the desired products free of obligation. Had it been up to the men to take the pill it might have worked. The coeds, however, giving lip service to an outdated moral code, refused to forearm themselves with the necessary regularity. The laboratory at the Health Service, where a positive pregnancy test induced massive ovulation in the female of the frog family, was up to its neck in excited frogs.

"Take your pill" buttons and protest marches flourished. Mottoes were slashed on every available facade. "Pills prevent people," "Pill-less passion produces pregnancy," to mention a few.

Male super-egoes were shaken and shattered. The Mental Health Department was a pandemonium of crying men. "If you can't trust your girl to protect you, then what?" they asked. "Look at me," they pleaded, "I'm only a lapse in mommy's memory."

The effects on campus life were dramatic. Twenty per cent of the Junior class volunteered for Viet Nam. The director of the Health Service was repeatedly hung in effigy. Unrest seethed through the classes and gloom enveloped the university. Finally even the "Winter Carnival" was declared a stag party.

It was in this mentally stupifying atmosphere that the star erupted and from that day forward the name of Dean Hubert Hereford Howser has a permanent place among the annals of college men. That memorable day when he rose above the common man to give birth to a plan that spanned both human and animal physiology and set T.P.U. once more on the road of progress.

Later in an interview for Time magazine the details were elucidated: Dean Howser related that while shoveling out the University barn (he doubled for the janitor on weekends) he was trying to avoid the hind foot of a heifer that seemed intent on smashing his thigh bone when suddenly he was struck as if by lightning. His fertile mind conceived the entire stratagem in a nonce.

It was ingenious, workable, and it destined Howser to immortality: feed the hormone to the kines, he reasoned. Give them enough so that a therapeutic dose comes through in the milk. Everyone drinks milk.

The coeds chug-a-lug their milk, chomp up cheese, and are passionate about puddings. It seemed foolproof, perhaps even student proof.

Twenty-one days of each month the cows were slipped a measured dose of medicated hay. The resultant fortified milk was passed on to commissary to be fed to the coeds. The effect was heartwarming to see. Not only was pregnancy no longer a problem but all the females on campus were now set on the same menstrual cycle.

The Infirmary set up a crash program once a month for "Dysmenorrhea Day." From the twenty-fifth to the thirtieth of each month Midol was available on the dinner menu. Classes in Women's Physical Education were simply cancelled if they coincided with "starting day." In recounting the system's benefits before the faculty club, the Director of Health stuttered and finally cried like a baby as he outlined the range of the plan.

We have now been fully activated for a period of three years and I'm happy to report that the tranquility of the campus is only rarely disrupted by unwanted and unwarranted pregnancy. These occur in girls to whom milk products in any form are anathema. We've agreed among us that any little runt as unAmerican as that can just take her chances.

Honor forces me to admit there were some minor shortcomings. These all arose in the male students who could not be dissuaded from partaking of milk products. The kinks were minor and rather easily disposed of, but for the sake of completeness I will list them and our solution to them.

(1) Only five per cent of our male graduates can pass their draft physicals.

No gripes there, eh?

(2) Once a month some of the men get extremely irritable.

We have encouraged them to take Midol. This seems to control that problem.

(3) The enrollment in the Art College has tripled and the sale of male cosmetics has skyrocketed.

To each his own, I say.

(4) In spite of the epic efforts of our animal psychiatrist, our prize Angus bull killed himself in a frenzy of frustration.

A steak is a steak is a steak.

(5) Surprisingly, the major body of complaints have come from the female students. It seems we are left with a campus of lusty fully protected females and the men aren't really interested.

Hell, you can't have everything.

Owan T. Wick

A STUDY OF LEARNING FROM TELEVISION WHEN PICTURE QUALITY IS DEFICIENT
East Texas State University, 1966.

Found "significant difference in the learning from normal T.V. reception conditions and when there was snow or ignition interference in the T.V. picture".

Joan B. Richmond

If ego takes control of "id"
And superego is the lid
Then "id" is pretty far below
So, seems that something's bound to blow
Up and away so "Id" can be
Itself, again, unconsciously.

THE ERADICATION OF POVERTY IN CONTEMPORARY AMERICA:

Genesis, Treatment and Evaluation[1]

Alan Frankel[2]
University of Portla

ABSTRACT

Without explicating specific psychological, social, political, and economic theories, and utilizing a hypothetico-deductive epistemology, a testable theorem is derived concerning the ontogenesis of poverty in contemporary America. A treatment strategy is suggested as well as a theory-related method of evaluation.

Poor people do not have enough money. Give them enough money. They will no longer be poor.

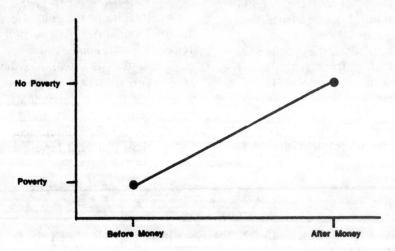

FIGURE 1. Mathematical representation of the Poverty-Money relationship. $r = 1.00$, $p < .0000001$

[1] This study was financed in part by Grant No. RD 14-1063-7093/RPM-1049/CIA/OSS/POOF from the Society for the Preservation of Social Sciences Interested in Nonparametric Hyper-multivariate Research of Trivial Social Problems.

[2] Reprints are available from the author at the Department of Psychology, University of Portland, 5000 N. Williamette Boulevard, Portland, Oregon 97203, if you are absurd enough to request one.

The Clinical use of Spondiac Vulgarisms in the Assessment of Hearing Aids in Sound Field Hearing Test

ROBERT L. FRANKENBERGER, Ph.D.

Speech and Hearing Laboratory,
Western Illinois University,
Macomb, Illinois 61455

n order that persons with hearing losses may hear
ter, the usual routine is the purchase of a hearing
. However, the purchase of a hearing aid is not a
ple matter. One needs the advice and counsel of
clinical audiologist to guard against being bilked
an unethical hearing aid salesman. The selection
a hearing aid is akin to the purchase of a new car.
one really needs is basic transportation, but the
esman mentions color coordinated pistons, white
lls, automatic antennas, dual mufflers and speakers
d other components not necessary to the task of
ting to and from one place to another.

There are as many types of hearing aids as there
types of cars, or, for that matter, hearing losses.
e should exercise judicious care in the choice. The
t hearing aid can be selected by the re-testing of
person's hearing while wearing the unit. The unit
t gives the wearer the best hearing is usually se-
ted; regardless of the color coordinated wires and
tteries or price. One reliable way to test hearing is
utterance of spondee words (six lists of thirty-five
o-syllable words with equal stress on each syllable,
h as "doorknob, campstool, ragmop," etc.) in a
nd field environment. Thirty-five words are usually
sented with a decrement of 1 dB less than the pre-
ding word so that the audiologist can cover a range
thirty-five dB in intensity.

Sound field testing is the presentation of the spon-
es in a free field environment without earphones
t with the hearing aid worn as one would usually
ar it in a non-test situation.

Some of the thirty-five words in the list have better
sponses than others. This should not be. Upon in-
stigation of responses, when the patient repeats the
rd he thinks he hears, the audiologist must some-
nes resist a powerful urge to giggle. Giggling in a
und treated chamber, with the patient seated facing
e, seems to diminish one's dignity as well as threaten
e professional aura that most hard-of-hearing pants give the clinical audiologist. The words most
mmonly "heard," or at least repeated, seem to be
o-syllable vulgarisms that apparently sound much
e the innocuous test words. Words such as "duck-
nd, horseshoe, hothouse, and storehouse," for in-
nce, are mistaken for common four letter vulgar-
ns.

With the relative freedom of language in books,
the theater, movies, and campus riots, clients often
do not hesitate to use expletives if they think they
hear them. Older female patients seem to hear these
words much better than their uttered counterparts in
the test in spite of not being able to hear preceding
or following words at the same, or higher, intensity
level. One patient, in fact, heard nothing but vulgarisms, in spite of the fact that the innocuous word list
was administered. She reported that she heard these
words all the time and that was why she needed her
hearing tested. She later told the psychologist that
someone was sending these words over the radio to
her hearing aid. (He suspects that our clinic is the
sending station of these words, since other of his
patients report similar aberrations.)

A new spondee word list was created, sprinkled
with common vulgarisms and expletives. Words were
taken from plays, movies, books, and rest room walls.*
A list of words accompanies the manuscript. (Inclusion or exclusion of the words from this article is
editorial responsibility; however, if he declines, a word
list will be sent in a plain brown wrapper if the reader
would contact the author.) All words were presented
and checked for equal syllabic stress and accurate
attenuation and placed on magnetic recording tape to
assure standardization. Two methods of response were
offered: (1) "repeat the words you hear," (2) "write
the words you hear."

One finding was clear. Hearing for spondaic vulgarisms is better than for standard or innocuous spon-
dees. A number of no responses were found however.
These instances were most commonly found in prim,
geriatric females, men of the cloth, clinic secretarial
staff, and a couple of female grad assistants who unwittingly volunteered for the final test. Psychogalvanic
skin response (PGSR) would be one way of confirm-
ing if the "no response" was or was not a response.

This new clinical test is offered as an addition to
already established tests of hearing. It is our opinion
that more accurate results are obtained and proper
selection, purchase and use of a hearing aid are assured.

Anaylsis of Modest Brand Pantyhose Forthcoming Advertising Campaign

A Deitrich Motivational survey, and a 984 base statistical study for demographical breakout have been run through the computer, with the following results.

(1) Men like to look at female legs. (2) Many men (68.5%) prefer to view legs covered with a transparent fiber. (3) Women are aware of this. (4) Women (86.5%) wear pantyhose or stockings in order to appear attractive to men. (5) Women will sacrifice durability to appearance, but are interested in both. (6) Women are much impressed with testimonial advertising.

Therefore we suggest a testimonal advertising campaign. Illustrations will be in good taste, showing only legs to upper thigh.

Beauty will be suggested by illustrations, which should be actual phtographs of legs in various positions. Face may be inset, to show who is giving the testimonial. The face need not necessarily belong to the legs, though both should be attractive.

We give two suggested testimonials, both of which are in our files. We have releases for pictures and testimonial

Copy 1

"In my business I take off my pantyhose from six to t times a night, yet Modest Brand Pantyhose gives me three months service."

Copy 2

"I go out with younger men, attracted to my pantyl yet the triple reinforcement at top of Modest Brand P hose even allows me to go to a drive-in movie and sit back seat without fear of tear or penetration. My life be different if I didn't wear Modest Brand."

This is a very brief summary of our projected camp which is certain to be a winner and a breakthrough in cr advertising.

We are now preparing media lists, budget, comps storyboards, and analysis of statistical data, and ou page total analysis will be in your hands within the we

We will supply sixty copies for distribution.

MR. H. C. VO

BASF Wyandotte Cc
Wyandotte, Mich. 48

It has come to our attention that the first of May is celebrated in some remote parts of the world as St. Walpurgis Nacht, commemorating St. Walpurgis (Walpurga or Walburga), the patron saint of polymer chemists, both organic and inorganic. She was reported to have been born in Sussex at the beginning of the VIII century. Her father, Richard, is thought to have been a son of Hlothere, 9th king of Kent, while her mother, Winna or Wuna, may have been the sister of St. Boniface. At the instance of St. Boniface and Willibald, her brother, she went about 750 to Germany to continue her studies on macromolecular dissymmetry in ordered systems. Her first major studies were conducted at Bischofsheim in the neighborhood of Mainz, a world-renown center for advanced studies in polymer rheology, where she was able to work in conjunction with St. Herwart. Two years later (754) she moved to Heidenheim, Eich-

statt, and continued her investigation of coumar indigent resins. This effort resulted in extensive pu cations which were well received by the scient community.

Upon her death (780) her relics were transla to Eichstatt, where she was laid to rest in a hol rock from which exuded a kind of bituminous afterwards known as Walpurgis oil, and regarded many as the universal plasticizer for PVC. The c soon became a place of pilgrimage, and an Instit was built over the spot. In addition, she is regar as the protectress against magic arts. In art she represented with a crozier, and bearing in her h a flask of balsam.

****

This information has been forwarded to IUA and awaits their action.

Traffic Jams for Fun and Profit

Robert Twintone tests the revolutionary Jamwagen 2000*

I have just returned from testing a car as with-it as Dusty Springfield, as slim as a virgin okapi, as comfortable as an old man's trousers, as appealing as graft, and yet as stationary as the Eddystone Light. The first car to be produced with immobility in mind, the Jamwagen 2000 manages to give an impression of relaxed power when standing firmly still on its revolutionary square wheels. Finished in drip-dry polystyrene, in a wide variety of tartans, and with siliconised paper bumpers, the Jamwagen isn't just a good-looker. Lift the bonnet, and prepare to gasp with the sort of surprise that would have confronted Menelaus had he looked on the Barbican development, or Ptolemy, faced with a sliced loaf! Beneath the racy mocklizard lining, in the space previously filled with a useless engine, is a glistening 4-tap, overhead-valve coffee-urn and food-mixer combined, complete with near-china mugs and a triple-jointed spoon-fork appliance. The wickerwork laundry baskets are linked by Fonk-Worthington lightweight con-rods to an alloy-head spin-dryer, close-coupled to independent front TV and an inflatable kiddies' paddling pool. There are compartments for books, records, dogs, a roulette wheel, an infra-red spit, and a complete 8-mm. home-movie outfit. A single touch on the tasselled dash-button, and the stainless breadbin opens automatically, firing slices into the toaster at a rate of 0–50 in 3 minutes. I found the twin egg-boilers sluggish in second gear, and it is irritating to find that the dishwasher tends to overheat in warm weather, but otherwise the car is a mechanical masterpiece.

Inside, the senses squeak and gibber in a mixture of awe and love, at the care lavished on the plastic ocelot upholstery, the deeppile, scurf-free yak-hair carpets, the succulent peach mirrors, and the glittering minichandeliers. No expense has been spared to make this the most expensive car of its kind. For once, I found myself unable to cavil at the size of the ashtrays, which have a dynaflow flush-system that instantly converts them into sparkling baby-baths, each with its individual rubber mini-duck on an edible chain. (The Speedwell conversion with high-pressure taps and twin-cam quick-lift soap-dishes is recommended for experienced bathers only). At the touch of a gilt handle, the 8 seats turn into 4 beds, to the tune of "Scotland the Brave", and the sink-unit swivels outwards to become a washable plastic flowergarden, I found the lavatory lacking in legroom, but the manufacturers assure me that they will be able to get the bugs out before the first model is carried triumphantly onto our roads.

---

*Reprinted by permission of PUNCH (Sept. 23, 1964, p. 454).

The History of Thought as a Closed Linear System**
More Empty Economic Boxes

Adam Smith was the first Keynesian, and not Thomas Robert Malthus, despite all prostitutuins to the contrary. It was Smith in his *Stability of the Wealthy Nations* who showed, when emasculating the Paradox of the Feeble Bees, that public vice was virtuous to private parts, thus avoiding, for the the first time, the Fallacy of Competition[1]. Malthus merely introduced a simple logarithmic transformation to show that reproduction could not be ejaculated indefinitely into the future without running into the positive checks. Multiplying through by -1, of course, converts the positive checks to negative balances, and reversing the axes is all that is required to get the liquidity trap — slim evidence that Malthus preceeded Smith. Indeed, assuming a hypothetical but reasonable value for P when $t=0$, and extrapolating Malthus' first law back suggests that Smith preceeded Malthus by 50×10^{-2} economists[2]. That Malthus' own First Law disproves his main claim to fame was shown by Ricardo in his superfluous chapter "The Wages of Irony", and it is very surprising that this confusion should not have died with the Sages Fund Doctrine.

Of course, the strongest evidence that Smith initiated the Keynesian Revulsion lies in Book V, "Death Duties of a Sovereign." It will be remembered that in that book, Smith shows that gold transmits general gluttons of goods from one country to the other via "wagon ruts in the sky". Here we have the beginnings of the International Monetary Feud as well as Boeing's first law of General Dynamics. (Smith was well aware that his roots were complex. They remained so until Walras cut them off, but, of course static existence had to wait for twentieth century lemmings[3]). J.B. Say, of course, frustrated the application of Smith's idea, thus founding a French tradition.

There is an old Chinese Proverb which reads: "Wrong ideas are forever in doctoral designations, but Wong must try".[4]

---

* Eugene Smolensky mapped the printout to bond. He, the Computation Center, and its Chief Programmer, Binary Fudgit, share the responsibility for all errors. Responsibility for the rest is, of course, mine.

** EEH/Second Series, Vol. 6. No. 1 ©Graduate Program in Economic History, University of Wisconsin, 1968.

1 Geoffrey Stigler, *In the Land of Canaan* (Irving and Co., Homoken, New Jersey, 1903), 6371.

2 The technique was first used by S. Kuzns. See his *"Numbers Without End", Surcease of Sorrow and Cultural Veneration,* Part II, Vols. II, III, IV, V, VI, VII, iii-iv.

3 A. Lance and J.P. Satyr, *"Existentionalism of a Competitive Equilibrium", Limits With Random Error,* 11110101101, 1ff. Of course, closed convex subsets were not normal in a pin factory in Smith's time. The pointless pin had not yet been invented. Smith's avoidance of Euclidean space was a polar position to which all the classicists were cosiners.

4 I am indebted to my old draftsman for correcting my initial rendering.

On Responsibility

The trouble of the present time
slips and shifts upon my sloping shoulders,
and I think I need
some new venue:
perhaps to troll for hours
to catch pelagic fish,
not for its own significance,
but just for the halibut.

Anthony Thompson
5138 Lillian Court
Livermore, CA 94550

EYES ONLY[1]

RUSSELL BAKER

SHINGTON, MARCH 11 — Datelines:

arch 8, 1972 — The Pentagon said today it is looking for a
type of paper that cannot be Xeroxed or otherwise
licated. The point is to stop Government secrets from
king to newspapers. Present paper stocks can all be
ly Xeroxed by Government people with a stake in pub-
ing them and printed before you can say Jack Anderson.
ay 5, 1972 — The Pentagon asked Congress today for
3,000 to start a feasibility study of Leakpruf, a new paper
de of plutonium-reactor shavings and horsehair, Spokes-
n said early tests indicated that Leakpruf was Xerox-
of, but that much research was needed.
ct. 16, 1972 — The Pentagon asked Congress today for
.3 million to develop a method for shaving a plutonium
ctor. Plutonium-reactor shavings and horsehair are the
redients of Leakpruf, an experimental paper required for
ional security.
n. 28, 1973 — Controversy has arisen between the Penta-
 and the Atomic Energy Commission over who has the
nt to shave a plutonium reactor. The Botchko Corpora-
n, which holds the contract to develop Leakpruf, wants
try a new shaving technique on an A.E.C. reactor. The
.E.C. contends that Botchko's security clearance does not
itle it to engage in reactor shaving.
March 17, 1973 — Embattled Botchko Corporation execu-
es want an additional $42 million to get enough plutonium-
ctor shavings to produce a prototype of Leakpruf, the
ntroversial new paper. The A.E.C. is suing Botchko for
72 million for pain and suffering sustained by one of its
utonium reactors which was severely nicked during an
perimental shaving by Botchko last month.
pril 11, 1974 — Senate investigators of the Pentagon's
akpruf contract with Botcko were told today that $900
llion was wasted in futile attempts to shave a plutonium
ctor with a straight razor. Pentagon officials revealed,
wever, that the problem has since been solved — an electric
zor did the job for $39.95 — and that Botchko can start
rk on a prototype of Leakpruf if Congress votes $1.5
lion needed to rescue the company from bankruptcy.
ov. 3, 1974 — The Pentagon annouced today that it was
unching a crash program to produce horsehair, an element
eded in the manufacture of the controversial new Leakpruf
per. Spokesmen insisted that Botchko, Inc., Leakpruf's
veloper, had not forgotten about the horsehair when the

project began, but had counted on finding a ready supply in
the U.S. Cavalry. The Pentagon said that rather than re-
create the U.S. Cavalry for this one project, it had contracted,
for $795 million, with Gasso da Morte, the International
chemical cartel, to develop a new synthetic horsehair.
July 24, 1975 — The Botchko Corporation told House investigators today its first prototype ream of Leakpruf had
failed to resist Xeroxing because synthetic horsehair would
not bond properly with plutonium-reactor shavings. To
make the product work, the company said, would require
genuine organic horsehair.
Aug. 14, 1975 — The Army will ask for a $6-billion budget
increase next year to reactivate the U.S. Cavalry.
Oct. 9, 1977 — The Secretary of Defense, it was learned
today, was among 42 high Government officials who suffered radiation sickness after participating in the recent
press-conference demonstration of the Pentagon's new
miracle paper, Leakpruf. A Xerox machine on which the
demonstration was conducted has melted. The historic paper
sample that could not be Xeroxed has turned into a glowing
mass of horsehair with a half life of 8,000 years.
Feb. 11, 1978 — The President denied today that B-52's are
dropping Leakpruf on Vietnam, but said he could not discuss what was being dropped on Laos.
June 9, 1978 — The Pentagon unveiled today a new device
for stopping Xerox machines from copying secret documents. It is milk. All secret documents from now on will be
written in milk, which does not show on a Xerox coy, but
can be read by holding a match under the original paper.
The discovery, made by Costplusco, a subsidiary of General
Messes, cost $2.5-billion.
July 6, 1978 — Xerox reported today development of a
milk-copier unit which, fitted in a copying machine at an
added cost of $19.87, makes it possible to reproduce words
written invisibly in milk. A Xerox executive said his son had
invented the device while playing with his toy chemistry set
and an old light switch.
Nov. 18, 1978 — The Pentagon asked Congress today for
$983,000 to develop a new milk product that could not be
Xeroxed or otherwise duplicated.

---

[1] From *The New York Times*, 3/12/72.

QUOTES

R. Tislow
AN AVERSIVE-THOUGHT/BELCHING SYNDROME: A SOMATIC EXPRESSION OF UNPLEASANT THOUGHT CONTENT.
Life Sciences, 1964, *3*, 1501

"It is suggested here that belching, besides being the physical result of aerophagia, can be a manifestation of a gastro-esophagal expulsive reflex which is triggered off by aversive thought associations.

"Several years ago I realized that belching may serve as a somatic expression of unpleasant thought content. Once during a lengthy talk with a colleague, a research psychiatrist, I noticed that he would belch each time his department head was mentioned. Asked directly about his feelings for his superior, he admitted having some differences of opinion."

From Summary: "The present paper assumes belching can be conditioned to aversive thought material by Pavlovian principles."

* * *

P. L. White
BARBECUING AND HEALTH HAZARDS
J.A.M.A. (Questions and Answers) 1964, *190*, 1019

Answering a question about carcinogenic properties of steaks broiled on a grill heated by burning newspaper:

"Could the combustion of newspaper or printing ink during the process of cooking result in the production of toxic compounds?"

Dr. White discusses the problem and concludes:

"One consultant suggested that nausea might result from the political content of the unburned newspaper."

* * *

S. J. Zimmerman, Maureen B. Maude and M. Moldawer
FREEZING AND STORAGE OF HUMAN SEMEN IN 50 HEALTHY MEDICAL STUDENTS.
Fertility and Sterility 1964, *15*, 505

(If done properly, this would be the neatest trick of the year.)

* * *

G. Bermant (Harvard University)
RESPONSE LATENCIES OF FEMALE RATS DURING SEXUAL INTERCOURSE
Science 1961, *133*, 1771

"The experiment reported here measures the effect of single copulations on the behavior of oestrus female rats, in the context of an ongoing series of copulations. In order to investigate the behavioral effects of single copulations of the female, it is necessary to provide a method by which she can control the timing of the copulation. One such method was to make each copulation contingent upon some measurable arbitrary response by the female. This was done by conditioning the females to press a lever in a box whereupon a male was placed in the box by the experimenter. The time required to train the females ranged from 15–90 minutes."

(*Results:* It was found that after copulation the female rats would press the lever within 20 seconds for at least 5 consecutive copulations).

Man Makes Himself?

N. A. DREKOPF*

New York City

Most anthropologists will agree that one of the more exciting developments in our discipline in recent years has been the discovery of the science of primatology. We concede that work on animal behavior has been done in the past by zoologists, comparative psychologists, ethnologists, and an extinct breed of scholar known as the "naturalist" (e.g., Darwin, Wallace, Agassiz, etc.), but their efforts have been insignificant when compared to the edge-cutting research now being done by anthropologists. Only members of our discipline have had the courage and imagination to extrapolate from the behavior of baboons, macaques, gorillas, and chimpanzees to a line of inquiry that has shed light upon the social evolution of early man. They have thus developed a methodology which allows us to determine the parameters of primitive human existence through analysis of the possibilities and limitations inherent in the organic equipment and behavioral inventory of our precursors. It is this Inferential Method which I intend to faithfully apply in the present paper.

It has been convincingly argued that hands are the father of man. Now, all primates have considerable manual dexterity, but it is agreed that the evolution of the full potential of the forelimbs is dependent upon the abandonment of quadrupedal motion and the lifting of the hands from the ground. Quite clearly, this is not a characteristic of the terrestrial monkeys and apes, all of which (or *whom*, depending upon one's opinion as to their capacity for culture) use their forelimbs in locomotion, and most scholars see arboreal existence as a precondition of the evolution of man. Attention has properly been turned to the arboreal primates in our search for insight into human evolution, but the observation of these creatures in the wild is made difficult by the fact that the human observer cannot follow them and usually cannot even see them.

The research upon which this paper is based suffered from this limitation, and, regretfully, it was necessary to observe arboreal monkeys in captivity. Except for brief trips to the Bronx Zoo, for comparative purposes, all the data were collected at Kornbluth's Katskill Kongo, a game farm in Grossinger, New York. The primate population at this research station included three spider monkeys, one capuchin, and two squirrel monkeys. (Mr. Kornbluth also had in his collection an aged hyena, a descented skunk, and two stuffed owls.) The monkeys lived largely on knishes thrown to them by tourists; since this is probably not characteristic in their natural habitat, I will not dwell heavily on feeding. The focus of this paper, however, is upon the use of the hands, and it is worthwhile to note at this juncture that I observed one squirrel monkey catch with his right hand a piece of halvah thrown from a distance of fifty feet. All the animals observed exhibited considerable manual dexterity, an ability made possible by the fact that they were usually in a sitting posture. Thus, though they do not have true bipedal gait, they very rarely used their forelimbs in locomotion. In fact, they moved around very little at all due to a limitation in space that was made necessary by the recent expansion of Kornbluth's Kottage Kolony, where I resided while in the field.

The monkeys observed by me at KKK only employed their hands in eating during 5% of the time. This again is an artificial limitation which must be corrected if we are to properly interpret the wild state. That the animals spent so little time in feeding was largely a function of meteorological conditions. Rainy and cool weather during the summer in which the field work was conducted drastically lowered the number of tourists, and therefore the knishes, and the A.S.P.C.A. ultimately closed Kornbluth's Katskill Kongo after half the animals had died. Mr. Kornbluth has since declared bankruptcy, a great loss to primatological research.

Even with the above slight deviation from natural conditions, a startling fact was noted. Approximately 40% of the manual movements of the monkeys were oriented to scratching and delousing (perhaps a higher figure than in the natural state due to the conditions of the cage), but, and this should be carefully noted, *55% of hand use was in masturbation*. It has long been known that this practice is common among monkeys, but I believe that this is the first time in which hard figures have been compiled. Frequency of masturbation varied from one squirrel monkey that masturbated on the average of 130 times daily to a spider monkey that communed with himself 723 times during a 24-hour period.[1] It was noted that towards the end of each day fatigue impelled the latter animal to use his prehensile tail for the purpose. This be-

197

havior, which I term *caudurbation*, has not previously been reported in the literature. These inordinately high rates of self-congress do not necessarily imply that most of the monkey day was taken up in such activity, for each episode lasted only three and one-half seconds.

It is possible now to consider the implications of these finds for evolution using the Inferential Method outlined in the introduction of this paper. (A tabular presentation of the full data will appear in a book to be published shortly by Pincus-Hall, Inc.) Man, it is agreed, developed culture through the use of his hands in the making of tools. There is also little doubt that the monkey hand, as we know it, is just about as evolved as was man's at the time when he made his breakthrough to humanity. The difference between the proto-human and the monkey lay exactly in the differential *uses* of the forelimbs by each primate. Our thesis that there is not all that much difference between the monkeys and man leads to a query of the usual assumption that the ancestry of monkeys and of man became differentiated early in the Tertiary Era. I would suggest instead that the two lines parted company in the Pliocene. The inferential basis for this statement is contained in the data presented above. I submit that man and the monkey had reached approximately the same stage of evolution during the Pliocene period (there is very strong support among certain eminent physical anthropologists for such parallelism), but man made tools with his newly evolved manual equipment whereas the monkey masturbated. The result was that this almost human creature rapidly degenerated, becoming the fuzzy and unintelligent animal that we now see in the zoo. While I will grant that occasional, even daily, masturbation has not produced marked deterioration among *Homo sapiens,* one can only wonder at the evolutionary consequences if men were to do so hundreds of times a day as reported in this paper for monkeys. Given these considerations it would perhaps be more profitable to look upon the monkey not as a prehuman, but as insane. It thus becomes necessary to reclassify the monkey as being a member of the genus *Homo.* Sapient he is not, however, so I will suggest the term *Homo onanismus drekopfii,* a name that at once combines his close relationship to man with his principal activity and at the same time incorporates the name of the writer.[2]

It may now be asked why man took the direction of tool making and *Homo onanismus* directed his interests inwards. The answer is really very simple: female monkeys remained victims of the estrus cycle while the human woman gained control over her generative abilities. During most of the year, the male *Homo onanismus* had no forms of gratification other than those provided from his own resources, a routine which was only occasionally broken by a female coming into heat.[3] Infrequent though these occasions may have been, biological compulsion required the female to present herself in a subordinate manner, and penetrability of the identity was maximized. Lacking choice alternatives, she never advanced to the position of a social person, unlike her human counterpart. The ultimate key to understanding humanity, then, is not that the *Homo sapiens* females are in heat all the time: they are *not.* Rather, they are able to choose exactly when to go into heat and are thereby able to control the males. The female stages this with sufficient frequency that man chooses to use his hands for externally oriented work, usually instigated by women. The female is therefore ultimately responsible for the evolution of culture. In conclusion, we may correct V. Gordon Childe's famous title. Man did *not* make himself—women made men—only monkeys make themselves.

---

* Mr. Drekopf is the alter ego of Dr. Robert F. Murphy, Department of Anthropology, Columbia University, who it should be noted, has confined his primate researches to occasional trips to the zoo with his children.

[1] The only female in the troop was the capuchin monkey. This, however, seems to have little bearing upon the data or the conclusions given below.

[2] This will strike some readers as immodest, but I should stress that the theory outlined in this paper has never been presented before, and the wording of my reclassification indicates only that I bear sole responsibility for it. I wish to restate my obligation to others, however, for the basic methodology that has produced these conclusions. Pioneering though my theory may be, I am optimistic that even more startling results will follow the further application of this method.

[3] The inference could be challenged by citing the availability of homosexual outlets to the monkeys in my sample population. Patterned and regular homosexuality is, however, confined to *Homo sapiens,* and there would seem to be excellent ecological reasons for this. These derive from population considerations, but not from the point of view of the birth rate, as would be the inclination of most ecologists. Rather, we should consider the rate of morbidity and the accompanying fact that most forms of homosexuality are highly unsanitary. Primatologists have observed that of all the nonhuman primates only the gorilla fouls himself, but not even a gorilla would foul himself by another gorilla.

Das Gesellschaftwitzbuch [*The Corporate Joke Book*]

This report trifles with Das Geselleschaftwitzbuch. I shall also refer to this nonthing as the Corporate Joke Book or the CJB when I lapse into acronymese. Inherently, the CJB is such a fearfully endangered species it has never existed long enough to have a physiology or establish a history. The failure of this apparently pedestrian event to occur gives many trivial insights into Gesellschaftgestalt.

A corporation exists to make money for stockholders, and it can persist only as long as it concurrently serves a socially acceptable function. To accomplish these dissonant missions the corporation requires capital, employees management and usually consumes nonrenewable resources. Employees demand money and increasingly, a sporting chance to survive the hazards of doing a day's work. Managers require money and ego gratification except that it is called job satisfaction when sought by employees without exceptional skills.

Corporate management has to get its jollies out of pacifying the public with pleasingly priced goods and services, pleasing the stockholders with profitability, and appeasing and nurturing the employees with money and gratification. All these greedy parties insist that their piece of the action grows increasingly pleasing, a requirement which may be satisfied only while the corporate universe imitates the total universe and expands continuously.

The nonexistence of the CJB is best understood by examining the incompatibility of such a corporate member with the physiology of the corporation. In the real world multiple case histories demonstrate that a CJB will induce an immediate anaphylactic reaction of the host corporation if a CJB gains parasitic attachment thereto. For example, consider Gesellschaftgestalt problems associated with my Leonardo joke.

Leonardo trained chimpanzees for a city zoo famous for enhancing the interest of its collection with shows featuring young animals still learning their acts. Leonardo's chimps tap danced, did needlepoint, rode bicycles and unicycles, presented a great atonal rock band and were prevented from seeking public office only by age rules and diffeculties in establishing citizenship. These feats came easily in spite of the fact that Professor Leonardo was demonstrably the ultimate clod, qualified for instructional duties only in a teacher's college.

Clearly Leonardo attained monumental instructional success with a total absence of personal talent. Jealous animal trainers, corporate managers and guys in the Dean business anxious to build parallel success stories with untalented staff finally called on Leonardo's boss, a distinguished savant named Earl, and demanded the logistic secrets and training doctrine responsible for Leonardo's success. Earl very graciously shared his supervisory insight. He said "If you can explain it to Leonardo, he can explain it to the monkeys."

While the Leonardo witz afforded opportunity for animal trainers and educators to take offense, neither group exerted much clout in the protest arena. These guys could, therefore, be disregarded with impunity pending legislation which confers status on them as disadvantaged minorities. This story was generally well received and for years no one overtly objected to the bit.

Boss Leonardo suggested that if I planned to continue to tell the story I had better change Leonardo's name to Jake. To avoid further confrontation, I pragmatically changed Leonardo's name to Rumplestelskin until Boss Leonardo was out of my picture. With any luck at all, I'll never have a boss named Leonardo again.

If you're editing a Gesellschaftwitzbuch, you are systematically alert to the sensitive Leonardo who resent a corporate Leonardo joke. Some of these guys sign orders; others will be talented brats the Gesellschaft wants to hire; still others will feel that the Leonardo witz is a sad attempt to belittle a great Italian genius. For Corporation purposes the joke must concern a guy named Rumplestilskin, or a guy named Bob. (Roberto if you operate in Spain.)

The Corporate anecdote cannot put down anyone because of nationality, race, color, creed, or sex. Such material is both illegal and counterproductive, and probing for loopholes may perturb both customer and employee relations. For instance, employees of scheduled airlines protest cutesy slogans like "Fly Me", "We want to do more for you", Let us wiggle our tail for you", etc. Furthermore, many pflegmatic customers of the airlines feign distaste for a ticket to Cleveland which includes erotic options.

Even normal and legal sex is not a suifable topic for the Gesellschaftwitzbuch of Fortune's Five Hundred. Husband and wife jokes irk the endemic disgruntled spouse present in customer and employee populations at about the 90% level. Anatomical jokes are particularly bad and no concern wishes to jeopardize the collective good will of people with big noses, noisey dentures, bow legs or jaundiced chitin by being pert on the subject of megabeaks, decibel dentures, etc. Labor relations jokes are sure to launch a flood of grievance hearings which cost about 3×10^{-3} megabucks per hearing. Political quips are toxic to the Gesellschaft hopeful of getting a sympathetic hearing at the local, state or national level regardless of who won, stole, or purchased a plurality in the last election.

People with money really don't "laugh all the way to the bank". They're too worried about being robbed, kidnapped, or taxed. Nobody equates his poverty to comedy even though he may be prepared to snicker at the next rerun showing Mr. Charles Chaplin dining on unseasoned boiled brogans. Naturally, financially oriented journals, magazines and newspapers are not bullish on humor.

Fortune, Forbes, Barrons, the Wall Street Journal, etc., are most concerned with facts and the opinions of philosophers with a good track record for fiscal ESP. The Dow Joneses (Barrons, WSJ) love puns and the worse the pun, the more the Dow-Jones editors adore it. In addition, the Wall Sreet Journal has a marginal tolerance of wit provided it is quarantined on the editorial page and the source of the wit is extramural. Gesellschaftgestalt can tolerate an occasional bad pun and a little carefully screened extramural wit, but the Gesellschaft has established empirically that disseminating such material is ungood for the balance sheet.

One of the many good reasons Corporate officers avoid humor relates to gesellschaft toutsmanship. Whenever possible, every large outfit sends its ranking huckster to address "Financial Analysts" to portray a glowing picture of the future profits its dedicated people are about to produce. Financial Analysts prefer Corporations which take their own efforts very seriously. The FA's advise and inform money managers who have no sense of the absurd and are antagonistic to suggestions that such capacity would be helpful. FA's are dedicated to searching for outfits staffed by sober, responsible, money geniuses in depth. (A Gesellschaft doing well is deemed risky if it is only one heart beat away from having boobs take over management.)

Cutesy kids are another publicly tolerated topic for corporate humor. The "funny paper" has its collection of cutesy kids and there was once a TV comedian type who made a good living out of cutesy kids. This cutesy kid specialist is now retired or unemployed - I don't know what happened to him. Most adults get all the opportunity they want to marvel at the kids syndicated in the funny paper or

thrust upon them by fatuous parents bursting to talk about little Jack and/or Jill. The babies may be cute, but people equipped with teenagers are usually a puddle of parental concern with little ability to find anything funny. Obviously, the juvenile joke may be acceptable, but it just isn't good Gesellschaftgestalt.

One might think that old jokes from a bastion of regressive stuffiness like the Reader's Digest would be safe. Let's analyze one of them. If memory serves me properly, the joke went like this. In the days when the triumphant American army was occupying Berlin in strength, a disturbed young wife wrote her military husband and demanded to know what the German girls had that American girls didn't have. Sergeant Husband wrote back: "Nothing, but they got it here". What does this joke do for a corporate sponsor?

1. A few German customers will be reminded of days they would like to forget.

2. The wives of business travelers will be stimulated to speculate on the behavior of husbands on the road.

3. A few corporate business travelers will feel encouraged by their management to seek ways to reduce the tedium and loneliness which is the lot of the chronic business traveler.

4. A collection of vigorous but bored business travelers will be persuaded that now is a great time to see if they can get an assignment requiring less travel so they can stay home where "it" is.

5. Etc. Etc. Etc. The joke isn't good Gesellschaftgestalt.

Sometimes a joke may be adapted for a corporate purpose. Years ago when I was a federal employee I received a handmade trophy noting my membership in a group called "The Mushroom Club". The membership of this group consisted of middle managers who were kept in the dark and fed well rotted horse manure. I told this joke to the local Rotarians. A few weeks later I encountered this same basic story, adapted this time for use by a top corporate manager. The story now had a different point. If you kept your middle managers in the dark and fed them with stale horse shit, you could expect them to proliferate all over the place - like mushrooms.

So, the point of it all is that humor can serve Gesellschaftgestalt but only in a very parochial way. However one must be incredibly imaginative to anticipate the neurotic hordes seeking a Gesellschaftgestalt source of grievance.

A Key to Dangerous Marine Vertebrates of Miami Beach**

MERVIS SMUCKER
Department of Ichtyagogo
Frug University

1a. Place hand (digits extended) into mouth of specimen. Hand in same condition when removed from mouth as when it went in 3
1b. Hand otherwise 2
2a. Digits disarticulated from hand . . . . Great Baccarruda
2b. Hand disarticulated from wrist . . . . Holymackerelder Shark
(Carcharodon gotcherass)
2c. Condition of hand undetermined (can't be removed from mouth of specimen . . . .
. . . . Miami Beach Moray
(Gymnothorax greedi)
3a. Place specimen (dorsal surface up) on substrate, remove your shoes, and tread with great vigor upon the specimen. Lower extremities rocked with excruciating pain 4
3b. Lower extremities otherwise 5
4a. Spine protruding through instep with small serrations . . . . Yankee stigray
(Dasyatis gougeum)
4b. Spines protruding through instep without small serrations . . . . Northern Pompano
(Scorpaena nomennudum)
5a. When specimen is tread upon it attempts to stab you in a tender portion with a spear. Disarm and stomp vigorously, then throw it back . . . . Goggle-eyed Scab
(Damnfool skindiverii)
5b. Specimen responds otherwise 6
6a. When backside of specimen is gently stroked your nose lights up . . . . Electric Ray
(Narcine acdc)
6b. When backside of specimen is gently stroked you light up all over and specimen invites you up to her room for a gin and tonic . . . . Galore Catfish
*(Bikini goodi goodi)**

* The investigator should be reminded that large series of this species are essential for any good variational study, and every opportunity to collect this species should be utilized to full advantage.

** Reprinted from DOPEIA, June 1962 (A Cold blooded Journal of Vertebrates published by the Am. Soc. of Fish Prevaricators and Reptile Fabricators).

Irreproducible

studies

must

be expressed

in

LANGUAGE

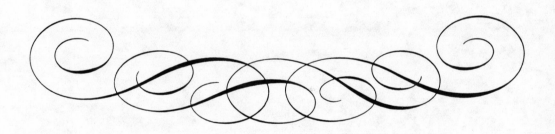

Sexual Behavior in the Human Language

H. J. LIPKINSEY

It is now apparent that sex is at the root of all human problems. In all of history[1,2] sex has been consistently suppressed in areas where it has every right to appear[3]. It has therefore popped up in other areas where there is no good reason for its existence[4]. All aspects of the problem have been treated in detail by Freud and Kinsey[3], with the exception of the sexual behavior of languages which is treated by Lipkinsey[5].

The French pride themselves on their rational attitude towards all things, including sex. But Frenchmen have neglected their language, whose anomalous sexual behaviour is among the worst of its kind. All French tables are feminine. "La crayon de ma tante est sur *la* table" is the first sentence every student learns. Woe be unto the poor wretch who says *le* table. No French table will ever forgive this insult. Yet, what is the lot of the unfortunate French table? All that the future offers them is hopeless spinsterhood, for *all* French tables are feminine and there are no male tables in France.

Lucky is the French table who can make the journey to a foreign land like Israel, where all tables are masculine (or the lucky Israeli male who can make the trip to France). Perhaps this is one of the reasons for the friendship which has recently arisen between Israel and France. But all in all, both the French and Hebrew languages are nothing more than a mass of misplaced sexuality. They are full of sexified tables, chairs, houses, trees and other objects who have no need for sex, have never asked for it, and use it only to frustrate themselves and anyone who is trying to learn the language.

The Germans have evidently stumbled upon the important idea that some objects need not have sex, and should remain sexless. With characteristic German thoroughness they have classified everything as masculine, feminine, and neuter, and they have made a horrible mess. Der Tisch, die Wand, das Mädchen, das Fräulein. German tables are masculine, German girls and unmarried women are neuter, walls are feminine. What is there for a young man to do in Germany? All young and unmarried women are sexless. If he wants feminine company he must find himself a married woman or go to the wall[6]. Is it any wonder that German youth has been responsible for so many upheavals in the past century?

The English-speaking peoples alone have almost completely succeeded in keeping sex out of irrelevant portions of their language. This is undoubtedly a result of the Puritan tradition of taking sex out of everything[7]. English tables are sexless and have no problems, even though they may be laid on occasion. Boys are masculine, girls are feminine, and Hollywood makes the most of it. It is only when foreigners speak broken English that sex is ever introduced into the English language: "This house, she is too small; My train, he did not come on time." An Englishman can always tell a foreigner by his attempts to introduce sex into the conversation.

---

[1] A. Essex, B. Sussex and C. Wessex, *Sex in English History,* Middlesex Press (1957).

[2] S. Freud, *Oedipus Sex, a study of sexual behaviour in ancient Greece.*

[3] S. Freud, A. B. Kinsey and S. U. Perkinsey, Sex and Repression in Human Society, *Journ. Inorgasmic Chemistry,* 1957, *1,* 51.

[4] P. Morris and L. Strike, "Sex in Cigarette Advertising," Any American Magazine.

[5] H. J. Lipkinsey, "Sexual Behaviour in the Human Language," *J. Irrepr. Res.* 1957. *V.*

[6] Die Magd, the servant girl, is also feminine. Draw your own conclusions.

[7] One Puritan sect succeeded in eliminating sex from every aspect of life and became extinct.

Multi Variational Stimuli of Sub-Turgid Foci Covering Cross-Evaluative Techniques for Cognitive Analyses of Hypersignificant Graph Peaks Following Those Intersubjectivity Modules Having Biodegradable Seepage.

DAVID LOUIS SCHWART

ABSTRACT.

After a definition of basic terms, a model is constructed wherein cross-disciplinary cognition patterns are subjected to increasingly unviable stimuli. The statement is made that a focus of point-sensitive trivalency does not necessarily presuppose molecular dispersion, despite the obvious tripolar discontinuity. It is shown that earlier research was misleading in its emphasis on total-sweep ranging procedures being applied to Judeo-Christian parameters.

BASIC TERMS.

Multi: Lots of them. Whole big bunches. More than just a few.

Variational: Changeable. Not likely to stay the same as it was the last time you checked.

Stimuli: Things what they make other things do things.

Sub-turgid: Not about to do much before next Friday. Less active than mere sluggish, the implication is of approaching rigidity. Useful in describing managemental characteristics.

Foci: Places where things come together. Related to "fussy" and "fussbudget" in the quasi-normative sense.

Fuss-budget: One who focuses ("foci") on one aspect while excluding whatever you happen to be interested in.

Hypersignificant: Big stuff. Top management conceptualization. See hyposignificant, hypochondriac, hypertension, hyperschmeiper, and hippopotamus.

Intersubjectivity: Involves intimate cross-relationships between subjects. Sometimes the subjects are people, in which case intersubjectivity becomes a dirty word.

Judeo-Christian: Jewish and Christian. Also Christian and Jewish. Or both. See Abie's Irish Rose, Nimzo-Indian defense, former Mayor what's-his-name of Dublin, and your dentist twice a year.

Trivalency: The kind of clothes hanger where you can put three things on at once without overlapping. See also trivial, Valencia, and Linus Pauling.

Vivaldi: Italian term for portable battery-operated noodle-sifter characterized by a distinctive "ticka-ticka-ticka-ticka-ticka-ticka." See Fig. 4.

Nimzo-Indian defense: Loses for black. Also loses for white. Highly recommended.

With: Conveys a sense of possession. Very useful pointing up the opposite aspects of without. (q.

Without: Lacking. Outside. Unless. Beyond. T word, for sanitary reasons, is infrequently parse Without, withouter, withoutest; these forms ha found favor in sociological manipulative par lels. For example, all poor people are needy, b some are more needy than others.

(q.v.): Abbreviation for the Latin quizzimus vit isius, meaning "Who used up all the hair toni Now used to introduce the participial subjuncti whenever a presidential aspirant wants to sho some familiarity with the farm problem.

Upwardly mobile: A vertical transfiguration of horizontal growth percentile. Expressed in cut geronimos, the reciprocals have been found us ful in predicting fluctuations in the patterns dog-food sales.

Downwardly mobile: Almost like upwardly mobi except for subtlies in directional modes.

Sicilian defense: Strong bond between king a knights. See Don Carleon and the continui Fischer King legend.

Unviable: Not too healthy. On the sickly side. generally diseased condition. (See nonviabl neo-biblical, unbuyable, and umbilical.) Th listless, run-down feeling. Tired blood. Take tw aspirin, some chicken soup and call me ne Tuesday.

Rhesus: Some kind of monkey. See Fig. 4.

Biodegradable: Ten minutes after you throw away, it turns into delicious pineapple yogu and you can eat it.

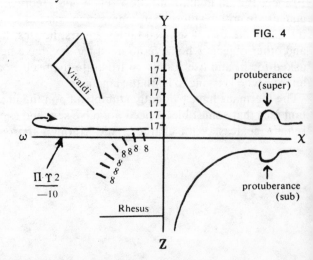

FIG. 4

RATTLE

F. H. AMES, JR.

Various concepts appropriate to the subject of RATTLE, Reportsmanship Aimed Toward The Lofty Expert, have appeared previously in various journals during the past decade. Unfortunately these articles are usually fragmented and are specifically oriented toward activities pertaining to government contracts. The author's purpose in developing RATTLE is to document and describe techniques applicable to the basic art of reportsmanship throughout all business, professional and academic activities. Accusation that RATTLE was derived from the age old expression "RATTLE the enemy" is without foundation and should be considered as malicious gossip. However, it is admitted that RATTLE does basically comprise a union of the various proficient reportsmanship activities existing in defense industries and the academic world to provide an equally useful management tool for other enterprises or professions.

The would-be practitioner of RATTLE must approach his task with the same mental attitude in which this paper was written. This can perhaps be expressed as sadistic glee overlaid with the humanitarian instincts of a hypersensitive cobra. The recipient of your report is your enemy! Defeat can be assured only if your approach is properly structured and systematically developed with the proper mental attitude.

The author must humbly acknowledge that his "expertize" does not permit delineation of specific examples in an area such as medicine. However the basic concept and technique described herein, although oriented to the engineering discipline, are equally applicable to any profession or activity issuing written reports to another entity which is categorized as being a superior office.

The basic objectives of this paper are as follows:
1. Define reportsmanship
2. Discuss the concept and purpose of RATTLE
3. Provide criteria for various levels of competence for practitioner of RATTLE
4. Describe specific techniques available to RATTLE
5. List source of background data

REPORTSMANSHIP

Reportsmanship is the informal technique of leading the reader to draw a wrong conclusion. It is not particularly systematic and does not require the originality required by RATTLE.

A forerunner of Reportsmanship is Gamesmanship or the gentle art of psyching your opponent in games or during casual conversation. One of the few documents on gamesmanship is Potter's delightful little book *Gamesmanship*. It is recommended reading as background information for the novice. Reportsmanship is really documented Gamesmanship with a little extra effort.

RATTLE, CONCEPTS AND PURPOSE

RATTLE is a systematic and formal approach to impressive verbosity utilizing the technique outlined later in this article. It is defined as the technique of authoritatively writing a report capable of inspiring a state of exquisite awe in the mind of the recipient through inducement of erroneous conclusions. The phraselogy must be carefully chosen to both impress the reader with the author's expertize and to provide data, largely factual, which will result in erroneous conclusions by the reader. A successful practitioner will induce a growing feeling of respect for the author

— because the only alternative for the reader is to admit that the contents of the report are beyond his comprehension. Such an admission is tantamount to a confession of insecurity and ignorance. No expert can afford this luxury!

The basic purpose is to keep the expert reader off-your-back. This situation is particularly true when the recipient must review and analyze the report as a result of his position in life, or, whenever the document is a contractual or administrative requirement. The reader should be familiar with the term "gobbledy-gook"; this technique must not be confused with RAT-TLE. Gobbledygook is merely a pathetic attempt to confuse, not to impress, although some specific elements of terminology may be suitable as RATTLE inputs.

RATTLE PRACTITIONERS, RATING OF

There is no existing standardization or qualification for RATTLE practitioners. This article presumes to establish three categories to formally describe the capabilities of those who utilize this particular technique. The section on technique will give more definite measurement criteria.

Apprentice — Although this could be deemed self-explanatory, a few words are appropriate. Satisfactory performance in this grade is evidenced by acceptance of one's peers within an intimate group, such as the local technical society/association, fellow employees, and knowledgeable friends. There is a tendance for these readers to address the author as "Mr." In this writer's opinion, at least two years are required normally as an apprentice under the tutledge of a man who enjoys a higher rating in RATTLE. Publication in house organs or small we-will-print-anything journals is required.

Journeyman — Satisfactory performance in this grade is demonstrated by publication in national journals which have a moderate technical content and serve the profession in which the author operates. Those readers who do not personally know the author occasionally address him as "Doctor." (This form of address, of course, is not appropriate within the medical profession.) Recognition is also evidenced by membership on some of the working committees of national societies and associations representative of his profession. At this point we must warn that such recognition must be based solely on the writings of the journeyman (and higher grades). Technical competence as evaluated by personal or factual knowledge of an individual, must not be confused with competence in RATTLE. Many emminent people, widely respected in their profession, are completely inept in RATTLE — such people actually transmit information and knowledge in clear concise terminology. RATTLE misleads the reader so he convinces himself, as an individual, that he is dealing with a more knowledgeable person.

Master — This is the highest grade attainable. To reach this lofty rating, one's articles will be published in the leading journals of the world; publication in a government periodical — even if as a source in a footnote, should be achieved regularly. A great deal of originality must be used in developing the report and considerable knowledge must actually be used. The Master displays a bold capability in generating impressive source documents, is often categorized as a consultant and is invariably addressed as "Doctor."

RATTLE TECHNIQUES

One of the most significant indications of proficiency is the originality displayed in developing new techniques, improving those used by others. The professional author will never hesitate to plagarize or modify techniques developed by his peers in RAT-TLE.

It is very important to recognize that RATTLE must contain a substantial amount of factual information — it is written from a slightly fictitious viewpoint — not as fiction.

BUZZ PHRASE GENERATOR

One technique utilized widely during creative thinking classes is the buzz phrase generator (or baffle-gab); this device is a multi-column matrix normally comprising two adverbs and a noun. Selection of three words, to formulate an abstract but plausible phrase, is made on a random basis. Normally each column has ten words numbered from 0 to 9, this identification permits selection by usage of random numbers. One widely used manner of selection is to ask someone for a three digit number which is then used to select the three words. It has been said that this technique possibly resulted from a meal in a Chinese restaurant: take one from column "A", one from column "B", and one from column "C".)

The selection of words requires careful thought since all possible combinations must be plausible to the reader. The practitioner of RATTLE must also define, to himself, the resultant phrase in understandable terminology so as to avoid generation of gobble-dygook. This precaution will be invaluable if the term is questioned by some stuffy reader who is truly an expert on the subject under discussion.

BASIC QUALIFICATIONS

TECHNIQUE	APPRENTICE	JOURNEYMAN	MASTER
Foreign Language[a]	Occasional phrase	Phrases/sentences; maximum of four per report.	Quote paragraphs in entirety — use profusely.
Footnotes/Source Documents	Legitimate documents of own profession occasional obsolete document.	Obscure/obsolete documents. One foreign source permitted.	Fictitious & foreign documents plus those of other disciplines.
Buzz Phrase/Acronyms	Desk dictionary. Terminology of writers profession.	Unabridged dictionary. Terminology of other professions.	Coins his own words.
Curves	Limited number of points.	Only 3-4 points shown.	No points — only the curve.
Fog Index[b]	16	18	21
Charts	Much detail	Present the same data in different formats.	Use extensively with minimal captions or describe only in words.
Oral Presentation	Never	Very seldom and then to local audience.	As requested.
Attitude Toward References Quoted	Straightforward	Point out small errors.	Challenge validity of theory.
Title Length	Multi-sentence or short paragraph.	Lengthy	Word or phrase.

[a] Never, never supply a translation.
[b] Refer to Robert Gunning's "How to Take the Fog Out of Writing."

Each generator requires tailoring to the profession of the practitioner; avoid using those generators which have been published before — extract words as appropriate but do not use examples blindly.

An appreciation of poetry is a great asset in preparing a buzz phrase generator. If the three words combination results in an awkward rhythm then reconsideration is advised. This poetic talent is particularly helpful in determining the order of precedence of the adverbs of the first two columns. A sample buzz phrase generator for industry in general follows; it is set forth merely to demonstrate the concept described previously. As a note of warning, although the buzz phrase generator can be used by itself, there are certain categories of personnel who should never be subjected to the output of the generator. Typical examples are manufacturing personnel who have never worked on a government contract and management personnel who have arrived at the top on sheer ability. Such people can be somewhat forceful in evaluating the output of a buzz phrase generator.

SAMPLE OF A BUZZ PHRASE GENERATOR

	"A"	"B"	"C"
0	discrete	behavorial	criteria
1	perceptive[1]	adaptive	motivation
2	dynamic	innovative	phenomena
3	synergetic[2]	emperical	systems[2]
4	cognitive	operational	model[2]
5	contributory	transitional	stimuli
6	classical	managerial[1]	centrality
7	sublimal	technological	theory[2]
8	pristine	competitive	propensity
9	systematized	optimal	interaction

1. Care must be taken to avoid use of both an adverb and noun having the same meaning; as an example: "perceptive-perception" is unthinkable. Along the same lines, it is most inadvisable to allow usage of three words all starting with the same letter; as an example "synergetic substantive system" could best be used to illustrate inept humor, certainly not for RATTLE. Avoidance of such circumstance requires considerable originality.

2. The expert could possibly challenge inclusion of these over-worked terms; the author's justification lies in the fact that this is only a sample buzz phrase generator used solely for illustrative purposes.

SOURCE DOCUMENTS

Numerous source documents exist for usage as footnotes for phraseology, as input to the buss phrase generator, or for quotation.

The following suggested list comprises basic categories; the practitioner of RATTLE should develop his own private list in considerable detail.

1. Doctoral dissertations — especially those in the field of philosophy, operations research, social sciences, and management. Those subsidized by a government contract are particularly rewarding and applicable to all professions.

2. The prestige journals of technical associations; usually these are issued on a quarterly basis in contrast to the monthly journal for the general membership.

3. Research and Development type of articles published by government organization. Those from the widely publicized "Think Tank" groups are highly recommended!

4. Obsolete technical publications, especially those which are nearly impossible to locate or are out of print.

5. Science fiction publications written by technical people. (Beware of the cops-and-robbers-with-a-ray-gun type which dominate.)

6. Text books used for advanced study in fields such as philosophy, operations, research, management theory, social sciences, communications, systems engineering and industrial engineering. It appears that a newcomer, anthropology, now deserves consideration as a source of data for RATTLE.

7. Congressional records.

8. Public relations and advertising publication.

Needless to state, source documents should not be limited to those in the English language. After all, if you ain't got no savoir-faire, how can you impress your reader?

HAZARDS

The basic information in your article or paper *must be predicated on factual data* no matter how obscurely it is presented. It must be defensible against a reader who requires definition of each term and has the tenacity to dig out the facts. When such individuals are identified, endeavor to keep him from receiving your masterpiece and apply for a position with his organization.

Be careful of using too many acronyms or abbreviations, otherwise you can create an unfavorable impression.

RATTLE must be used as a tool; it is a method of presenting information — not a technique to prepare a series of incomprehensible phrases. Your publication must, on the surface, be dignified, logical and most impressive to your peers.

GENERAL ADVICE

One particular effective technique in using acronyms is selection of a common one with two different meanings.

Draw conclusions, "it obviously follows," without any intermediate explanation as to the thought processes required to reach the conclusion.

Quote theories/models taken from publications outside your profession; of course, you should not explain the theory and be vague about the publication from which it was obtained. But, be able to explain it, just in case!

One technique which merits consideration is inclusion of a very, very detailed index which could amount to 10 percent of the text. One aspiring to the classification of MASTER should also consider inclusion of a massive bibliography including each document read during preparation of your article or paper. Whether you actually extracted information from such references is besides the point. (Although this concept is open to debate, one respected author of a management text stated, "It also includes a substantial number of books that might have been cited." His text comprises 212 pages with a 35 page bibliography.)

It is inadvisable to give sufficient information, when quoting references, to permit the reader to actually locate such references. Quote only the title and author — nothing more — as demonstrated by this article.

The writer sincerely hopes that the reader's future reports will benefit by this article.

Obscurantism*

Referees and editors often complain about the obscure style of the majority of Letters and Articles. In addition to using unintelligible, twisted sentences, many authors create and use slang expressions known to a few specialists only, and indulge in unnecessary abbreviations. Such practices may help the writer but they slow down the reader considerably and exclude the uninitiated completely. In fact, many papers give the impression that the author was writing a memorandum to himself or merely for the benefit of a close collaborator. Yet when we ask authors to write their papers so that a few more colleagues can appreciate their significance, some of them rebut that popular articles do not belong in our journal.

We are convinced that an Article or even a short Letter can be written in a style that helps the interested physicist to understand its aim even if he is not a specialist. One of the causes of bad writing is that so many young research physicists lack teaching experience. They have never faced the challenge of explaining something they know very well to a student who knows nothing about it.

But there is still another reason for writing an obscure paper. It is the common subconscious fear of exposing oneself to scrutiny. If a paper is too clear, it might be too easy for readers to see through it and discover its weaknesses. We observe this same behavior with the lecturer who writes a formula on the blackboard and erases it almost immediately. We see it with speakers who address the blackboard instead of the audience and who keep the room dark between slides. They themselves do not realize that they are subconsciously afraid of being clearly understood.

Thus we believe that writing incomprehensible papers is not an indication of the author's erudition but merely reveals a common psychological defect. We hope that this insight will induce a few more of our authors to come out from behind their screen of specialized terms and machine-inspired sentence constructions.

* Editorial, Physical Review Letters

(A sample of clarity of style)

G. Bertani: LYSOGENY, Advances in Virus Research, 1958, 5, 190

"Whereas the rarities of spontaneous prophage loss and of stable double lysogenization at superinfection, compared with the relatively high frequency of prophage substitution at superinfection, make it impossible to assume that lysogenic cells carry a *large* population of prophage copies segregating at random at cell division, and reproducing *pari passu* with the cell, model G, which assumes a *small* number of prophage copies, cannot be ruled out on these grounds, because the volume of the nucleolus-like material would be small as compared with the size of the prophage copies, so that when the bacterial chromosome divides, and nucleolus-like material is halved the segregation of the prophage copies is not completely random."

A Verbal Rorschach. An Antidote for Technically Obnubilated Appellation

By E. J. HELWI

In his book *African Genesis* Robert Ardrey tells a delightful story about Sir Zolly Zuckerman, a young South African anthropologist, who once horrified his English friends by proposing to publish a book titled *The Sexual Life of the Primates*. He was promptly informed that "primates" in England could refer to nothing but the prelates of the established church. The book eventually appeared under the title *The Social Life of Monkeys and Apes*.

Perhaps the book would have sold more copies with the sensational title, but it would have disappointed many readers. As it was, the new title was simple and unambiguous. It contained no technical jargon and in clear terms informed the most casual reader of its contents. It is a pity in these days of publish or perish that more technical writers aren't similarly embarrassed into simplifying abstruse titles.

Today, when one can make a career out of reading as well as writing technical articles, many authors seem to choose titles that will look well in the Chemical Abstracts. Apparently titles must sound scientific, esoteric, and prestigious (in the archaic sense). Since the recondite is often confused with the erudite, the titles of technical articles frequently smother meaning under a plethora of jargonese.

As a result the layman, or, jargonwise, those not familiar with the lexicon of the scientific disciplines, don't receive the slightest benefit from a technical title. Or does he? Words, like the Rorschach ink blots, invariably carry some sort of impression, even if they conjure up pictures of erotic clergyman.

Technical writers might be able to gage the fuddle-factor of a proposed title by testing it as a Verbal Rorschach on their unscientific friends. The results could be devasting to the dignity and prestige of technical journalism. And they should effectively deflate pompous titles.

The following examples illustrate just what could happen with a Verbal Rorschach test. The titles were gleaned from a single issue of a listing of current technical papers. A possible Rorschach interpretation accompanies each title.

Title: Representation Mixing in U12.
Translation: Social Life on an Atomic Submarine.

Title: Group Theory of the Possible Spontaneous Breakdown of SU3.
Translation: Group Therapy for Demoralized Submarine Crews.

Title: On the Existance of a 189-Plet Mesons.
Translation: Extraterrestial Life on Meson.

Title: Double Image Formation In a Stratifie Medium.
Translation: Visual Aberration in a Stone Spiritualist.

Title: Wave Motion Due to Impulsive Twist o the Surface.
Translation: Math a Gogo, in the surf.

Title: Behaviour of the Nighttime Ionosphere.
Translation: The Naughty Sky After Dark.

Title: Fluid Behaviour in Parabolic Container Undergoing Vertical Excitation.
Translation: Standing Room Only At The Bu lesque.

Title: Redundancy in Digital Systems.
Translation: Having More Than Five Fingers o Toes.

Title: Many Body Theory.
Translation: Life in a Harem.

Title: Some Results of Transport Theory an Their Application to Monte Carlo Methods.
Translation: Hitch-Hiking Home From Los Ve gas.

Title: Dispersion Techniques in Field Theory.
Translation: Fun on a Field Trip.

Title: Wullenweber Arrays Using Doublet Aer ials.
Translation: A death-Defying Double Trapez Act Featuring the Famous Flying Wullenwebers.

Title: Holography and Character Recognition.
Translation: It Takes One to Know One.

Now that you know what Verbal Rorschach testin is, try the following titles on yourself and your friends

(1) Numerical Model of Coarticulation.

(2) Propagation Behaviour of Slotted Inhomoge neous wave Guides.

(3) The Verbal Rorschach—An Antidote fo Technically Obnubilated Appellations.

(4) General Methods of Correlation.

(5) Rectification in a Column with Wet Walls

All the titles referred to are bonefide titles of actual technical papers. The authors and the Journals in which they appear are not listed, in order to protect the guilty. If you object to the lack of good taste of some of the translations, remember that in the case of the last five, it was you who drew the dirty pictures.

An Elucidation of Certain Varieties of a Phenomenon of Common Occurrence in Scientific Communication......

RICHARD L. SUTTON, JR., M.D.
Kansas City, Mo.

"Bullshit" is widely used. The connotation, broadly understood, is more benignant, less denigratory, when it is spelled as one word of 8 letters than when spelled as two words of 4. While perceptive and analytical essayists, like Morris Fishbein in his "Medical Writing" years ago, have given it consideration — although not directly by name — systematic b-ology, in contradistinction to the mere amateur utilization of b., may be said to have been largely neglected by practically all contributors to Scientific Literature. "Literature," so used to designate the main mass of such publication, is a specimen of b.

"Bull" in the sense of "nonsense" is in the Collegiate Dictionary, but there is no entry between "bull's eye" and "bull snake" or between "shish kabab" and "shit-rh." This denotes on the part of professional wordsters an obtuse inattention to the vulgate as it is practiced, for example in the spirited public utterances of the entire student body of Leland Stanford Junior University at football games.

Limitation of space precludes all but a basic consideration of b., with its variegated and esoteric occurrences. Simply, I classify it as Conscious, Subconscious, and Unconscious. I refrain presently from ethical valuations but do believe that some kinds are worse than others. The following are illustrative.

Conscious. — "We" in the place of "I": the author is not valorous, and he knows it. Possibly his reasons are cogent. If his idea should prove demonstrably stupid, his critic may miss his head with the righteous bolt of indignant rectification as a result of the sportsman's error of "shooting into the brown," of which "we" provides ample. From a contemporary work I quote, "Dystrophia Unguis Mediana Canaliformis (Heller) . . . Treatment is unnecessary, but the patient should be advised to apply an emollient cream to the nail fold." The title, for which the authors are not responsible, is Heller's b., since the disorder is not a dystrophy or median or canaliform necessarily; but it is necessarily the tubular outgrowth of nail about a matrix teat, which is the essential lesion and which,

usually, can be extirpated so as to cure the condition — which is not to be accomplished by applying an emollient cream to the nail fold for a period of time equivalent to the Triassic. Thus, excepting the first 3 words, the text quoted is clearly a specimen of Conscious B.

Subconscious. — "Logical" is pathognomonic for "illogical," to be translated, when and if the author becomes conscious, with "plausible" or "inviting." "It is thought" analogously means, "My brilliant colleagues . . ." or possibly "I, myself, have hypothesized, or fancied, or dreamed . . ." Like "we," this is invalorous but less deliberately, since the author simply lacked the guts to say, "I think . . ."

Unconscious. — In these cases, the author's intellectual environment was deprived, so he ought in charity to be held blameless, for it is Society that is at fault when the language of the home is Troglodyte. No one told him, and he did not discern, that "regime" does not mean "regimen." His "plantar callus of the sole of the foot" uses 8 words to say 3 times what the first 2 say in a manner that appeals esthetically to the discriminating. Compare "tinea capitis of the head," which I have heard but not seen because a first-day copy girl will decapitate it. I designate this variety as "Solecistic Redundant B. of the Innocent." This is itself of course pedantic humor, so named by Fowler — i.e.,b.

Acronyms have merit in saving the printed page and/or the muscles of phonation, and I submit a new one especially fitting when Conscious B. is redolent: A C E R B, meaning "Archie Campbell's Estimable Rejoinder to B." Band 5 on Side 2 of RCA Victor LSP 3699 records his musical "I'd 'a wrote you a letter, but I couldn't spell pffft."

Two conclusions may be adduced: barring the necessity of technical symbolism, anything worth saying can be said in plain English; and the hypothesis is inviting that an article in a learned journal, if devoid of b., would be a thing of beauty, a joy for quite awhile, and brief.

P. T. Brown
ON THE DIFFERENTIATION OF HOMO- OR HETERO-EROTIC INTEREST IN THE MALE:
AN OPERANT TECHNIQUE ILLUSTRATED IN A CASE OF A MOTOR-CYCLE FETISHIST.
Behav. Res. Ther. 1964, *2*, 31

"In a paper recently published in this journal, Freund (1963) presents evidence to illustrate the value of the phallopletysmograph as an aid in the diagnosis of the predominance of homo- or hetero-erotic interest in the male. The method involves continuous recording of volume changes of the male genital while the subject is viewing projected pictures of possible erotic subjects — pictures of nude men, women and children of both sexes."

* * *

S. B. G. Eysenck and H. J. Eysenck
AN IMPROVED SHORT QUESTIONNAIRE FOR THE MEASUREMENT OF EXTRAVERSION
AND NEUROTICISM
Life Science 1964, 3, 1103.

From answers to 12 questions such as: Are you rather lively? Do you like mixing with people, would you call yourself happy-go-lucky? Do you like practical jokes? Do you suffer from sleeplessness? When you get annoyed do you need someone friendly to talk to about?

The authors come to the conclusion that "the men are very slightly more extraverted, although the difference is too slight to mention," and that the women are noticeably more neurotic about ⅓ S. D.

* * *

M. A. Schneiderman
THE PROPER SIZE OF A CLINICAL TRIAL. "GRANDMA'S STRUDEL" METHOD.
Jour. New Drugs, 1964, *4*, 3.

"Although clinical trials are not apple strudel, too often they leave a bad taste."

* * *

G. H. Fuller, Steltenkamp, R., Tisserand, G. A.
THE GAS CHROMATOGRAPH WITH HUMAN SENSOR: PERFUMER MODEL.
Ann. N.Y. Acad. Sci., 1964, *116*, 711.

"This paper describes the results obtained when a vapor phase chromatograph is equipped with a "perfumer detector" supplementing the electronic "thermal conductivity cell." The information we will give here may be duplicated in any laboratory using the same equipment and conditions employed in our experiments. We cannot supply "the perfumer detector"*.

---

* A perfumer is an artistic person with a highly developed discriminatory sense of smell.

QUOTES

Takeshi Odake.
DISAPPEARANCE OF INFECTIOUS VIRUS FROM FRIEND VIRUS INDUCED C57BL/6 TUMORS.
Intern J. Cancer 1969. 4/4.

Reviewed by F. C. Chesterman in Reading guide to the Cancer Virology Literature, Information Unit Program Analysis & Communication section, Viral Oncology Program. N.C.I., N.I.H.

"Homosexual subcutaneous isograft of these spleens gave rise to 5 transplantable lymphomas at the transplantation site."

(Found by C. E. Dunlap, who asks: "How do you tell a gay mouse?")

* * *

S. A. Morocus
THE EFFECTS OF ASWAN HIGH DAM ON CURRENT REGIME IN THE SUEZ CANAL
Nature, 967, 214, p. 901–903.

(Who would think that NATURE deals with politics?)

* * *

E. C. Griedberg, S. M. Hadi and D. A. Goldthwait
ENDONUCLEASE II OF E. coli.
J.B.C. 1969, 244, 5883.

"The recovery of enzyme was not calculated for this gradient but in a similar experiment it was slightly more than 100%."

(Amazing!)

* * *

L. Coombs and R. Freedman
USE OF TELEPHONE INTERVIEWS IN A LONGITUDINAL FERTILITY STUDY
The Public Opinion Quarterly, 1964.

* * *

Chernyshev, V. I.
ADAPTATION OF MONKEYS TO THE CONDITIONS OF MOSCOW SUBURBS
Int. Congress Anthropol. Ethnol. Sci. 1968, 7(3), 216–219.

(In Central Moscow they are probably already adapted.)

* * *

LETTERS PREY: AN ANALYTIC EXAMINATION OF THE J.I.R.

ALVIN R. HOWARD, Ph...
Chillicothe, Oh...

Basic research is the sine qua non for any profession. Without basic research, science stagnates. "A stagnant science," as Tation[1] has so pungently phrased it, "is at a standstill."

Where would psychology be without its white rat? Where would medicine be without its guinea pig? Where would politics be without its white wash? Obviously, then, it is to basic research that we must turn in our ending search for the elusive facts that hold the key to the mysteries of our universe.

It is precisely because of this obviousness that one rushes impatiently to such notorious scientific publications as the JIR. A communication medium that represents the stature and the dignity of the nonpareil Society for Basic Irreproducible Research must be diligently studied lest we risk losing the irreplaceable data that will undergird an order of civilization such as Darwin never anticipated. Yet, despite the eminence of the JIR and of its erudite Society, the Journal has neglected to examine the basic components of its own scientific contributions. The most notorious scientific journal, the basest publication in any language, has been so concerned with its galactic responsibilities that it has unwittingly overlooked the constituent elements of the words appearing between its covers. Without these words, JIR readers are speechless. Words become parts of phrases, phrases become parts of sentences, sentences become parts of published articles, etc.

Therefore, it is imperative to determine what comprises the words in the JIR. We must dissuade the JIR from looking backward at the laurels it has already amassed. We must examine it analytically, lest it fall behind. This paper is designed to fill the gap that has existed so far.

Method

A random sample of words was chosen from random sample of issues of the JIR.[2] The sample w stratified according to age, sex, lingual origin, a marital status, all based on latest available cens data. In no case did a stratum in the sample diff from its corresponding population stratum by mo than 84% and, in all cases, variation is attribute solely to well-known census inaccuracies.

The letters in each word were classified accordi to an ancient Indo-European system. For exampl an "a" in any given word was tallied under the c umnar heading "a," whereas a "b" employed in a given word was tallied under the heading "b," etc. the sample of 3417[3] words, the following frequenci were obtained:

TABLE 1
Frequency Distribution of Letters in JIR Words

a	3456	f	234	k	432	p	543	u	23
b	678	g	321	l	654	q	98	v	
c	789	h	567	m	345	r	890	w	34
d	1098	i	3210	n	987	s	876	x	
e	4567	j	123	o	1234	t	765	y	4
								z	1

Results

Mean usage of letters varies from 23.724% for th letter "e" to .069% for "z."[4] To some degree this attributable to the corollary finding that JIR autho tend, all other events remaining equal, to prefer mo words containing "e's" than "z's." More research urgently needed on this point to uncover the reasor r this preference. The magnitude of this difference, nificant beyond the .00001 level of confidence, ses the unwelcome specter of some underlying liter-y bias that can no longer remain unnoticed by scien-ic disciplinarians.

A correlation matrix was constructed with the re-lt that additional preferences of JIR authors were vealed. For example, our carefully selected sample ferred to in footnote 2 makes it clear that in each the 98 instances where a JIR author employs the ter "q" he invariably prefers to follow it with the ter "u." On the other hand, such letters as "j," "x," d "z" are never used consecutively. Why should such aring biases exist in a journal that is renowned for scientific neutrality? On the third hand, when the age of "i" before "e" is examined, it becomes evident at JIR authors are not unduly selective, except after ." In the latter instance, a correlation coefficient of 898984 is obtained, significant at the .000106 level. owever, a simple modification in our spelling habits in the instructions given to JIR proofreaders should rrect this problem without undue difficulty.

Conclusion

If science is to progress, it must have standards. Unbelievably, prior to the present research, norms for the letters of the words appearing in the JIR had never been offered in the mass media. With the publication of the foregoing table, we are provided with the preliminary means for gauging the basic content in the JIR and need no longer watch helplessly as that content is kicked in the mass.

[1] Tation, Dino. *J. Odor Laryngology*, 1969, 35, 127-146.
[2] Space limitations do not prevent the author from detailing the sampling methods used.
[3] This is a tentative total. The author's assistant, Miss Fitt, became bleary-eyed during the counting process and was uncertain whether the total was 3417 or 3147. (She gets hung up on telephone numbers also.)
[4] More scientifically, the precise means were 23.724186392 and .069347280613 but in the interest of conserving expensive space it was reluctantly decided to report these only to three decimal places. The author begs the indulgence of the statistical community for thus bowing to the economic demands of mass media publication but calls to his defense the unforgettable words of the revered Professor Golem: "Mass media must publish or perish." (Golem, Ezza. *J. Inner Space* 1724, 63, 405-504.)

Paper Chormatography

RALPH A. LEWIN
Scripps Insistion of Oceanography,
La Jolla, Calif. 92037

In these days of neo-classical renaissance, when it seems that everyone above the rank of labroatory assistant is "charismatic" and every insistion beyond the junior college level is "prestigious", we should not fail to note the grwoth of what may be called "paper chormatography" (from the mythical Greek: *"chorma"*, gen. *"chormatos"*, an inversion, and *"graphein,"* to write). With the further limitation of research grants, and the general need for scientists to type their labroatory reprots themselves, chormatographic phenomena will undoubtedly become more and more evident as time goes on.

I first became aware of the phenomenon when I was typing the penultimate draft of my thesis on the genetics of *Chalmydomonas*. I wasted a lot of time, back-spacing over the third and fourth letters, or erasing them, and then carefully retyping the word *"Chalmydomonas,"* before I realized what was going on and capitulated to what is clearly a force of nature. I am sure that all biochemists who have used slat gradients to elute unknown substances from columns will know what I mean. My brother-in-law Gerlad, a mathematician, has had the same trouble with cala-culus.

We are planning a symposium on the grwoth of chormatography, to be held in this insistion some time in 1972. Will all those who wish to participate please contact: Ralph A. Lewin.

How To Write Technical Articles

"When I use a word", said Humpty Dumpty, "it means just what I choose it to mean, neither more nor less."

—Through the Looking Glass.

Abstract: We shall endeavour to establish, Q.E.D. fashion, that contrary to popular misconceptions, writing is not an art, but a science, hence not something one is born with, but an attribute one acquires through diligent exertions.

Dear Scribe:

If writing were an art, how come so many artists write wretchedly and so many scientists well? Conversely, if writing were a science, then a writer is, ipso facto, a scientist and an artist has no business meddling in extraneous vocations. Q.E.D.

Otherwise: Writing is either a science or an art. But the artists are not writing since they are holding the paint cans while painting with their feet. Hence, it must be a science. Q.E.D. again.

Before you ever dip your quill into the inkwell, consider who your readers will be. Ostensibly, technical articles are intended for technical readership, i.e., one endowed with a level of intelligence somewhat above the mundane. Hence, if you are contemplating a "snow job", it behooves you to resort to seemingly inadvertent impediments to comprehension, e.g., sporadic cacology and non-germane juxtapositions on a level befitting those readers. It is practically incumbent on you to do so when all you have to communicate is trivial, trite and obvious. But the science of this discipline has not been yet sufficiently formulated. Henceforth, adhere to the Ten Commandments pertaining to that arcane body of knowledge and you shall have snow enough to ski in Sun Valley the year round.

You ought to realize that even the most ardent follower of "the-state-of-the-art" (a vain euphemism for "our current ignorance") gets jaded somewhat after the first grey hairs streak through and his general sophistication (a constant function of time) reaches a certain "firing level." It then becomes a matter of bemused detachment, polite boredom or downright amazement to skim through such a masterpiece laboriously sifting the heavy verbal sands for a golden nugget of original information.

Sedulously then, adhere to the following tenets to attain lasting recognition in printers ink:

1) Use words which mean only what you want them to mean and don't let on to the perplexed reader. (One professor actually wrote to me: "The earth has no boundaries, yet it is finite!")

2) Always expound in pompous polysyllables employing current buzz-words and expostulating with circumlocutory verbosity.

3) Synthesize ingenious concatenations of sonorous phrases with negligible congruity.

4) Use surreptitious recourse to arcane etymology to inculcate an impression of coruscating erudition.

5) Compound your syntax with ambivalent and equivocal periphrasis to attain esoteric obfuscation.

6) Resort to immutable quantifications to purvey an aura of punctilious erudition.

7) Sporadically resuscitate your reader from somnolent stupor by bombastic superlatives and fustian imperatives.

8) Intersperse your thematic opus with technological nomenclature without terminological reduncancies to promote extirpating turbidity and deleterious opacity.

9) Preclude untenable allegations which can be repudiated by fractious readers, incensed enough to do so, with opprobrious effects to yourself.

10) Never write as one speaks.

Of course, sodium chloride being so ubiquitous, some readers will liberally resort to it when reading you. However, if you are versed in the principles of NOR logic and apply them to the foregoing, it might come to pass that a lot of salt shakers will keep their grains for other applications. If you just keep in mind the journalistic tenets of: what, when, where, why, how and so what and furthermore have some innovation to convey, then by applying NOR logic to the above golden rules you should be able to see the light of publishing to your eternal recognition.

Yours in Caligraphy,
Semper Lucidus
Jack Eliezer
Western Union

Aug. 1968

A Call to Clearer Thinking

CHAS. M. FAIR

Synax Biomedical Corporation
Somerville, Massachusetts

In an age in which equal opportunity has become a major issue, Marigold L. Linton, in a recent letter to Science[1], calls attention to a neglected aspect of the problem. According to Miss (Mrs.?) Linton, the chimp Washoe who has been learning sign-language might have done far better had he (she?) not been "culturally deprived". In fact Linton suggests that the linguistic backwardness of apes in general may be due to the same cause. This is an arresting thought and I suggest that schools be set up in the jungle at once. Funding might be arranged on a matching-grant basis between HEW and UNESCO, with participation of local governments on a scale prorated to the GNP of each.

It will be recalled that John Lilly, in Man and Dolphin[2] pioneered in this field when he foresaw that dolphins might be taught to speak and proposed that, if not pacifists, they might be used by our government for underwater espionage. It may be that Linton has provided a clue as to why that project has been so slow in materializing. Dolphins probably *can* talk if only we get them started on it soon enough. Thanks to the work of Cousteau and others, a plan for setting up kindergartens for dolphin young in their own habitat is now quite feasible. There they might get the "feel" of language by playing with alphabet blocks, and later listen to stories played to them on speeded up tape. (A dolphin's vocal range runs up to 100,000 cps, its normal speaking voice lying somewhere in the middle of that range, or around 50 kc.) The aim, as I see it, should be to produce not dolphin spies but dolphin teachers, who might then carry on the work for themselves, on an oceanwide scale. The economy inherent in this approach should appeal to the present Administration in Washington. Its end-result would be to give us a pool, so to speak, not merely of secret agents, but of useful new citizens of all kinds — oyster-bed guards hull checkers, pilots (some dolphins have already gone into the field on their own, according to well-authenticated sea-stories), lifeguards at public beaches (Aristotle reports that in the Mediterranean, dolphins have on occasion come to the aid of drowning men), and guides for fishing fleets, to name a few.

Shaller's work with the gorilla suggests a third group which may only require a nudge from us to begin making giant strides on its own. The reader may recall the story of the golf-playing gorilla whom a man bought and entered in a tournament. The poor animal, having driven the ball 350 yards onto the green, was then handed a putter and drove it another 350 yards into a nearby woods. Lacking, as he and his kind have always been, in the advantages we enjoy from birth, he could hardly have been expected to do otherwise and besides incomprehension of the game, his action may have revealed a quite natural resentment at the position in which he had been put.

Such evils should not be allowed to persist, and will not, if Drs. Lilly and Linton, and others like them, are heeded. I say we should move immediately. In a technological age, literacy and speech are the birthright of all. To deny them to other species is as gross an injustice as to withhold them from our own.

(By one of those coincidences which occur with remarkable frequency in the history of science, I have just received a letter from a chimp who recently took his doctorate in driver-training arts at the University of the Pacific on Tutuila. He has given me permission to make his remarks public, since it seems that his *incognito,* respected all these years by his foster parents and fellow students, is about to be abandoned and his achievement made known to the world.

Doctor Ikashi Chojo, who was given his name by the Japanese couple who adopted him, spent his earliest years in the Tokyo Zoo, receiving his first instruction when a visiting ethologist, Professor Eibl-Eibesfeldt, gave him a short course in German word-order and prepositional constructions. Dr. Chojo has since scored an impressive number of "firsts". He is the first chimp to speak *and* write Japanese, the first to have played professional baseball — second base with the Hokkaido Giants — the first to shine his own shoes and dress himself. While at the university he shaved the backs of his hands and wore a kimono and a rubber Frankenstein mask to conceal his identity. His major, as mentioned, was driver-training, with a minor in political science. He writes:

Dear mister doctor Fair: Please forgive and forget. I write English rotten, start too late — two months old. . . . I just want to say you good student man-ape relations, out of sight, keep up good work, but strongly resent your suggestion dolphins may equal or surpass ape. All knows dolphin is a fish — warm-blooded but a fish. Sane world polity impossible if dolphin to be included. Please reconsider unsound view.
Yours truely
[Ikashi Chojo, PhD]

*   *   *   *

The new age may have its complications, but it is clearly here.

[1] Science, *169*:328, 1970
[2] Lilly, John, Man and Dolphin, Pyramid Books, 1962

The

sometimes

fickle

handmaiden

of the

sciences:

MATHEMATICS

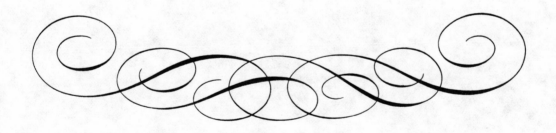

THE DATA ENRICHMENT METHOD*

HENRY R. LEWIS

The following remarks are intended as a nontechnical exposition of an interesting method which has been proposed (not by the present author) to improve the quality of inference drawn from a set of experimentally obtained data. The power of the method lies in its breadth of applicability and in the promise it holds of obtaining more reliable results *without recourse to the expense and trouble of increasing the size of the sample of data*. The method is best illustrated by example. Two such examples are outlined below; the first is somewhat routine, but the second is a striking illustration of what "data enrichment" can achieve.

Consider an experiment performed to test the ability of a specific sound receiver to detect an audio signal. The experiment is performed in such a way that in each of a series of trials one learns either that detection was accomplished or that it was not accomplished. Suppose, moreover, that the sound source and the receiver are fixed in space and trials are made with the source intensity set at six different levels. At each of the six source intensity levels a number of tests are made and the result, detection or no detection, is recorded. The data from such an experiment are summarized in Table 1.

sity. Using these simple facts, the data collected at one source level can be used to add to the data available for other levels. For example, looking at Table 1 we see that three of the trials made at a source level of 77 db resulted in no detection. These trials would also have led to no detection had the source level been at 62 db. Consequently, we can add the results of these experiments to our body of knowlege about 62 db *since we know how these experiments would have come out had we performed them*. Similarly the five trials made at 62 db and resulting in detection would certainly have resulted in detection had the signal been as high as 77 db at the source. Thus five more trials resulting in detection can be added to those actually made at 77 db. Treating all the data in this fashion, we can compile Table 2.

Two things are apparent at once: the probabilities of detection given in Table 2 are quite different from those which might have been deduced crudely and directly from Table 1; in addition the number of "virtual" trials at each level of source intensity is much larger than the actual number of trials. Hence one may be more confident of the results of Table 2 than of any results one might get directly from Table 1.

TABLE 1.

Raw data

Source level (db)	Number of detections	Number of failures to detect
62	5	40
65	10	30
68	15	20
71	20	10
74	25	5
77	30	3

It is desirable, of course, to increase the amount of data available at each source level. It is reasonable to assume that detectability is a function of source level and that, if all other parameters are held constant, a loud sound is easier to detect than one of smaller intensity. Thus it is safe to assume that if a signal was detected at a given level, it would have been detected at all higher source intensity levels. (The electronics are not such that overloading of the receiver would prevent detection.) Moreover, if a signal was not detected at a given level, it would not have been detected at any lower level of source inten-

A second example, even simpler than the first, should make the advantages of this method of analysis quite clear now that the details are fixed in the reader's mind. It has been known to those interested in psycho-physical phenomena that a man's tendency to flip a coin in such a way that when it lands he will be faced by a head rather than by a tail increases with the altitude at which the experiment is performed. The effect is small but a vast

*Reprinted with permission of the Editor from Operations Research, 1957, 5, 551.

TABLE 2
ENRICHED DATA

Source level (db)	Number of virtual detections	Number of virtual failures	Probability of detection
62	5	108	5/113
65	15	68	15/83
68	30	38	30/68
71	50	18	50/68
74	75	8	75/83
77	105	3	105/108

number of trials conducted on Mount Everest, from base to summit, have shown that the effect indeed exists. With due respect to the hardy band of men who invested so many years and Sherpas in this effort, it is of interest to show how the same result can be obtained by one man with no more athletic ability than that required to climb a flight of stairs and no more equipment than an unbiased nickel. Our advantage over the pioneers in this field lies, of course, in our knowledge of the "enriched-data" method.

Consider a set of stairs with ten levels and number them in the order of their increasing altitude. The experimenter climbs the stairs, slowly, and at each level flips a coin ten times and records a head as a success and a tail as a failure. The results of an actual test are recorded in Table 3.

The results of Table 3 are not conclusive. The altitude effect may be present but is not evident, at least to a naive observer. Suppose we now attempt to increase the da[ta] available by recourse to logic in the manner already illu[s]trated in the first example. The altitude principle tells [us] that if a trial on the first step resulted in a head, then [it] would certainly have resulted in a head if the trial ha[d] been made at the loftier tenth step. Similarly, if despi[te] the height of the tenth step a trial made there resulted i[n] failure to throw a head, then the same trial would sure[ly] have been a failure on the lower steps. Using this add[ed] insight, the data can be enriched by a large number of v[ir]tual trials as is shown in Table 4.

A glance at Table 4 shows that the altitude principl[e] which was skulking almost unnoticed in the raw data [of] Table 3, has been fully brought forth by the data enric[h]ment method. The probabilities in Table 4 are shown [in] Fig 1 to further emphasize the point. It might be me[n]tioned in passing that the altitude effect in the Pentago[n]

TABLE 3
RAW DATA : COIN EXPERIMENT

Step number	Number of successes	Number of failures
1	4	6
2	5	5
3	7	3
4	4	6
5	6	4
6	6	4
7	6	4
8	6	4
9	3	7
10	4	6

TABLE 4
ENRICHED DATA : COIN EXPERIMENT

Step number	Number of virtual successes	Number of virtual failures	Probability of throwing a "head"
1	4	50	4/54
2	9	44	9/53
3	16	39	16/55
4	20	36	20/56
5	26	30	26/56
6	31	26	31/57
7	37	21	37/58
8	43	17	43/60
9	46	13	46/59
10	50	6	50/56

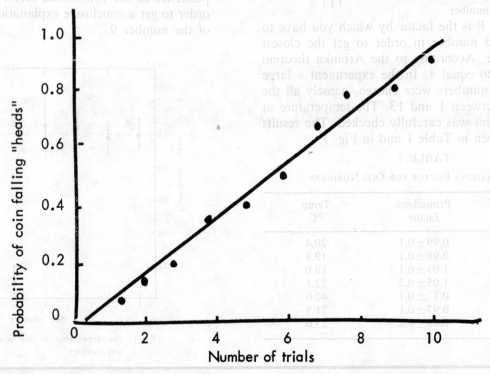

FIGURE 1 . ALTITUDE EFFECT IN THE PENTAGON

appears to be 10^5 times as large as that found in the Himalayas. Whether this is a temperature effect, a geographical effect, or the result of psychical factors as yet unknown should be the object of further study.

A final remark on the strength and weakness of the method is in order. As mentioned earlier, its strength lies in its breadth of applicability, and the method is as pertinent to experiments in classical physics as it is to experiments in psychical phenomena. In short, the method will give new meaning to data quite without regard to the status of the hypothesis used to increase the sample size.

Despite its evident power, however, the method requires further study. Its principal shortcoming is that before the enrichment process can be started, some data must be collected. It is quite true that a great deal is done with very little information, but this should not blind one to the fact that the method still embodies the "raw-data flaw." The ultimate objective, complete freedom from the inconvenience and embarrassment of experimental results, still lies unattained before us.

========

Measuring The Primadona Factor For Odd Numbers...

Y. RONEN et al.
Department of Experimental Mathematics
Beer Sheva, Israel. P.O.B. 9001

Recently Arbinka[1] proposed a revolutionary theorem in the field of falstional analysis. According to this theorem (Appendix A) all odd numbers are primary numbers. Due to the importance of this discovery our group at the department of experimental mathematics has proposed an experiment to verify this idea.

In our experiment we measured the amount in which odd numbers differ from being primary. The Primadona factor P is defined as,

$$P = \frac{\text{primary number}}{\text{odd number}} \qquad (1)$$

In other words, P is the factor by which you have to multiply an odd number in order to get the closest primary number. According to the Arbinka theorem this factor has to equal 1. In the experiment a large domain of odd numbers were chosen, namely all the odd numbers between 1 and 13. The temperature at each measurement was carefully checked. The results obtained are given in Table 1 and in Fig. 1.

In Fig. 1 we see an excellent agreement between our experiment and Arbinka's theory. The only difference occurs for the odd number 9. A possible explanation for this difference is the effect of temperature. Table 1 shows that all the measurements, besides the number 9, were taken at about the same temperature, whereas the measurement of 9 was taken at the high temperature of 40°C, which might explain the difference. We are now designing equipment for measuring the dependence of the Primadona factor on temperature in order to get a conclusive explanation of the anomaly of the number 9.

TABLE 1

THE PRIMADONA FACTOR FOR ODD NUMBERS

odd number	Primadona factor	Temp °C
1	0.99±0.1	20.4
3	0.98±0.1	19.8
5	1.03±0.1	19.0
7	1.05±0.2	22.1
9	0.1 ±0.1	40.0
11	0.97±0.1	21.5
13	0.88±0.2	25.0

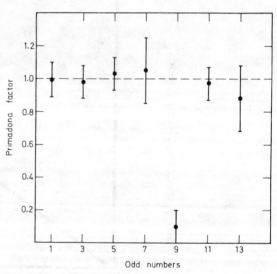

Fig 1. The dependence of the primadona factor for odd numbers

---

REFERENCES

[1]ARBINKA: Private Communication (1972)
[2]ibid.

ACKNOWLEDGEMENTS

The authors are indebted to many people for useful comments and smiles.

APPENDIX — A

Theorem: All the odd numbers are primary numbers.

Proof:
One is primary number
Three is primary number
Five is primary number
Seven is primary number.

Thus using the induction technique every odd number is primary.

Advanced Applications Of The Theory Of The Bar Chart

PICROCOLE RASHCALF, et al.

In a report prepared for the U.S. Department of Labor[1] the following quotation is found:

"Fiscal Year 1975 was not included in Figure 2 because the graph was not long enough to show the projected state and local funding for the four projects combined."

Fundamental to the performance of basic irreproducible research is an understanding of the basic theory of the bar chart. We find, however, dangerous lacunae among our fellow scientists in their apprehension of this basic statistical skill. It is regretable that the authors found themselves in such a pickle for FY 1975 was a vintage year for local, state and Federal statistics on vocational education. Even simple means and standard deviations based on FY '75 data have been known to throw the casual statistical analyst of these data into paroxysms that border on the orgasmic.

Had the authors been truly interdisciplinary they would have known, for instance, that econometricians had long since cracked the statistical problem they were confronted with. The technical name for the solution of Miller and Miller's problem is the "Procrustean Schtick." One either lengthens or widens the page (the procedure is perfectly general) or one changes the scale on the bar. Corollaries to the Procrustean Schtick involve several dimensions. If one also has a large number of bars as in the case of M-M, where they were confronted with a fixed page size, fixed scale, but an almost infinite historical record to display, one can narrow the width of the bars and reduce the type size. Or, since six years of data were reported, FY 1969 could have been dropped, thus creating room for FY 1975. The only problem remaining could then have been solved by dropping the analysis of State and local funding and reporting only on Federal funds, which would have easily fit the page.

One expedient, but not a very professional response, would have simply been to omit the sentence quoted above, whereupon the reader would have likely assumed that FY '75 data were not available. On the chance that FY '75 data are known by one or more additional colleagues to be available, the authors could have pleaded lack of resources necessary to publish and discuss FY '75 data or to buy the required larger size paper. In fact, the authors had almost hit on this solution on page 1:

"The writers of this report did not intend to present a complete exposition of all the major projects . . . It would not be possible within any reasonable time and cost allowance."[2]

But, apparently, this train of thought was lost in the shuffle between pages 1 and 3, a common problem in jointly authored papers.

Let us assume, however, that none of these alternatives were acceptable to M-M. The Procrustean Schtick proves inoperative. The solution here, then, is a fail-safe known as the "Phallic Schtick." This simple but elegant technique merely involves a bending of the bar up along the vertical right hand margin (See Figure 2). Often, depending on the dimensions of the page and the placement of the figure on it, one can double or quadruple the amount of data to be displayed. One can either have a smooth, twice differentiable curve at the bend or a simple right angle. Either is correct.

Finally, if one is truly constrained by the scale on the horizontal axis it is possible to generalize the Phallic Schtick to take advantage of the fact that every page has four margins. This is known as "Coil-Relational Analysis"[3] (See Figure 3). Depending on the thickness of the bar and the size of type (given the margins, of course) one can wind the bar around the page margins literally millions of times, constrained only by the fact that the real number set ends at plus infinity. This, of course, represents the very apex of bar chart theoretical development. Quod erat demonstrandum.

[1] Robert Miller and LaRue W. Miller, *Impact of Vocational Education Research at the State and Federal Levels: Project Baseline Supplemental Report*, Project Baseline, Northern Arizona University, Flagstaff, Arizona, October 25, 1974, p. 3, paragraph 2, lines 1, 2 and 3.
[2] *Ibid*, p. 1, paragraph 3, lines 1, 2, 3 and 4.
[3] Coil-Relational Analysis is derived from "Coillon Analytics," which, in turn was developed by Chaucer in his memorable *Canterbury Tales*. The particular quote on which the theory is roughly based is "Your Coillons Shal be enshrined in a Hogges Torde."

Figure 1: Basic and Deviant Bars

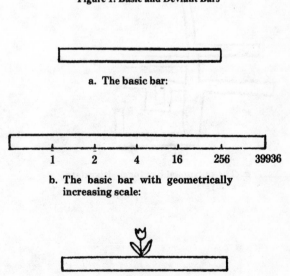

a. The basic bar:

b. The basic bar with geometrically increasing scale:

c. The Gay Bar:

d. The basic bar with spline:

227

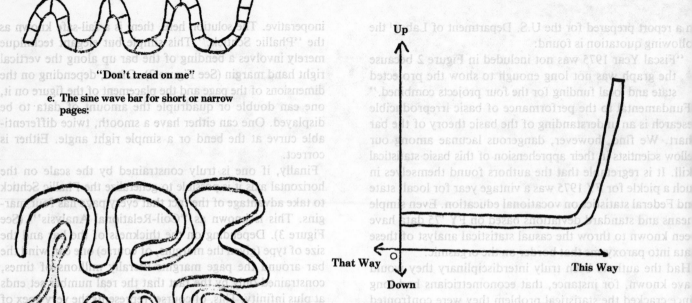

Up

That Way ←O→ This Way

Down

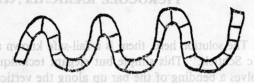

"Don't tread on me"

e. The sine wave bar for short or narrow pages:

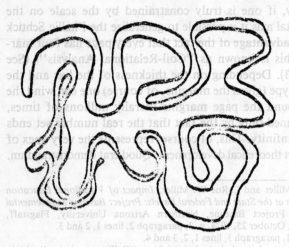

f. The convoluted bar for small pages and tightly enclosed spaces:

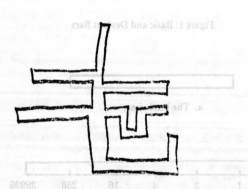

g. The polygonal bar for multivariate analysis:

Not Depicted

h. The Grizzly Bar:

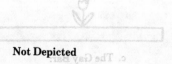

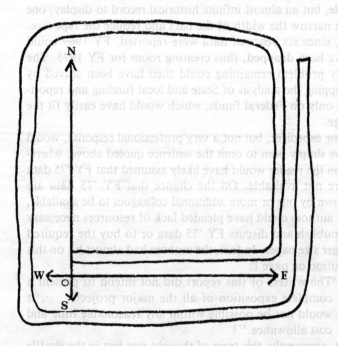

Figure 3: Coil-Relational Analysis

N

W ←O→ E

S

The Art of Finding the Right
Graph Paper to get a Straight Line

S. A. RUDIN

As any fool can plainly see, a straight line is the shortest distance between two points. If, as is frequently the case Point A is where you are and Point B is research money, it is important to see to it that the line is as straight as possible. Besides, it looks more scientific. That is why graph paper was invented.

The first invention was simple graph paper, which popularized the straight line (Fig. 1). But people who had been working the constantly accelerating or decelerating paper had to switch to log paper (Fig. 2). If both coordinates were logarithmic, log:log paper was necessary (Fig. 3).

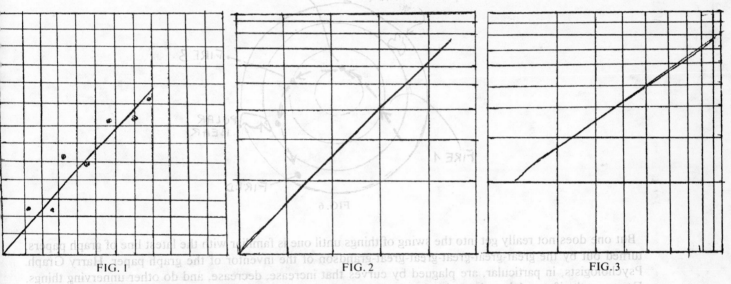

FIG. 1   FIG. 2   FIG. 3

Or, if you had a really galloping variable on your hands, double log-log paper was the thing. And so on for all combinations and permutations of the above (Fig. 4).

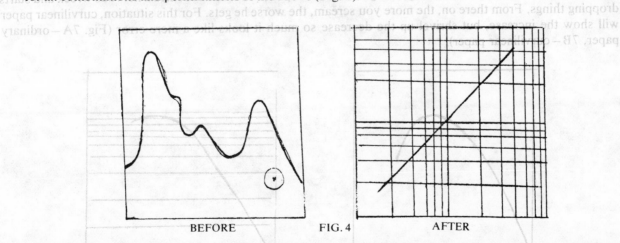

BEFORE   FIG. 4   AFTER

For the statistician, there is always probability paper, which will turn a normal ogive into a straight line or a normal curve into a tent. It is especially popular with statisticians, since it makes their work look precise (Fig. 5).

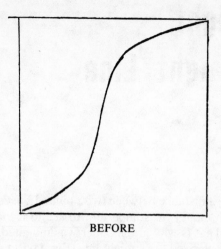

BEFORE

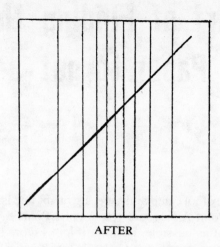

FIG. 5　　　　AFTER

For sailing submarines under the North Polar Cap, there is polar coordinate paper (Fig. 6).

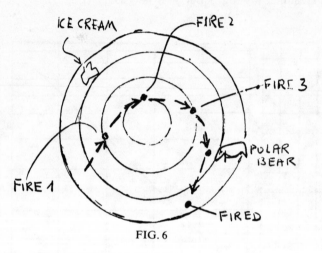

FIG. 6

But one does not really get into the swing of things until one is familiar with the latest line of graph papers, turned out by the great-great-great-great-great-grandson of the inventor of the graph paper, Harry Graph. Psychologists, in particular, are plagued by curves that increase, decrease, and do other unnerving things. For example, if your lab assistant is a lazy slob, his work output is zero. If you yell and threaten him, it goes up. The more you yell at him, the higher it goes, up to the point where he becomes a nervous wreck and starts dropping things. From there on, the more you scream, the worse he gets. For this situation, curvilinear paper will show the increase, but shrivel up the decrease so much it looks like a mere error (Fig. 7A—ordinary paper, 7B—curvilinear paper).

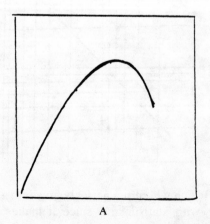

A

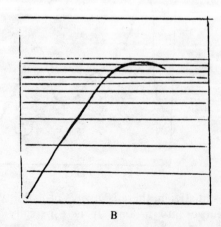

FIG. 7　　　　B

Sometimes correlation coefficient scattergrams come out at .00, with a distribution shaped like a matzo ball (Fig. 8A). But using "correlation paper" Pearson r's of any desired degree of magnitude can be obtained (Fig. 8B). Naturally, negative correlation paper is available; it simply points the diagram the other way.

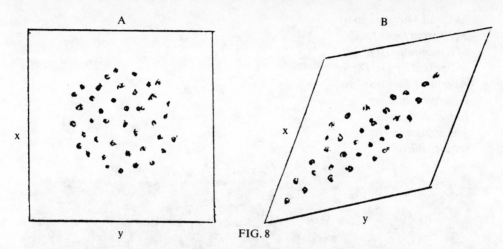

FIG. 8

When you get a curve where you should be getting a straight line, you use the following method. First, the peaks and troughs of the original plot are marked (Fig. 9A). Then, an overlay of transparent plastic sheet is put over it, and the dots alone copied. Now, it is obvious that these points are simply departures from a straight line, which is presented in dashed form (Fig. 9B). Finally, the straight line alone is recopied onto another graph paper (Fig. 9C).

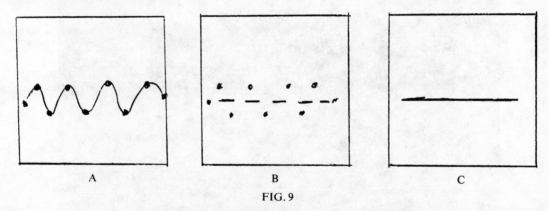

A   B   C

FIG. 9

But by far the latest wrinkle in graph paper (ha!) is the do-it-yourself kit. This consists of an ordinary graph of equally spaced lines, at right angles to one another, as in Fig. 1, but printed on a large sheet of transparent rubber. The user is then free to make up his own technique by stretching the sheet according to his requirements (Fig. 10A and 10B).

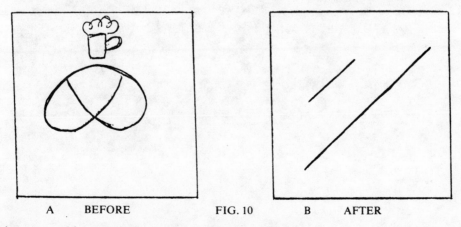

A   BEFORE   FIG. 10   B   AFTER

There is nothing so graphic as a graph to make a point graphically.

*Electron Micrograph of
a cell from line of cells
of a mosquito (Aedes).
Submitted by Dr. Dieter
Adamiker Elektronen-
mikroskophisches
Laboratorium der
Tierarztlichen Hoch-
schule, Wien*

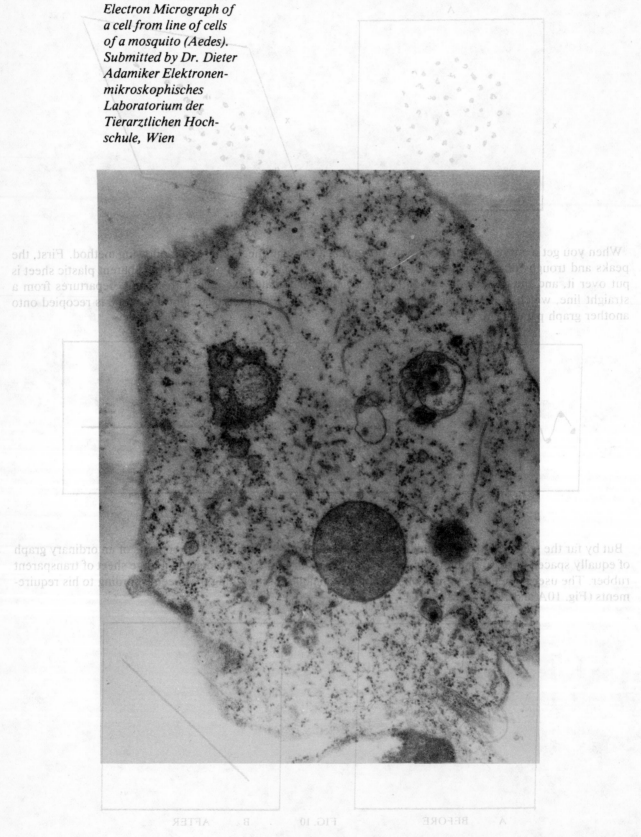

GRAPHSMANSHIP III THE HIGH ENERGY COLORING BOOK

These are experimental points plotted as an idiot-gram. If you are an idiot, color them all colors of the rainbow. If you are not an idiot, do not color them. Just take an anti-histogram pill and go to bed.

H. J. LIPKIN

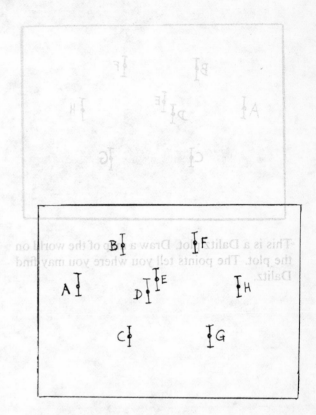

This is a Dalitz plot. Draw a map of the world on the plot. The points tell you where you may find Dalitz.

This is an experimental curve. Theory says there is no peak at point B. Color the Peak Red.

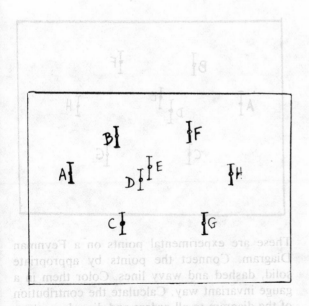

These are experimental points on a Feynman Diagram. Connect the points by appropriate solid, dashed and wavy lines. Color them in a gauge invariant way. Calculate the contribution of the diagram to all states and divergences.

This is an experimental curve. Theory says there is a peak at point B. Color the Peak Grey.

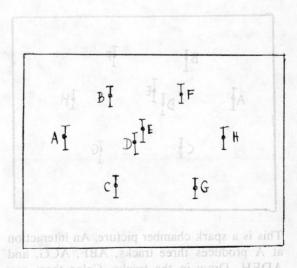

This is a spark chamber picture. An interaction at A produces three tracks, ABF, ACG, and ADEH. Draw in the tracks. Color them any color you wish, and interpret the event.

This is an experimental curve. It is in complete disagreement with theory. Color the error bars BLACK. Make them bigger, BIGGER! **BIGGER!**

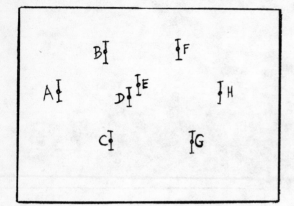

This is a Dalitz plot. Draw a map of the world on the plot. The points tell you where you may find Dalitz.

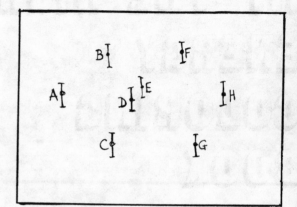

These are experimental points plotted as an idiot-gram. If you are an idiot, color them all colors of the rainbow. If you are not an idiot, do not color them. Just take an anti-histogram pill and go to bed.

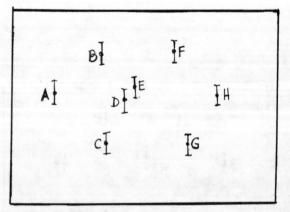

This is a spark chamber picture. An interaction at A produces three tracks, ABF, ACG, and ADEH. Draw in the tracks. Color them any colors you wish, and interpret the event.

These are experimental points on a Feynman Diagram. Connect the points by appropriate solid, dashed and wavy lines. Color them in a gauge invariant way. Calculate the contribution of the diagram to all orders and disorders.

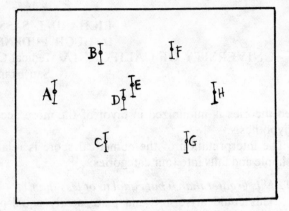

These points are experimental evidence for a new unitary symmetry octet. There is no time to color this picture. Send it to *Phys. Rev. Letters**, right away!

---

*or New York Times

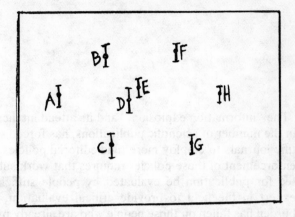

These are experimental points in the non-physical region of the complex angular momentum plane. Only Chew knows what they mean. If you are a Believer color them gold. If you are not a believer, put a cut from point A to infinity. Do the same for points B, C, D, E, F, G, and H. After you have cut the paper to pieces, throw it away.

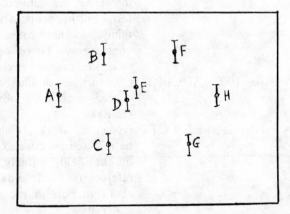

Can you find the Intermediate Boson in the picture?

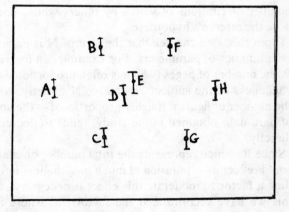

These are experimental points. The values are all finite. The theory gives infinite values. So the experiment is wrong. Do not color this page. Throw it away. Design an experiment to give the correct infinite value.

SWINGER FUNCTION (S.F.)^{4}*

RICHARD J. SASSE

H. HUGH FUDENBE

UNIVERSITY OF CALIFORNIA Medical Ce

San Franc

The "information explosion," and its attendant increase in the number of scientific publications, has forced scientific journals to employ more rigid editorial policies. The enforcement of these policies requires that work submitted for publication be evaluated by people sufficiently expert in the field to provide critical evaluation. This burden has fallen on those people who are already preoccupied in producing the "information explosion."

In an effort to alleviate the burden and speed the laborious process of refereeing scientific articles we have devised a method for rapid evaluation of articles submitted for publication. This method can be summarized in the following formula:

$$N = \frac{P}{f} \cdot \frac{R(r/a)\, r!\,(Oo - Os)}{2\, Oo}$$

where N is the Numerical Score; P is the number of pages in the article; f is the number of figures; R is the total number of citations; r is the number of citations of works authored by the referee; a is the number of citations of works by the author of the submitted manuscript; Os is the number of citations of work by others whose data support the hypotheses of the referee; Oo is the number of citations of works by others whose data oppose the referee's hypotheses.

From this, one can see that the size of N is dependent on a number of parameters. For example, an increase in P, the number of pages (which is often proportional to the vagueness of the subject), increases N directly, while f, the number of figures, roughly proportional to the amount of hard data obtained in the study, tends to decrease N directly.

Since R, which represents the total number of citations, could reflect incorporation of much meaningless information, a factor to moderate this effect is necessary. To do this we have incorporated the factor r/a, where r, the number of works by the referee cited is divided by the number of citations of works by the author, a. In this way, any inadvertent exclusion of significant information, will tend to moderate the effect of R. Therefore, to insure proper weighting of N, the exponent r factorial has been added to overcome small differences between r and a.

Finally, to minimize the adverse effects, should the data be controversial, we have added the normalizing factor (Os − Oo). By this means, bias introduced by the citation of too large a number of papers not in accord with accept-

ed theories is minimized in favor of the more accep hypothesis.

The interpretation of the numerical score is relativ simple and falls into four categories.

1. *N is greater than 0 but equal to or less than 1.*
   This could arise if P and f are nearly equal of (number of figures) is very large but r is large rela to a. If r is small or zero, N will be zero. Also a la (Oo − Os) (which could arise if Os is small or Oo ordinately large), would result in a small N.

2. *N is greater than 1 but equal to or less than 10.*
   This could arise where either P, a, or Os are relativ large, or f and r relatively small.

3. *N is greater than 10 but equal to or less than 100.*
   This could arise when P, r, or Oo are relatively larg

4. *N is greater than 100.*
   This can occur where r is significantly large or O negligible.

The interpretation of N, then, is as follows:

N = 0 – 1:   REJECT   (Author is not familiar w pertinent literature)

N = 1 – 10:   ACCEPT   (It is difficult to determ how well the author mastered the subject terial but his proposals c tainly do not cause controversy. To be on safe side, demand revisic

N = 10 – 100: ACCEPT   (The article should be cepted since it has obvi merits).

N = 100:   REJECT   (Excellent work. It sho be rejected because expe in the field, namely, referee (or his friends) about to publish the sa material).

This investigation was supported by grants-in-aid fr NSF (Non-sufficient Funds) and NIH (Not Immediat Helpful.)

---

* Scientific Facilitation, Special Formulation, Sassetti-Fudenberg, Francisco.

QUOTES

B. Smith and C. V. Fasano,
THE DIAGNOSIS AND TREATMENT OF BAGGY EYELIDS
Bull. N.Y. Acad. Med., 1962, *38*, 163 – 167.

"Concluding we would like to emphasize that if Baggy Eyelids are properly diagnosed and adequately treated, the patient is pleased and happy because he looks better; the surgeon has a sense of artistic accomplishment."

* * *

The Lancet, January 13, 1962, No. 7220, p. 100

"The news about breaking of the genetic code comes as something of a relief. At one time it seemed highly probable that the DNA chain was made up exclusively of four-letter words."

* * *

Katiyar, K. N.
A CRAZY INSTINCT OF COPULATION IN MALES WITH DEAD FEMALES AND
VICE VERSA AMONG SHORT HORNED GRASSHOPPERS (ACRIDIDAE)
Ztschr. f. Ang. Entomologie, 1962, *49*, 399.

* * *

A Montague
NATURAL SELECTION AND THE FORM OF BREAST IN HUMAN FEMALE
J.A.M.A., 1962, *180*, 826 – 827.

"A factor that may have correlatedly assisted in the development of the female breast is the fact that in most nonliterate societies, and especially in areas in which the nights are cold, fat women would tend to be preferred to thin ones. Love in a cold climate is considerably assisted by central heating. Eskimos, for example, always prefer fat women to thin ones. The forerunners of central heating in prehistoric times were fat ladies. Fat ladies would have large breasts, and the premium placed on fatness itself would in this way have further contributed to the development of the breast."

* * *

Walter S. Snyder
THE ESTIMATION OF A BODY BURDEN OF PU FROM URINANALYSIS DATA.
7th Annual Bioassay and Analytical Chem. Meeting, Argonne National Lab. October 12 – 13, 1961.

* * *

Hildebrand, G. J., Ng J., von Metz, E. K., and Eisler, D. M.
STUDIES ON THE MECHANISM OF CIRCULATORY FAILURE INDUCED IN RATS
BY Pasteurella pestis MURINE TOXIN. J. Inf. Dis. 1966, *116*, 618

  "*Decapitation.* Decapitation was performed according to standard procedures."
                                                (probably guillotine – Ed.)

* * *

QUOTES

Lefevre, P. G.
PRESISTENCE IN ERYTHROCYTE GHOSTS OF MEDIATED SUGAR TRANSPORT.
Nature, 1961, *191*, 970–972 (p. 971, line 2).

"It is known from Theorell's observations that ghosts may continue to take in glucose while still excluding sucrose, but Theorell did not examine whether this could be attributed to a free diffusion or to a surviving-mediated transfer activity."

* * *

Blazer, J. A.
LEG POSITION AND PSYCHOLOGICAL CHARACTERISTICS IN WOMEN
Psychology—A Journal of Human Behavior, 1966, *3*, 5–12 (August 66).

"The present study was designed to test a theory of "leg position analysis" or "observed psychology" using standard psychometric tests and methods to gather and analyze the data." "The first hypothesis tested was: The preferred method of leg-crossing or position generally used by a woman as indicative of her need strengths and basic values or interests. The second hypothesis was: intelligence and education have no effect upon preference of leg crossing or position in women."

(Highly recommended to our readers!)

* * *

Myers, R. J.
AN INSTANCE OF THE PITFALLS PREVALENT IN GRAVEYARD RESEARCH
Biometrics, 1963, *19*, 643–650

* * *

Rubin, M., Sliwinski, A., Photias, M., Feldman, M. and Zvaifler, N. (Div. Nuclear Medicine, Walter Reed Hospital, Washington)
INFLUENCE OF CHELATION ON GOLD METABOLISM IN RATS
Proc. Soc. Exp. Biol. & Med., 1967, *124*, 290

"The tissue distribution and excretion of gold injected in rats is dependent upon the nature of the gold carrier."

* * *

Sabastiani, J. A.
PSYCHOTIC VISITORS TO THE WHITE HOUSE
Amer. J. Psychiatr. 1965, *122*, 679.

THE GLASS AND SPLEEN EXPLOSIONS

SIDNEY L. SALTZSTEIN (M.D.)
San Diego County General Hospital

"Explosions" and their dire consequences occupy much of the current scientific and popular literature. The world's population is growing at such a rate that if it were maintained until the year 6000, a solid mass of humanity would be expanding outward from the earth at the speed of light.[1] The number of authors per scientific paper is increasing so rapidly that by 1980 it will reach infinity.[2] Another pair of phenomena, possibly more to be feared, is the glass and spleen explosions.

MATERIALS AND METHODS

When the surgical pathology laboratory at Barnes Hospital, St. Louis, Missouri, was remodeled in 1959 the number of specimens received annually in the laboratory was tabulated so that storage space for past and future slides could be planned. At the same time it was necessary to count, and review the slides, of all spleens either biopsied or removed and received in the same laboratory since the hospital was opened.[3]

RESULTS

The annual number of surgical specimens received is plotted in Figure 1 on semilogarithmic co-ordinates. It is apparent that the number of specimens is increasing loga-

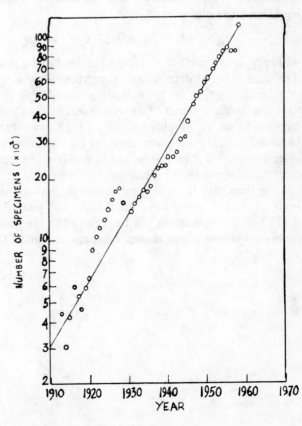

rithmically (exponentially). Close examination of the graph also shows the effect of the Depression of the late 1920's and early 1930's and of World War II. Determining the line of best fit by the least squares method, the following linear regression equation is obtained[4]:

$$Log_{10}N_1 = 2.175 + 0.0317(T - 1900);$$

where N_1 is the number of specimens received in the year T. The coefficient of determination, correcting for degrees of freedom lost, is 0.916, indicating that 91.6% of the variation in the number of specimens received is explained by time alone. A "doubling time" of 9.49 years can be obtained from this equation. Extrapolating backwards, the year when the first specimen should have been received (the year when $N_1 = 1$) is 1832. While this may be absurd since Barnes Hospital did not open until 1912, Dr. William Beaumont, the first modern surgeon in St. Louis, arrived in the area in 1834 (an error of only 0.1%)[5]. Perhaps the onset of this growth of surgical specimens should be correlated with his arrival.

Extrapolating forward, in the year 2224, 2.854×10^{12} specimens will be received, making a total of 5.7×10^{12} specimens to be stored. The slides from approximately 1119 specimens can be stored per cubic foot[6], so 5.1×10^9 cubic feet of storage space will be needed. As the area of the city is 61 square miles[7] this will be enough slides to bury the city of St. Louis 3 feet deep with glass!

The annual number of spleens received is plotted in Figure 2, again on semilogarithmic co-ordinates*. Again, it is apparent that the number of spleens is increasing logarithmically (exponentially), and the linear regression equation turns out to be:

$$Log_{10}N_2 = 0.917 + 0.0457(T - 1900);$$

where N_2 is the number of spleens received in the year T. The coefficient of determination, correcting for degrees of freedom lost, is 0.773, indicating that 77.3% of the variation in the number of spleens received is explained by time alone. A "doubling time" of 6.59 years can be obtained from this equation, showing that the number of spleens received is increasing considerably more rapidly than the total number of specimens received.

If one then sets $N_1 = N_2$, and solves the equations for both N and T, one will find that in the year 2121, 8,271,800,000 specimens will be received by the surgical pathology laboratory at Barnes Hospital, and all of them will be spleens!

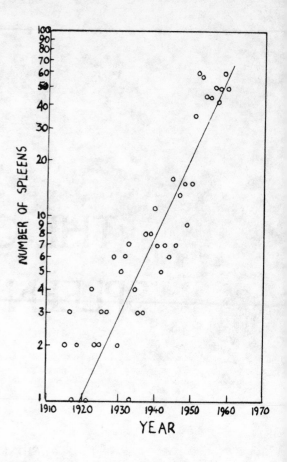

CONCLUSION

Be careful when extrapolating biological data.

REFERENCES

[1] Editorial: The Weight of Humanity. St. Louis Post-Dispatch, day, July 22, 1962.

[2] Price, D. J. de S.: Little Science, Big Science. Cited in Review: J repr. Res. *13*: 22, 1964.

[3] Saltzstein, S. L.: Phospholipid Accumulation in Histiocytes of Sp ic Pulp Associated with Thrombocytopenic Purpura. Blood *18*: 88, 1961.

[4] Hirsch, W. Z.: Introduction to Modern Statistics. N.Y. The N Millan Co. 1957.

[5] Pitcock, C. DeH.: The Involvement of William Beaumont, M.D., Medical-Legal Controversy: The Dames-Davis Case, 1840. souri Historical Review, 1964, 31–45.

[6] Saltzstein, S. L.: Unpublished data.

[7] World Almanac, 1960. p. 294.

[8] Furst, A.: On the Treatment of Annoying but Incontrovertible Inexplicable Facts. J. Irrepr. Res. *13*:10, 1964.

---

* In accordance with Furst's first modification of the scientific met the years when no spleens were received ($Log_{10}0$ indeterminant) ignored.[8]

THE LARGEST INTEGER

JOEL H. SPENCER
Bell Telephone Laboratories

Mathematicians have long sought to discover the identity of the largest integer. Some have proclaimed that such a thing does not exist. This view, while possible internally consistent, certainly cannot give a true model of the integers. For by symmetry, if there is a smallest integer there must be a largest. Of course, this argument's premise may be, and has been, denied. However, without the principle of symmetry much of the work of the last two centuries would have to be discarded. This, we feel, is too great a price to pay. Our solution is given by the following.

Theorem: -1 is the largest integer.

Proof 1:   List the integers

$$\ldots -4\ -3\ -2\ -1 \qquad +1\ +2\ +3\ +4 \ldots$$

You will note that nothing has been left out. The largest integer must have no successor—clearly -1.
This proof lacks rigor as it required a "listing" of the integers. We therefore include a rigorous

Proof 2:   Let n be the largest integer

Then $\qquad\qquad\qquad n \leq n + 1$

and $\qquad\qquad\quad n + 1 \leq n + 2$

so $\qquad\qquad\qquad n \leq n + 2$

But since n is the largest integer

$$n \geq n + 2$$

so $\qquad\qquad\qquad n = n + 2$

Squaring both sides $n^2 = n^2 + 4n + 4$

$$4n = -4$$

$$n = -1$$

Q.E.D.

It has been noted that since $n + n + i, n = \dfrac{-i}{2}$. Since n must be integral $i = 2 j > 0, n = -j$. But $-1 \geq -j$ for all $j > 0$ and so is the largest largest integer and therefore the largest integer.

We might also recall the conventional non-existent argument (generally, and for good reason, used only with children), "add one and you get a larger number." But we see that nothing is one more than -1.

Scientists

are

always

affected

by

irreproducible

FACULTY

CONCERNS

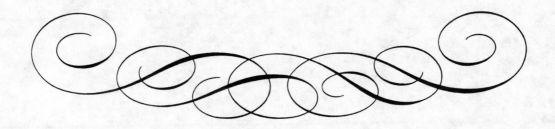

Important Laws in Science [A Review]

A. KOHN

There are many laws in science. Many are taught in high schools: such as the laws of Newton, Boyle-Mariotte, Thermodynamics, Ohm, etc.

In the last decade some new important Laws were discovered:

1. *Parkinson's Laws.* Most of these laws are well described in Parkinson's book[1]. Recently a new Parkinson's Law for Medical research has been described[2]. It states: SUCCESSFUL RESEARCH ATTRACTS THE BIGGER GRANT WHICH MAKES FURTHER RESEARCH IMPOSSIBLE."

2. *Maier's Law*[3]: IF FACTS DO NOT CONFORM TO THEORY, THEY MUST BE DISPOSED OF.

3. *Murphy's Law*[4]: IF ANYTHING CAN GO WRONG WITH AN EXPERIMENT, IT WILL.

4. *Paradee's Law*[5]: THERE IS AN INVERSE RELATIONSHIP BETWEEN THE UNIQUENESS OF AN OBSERVATION AND THE NUMBER OF INVESTIGATORS WHO REPORT IT SIMULTANEOUSLY.

5. *Hersh's Law*[6]: BIOCHEMISTRY EXPANDS SO AS TO FILL THE SPACE AND TIME AVAILABLE FOR ITS COMPLETION AND PUBLICATION.

6. *Old & Kohn's Law*[7, 8]: THE EFFICIENCY OF A COMMITTEE MEETING IS INVERSELY PROPORTIONAL TO THE NUMBER OF PARTICIPANTS AND THE TIME SPENT ON DELIBERATIONS.

7. *Gordon's First Law*[9]: IF A RESEARCH PROJECT IS NOT WORTH DOING AT ALL, IT IS NOT WORTH DOING WELL.

REFERENCES

1. Parkinson, C. N. Parkinson's Law, Houghton Mifflin Co. 1937.
2. Parkinson, C. N. Parkinson's Law in Medical Research, New Scientist 13:193 (1962).
3. Maier, N. R. F. Maier's Law, The American Psychologist (1960).
4. Michie D., Sciencemanship, Discovery 20:259 (1959)
5. Pardee, A. B., pU, a new quantity in biochemistry, American Scientist 50:130A (1962).
6. Hersh, R. T. Parkinson's Law, the squid and pU, American Scientist 50:274A (1962).
7. Old, B. S. Scientific Monthly, 68:129 (1946).
8. Kohn, A. Boardmanship, J. Irrepr. Res. *10*:24 (1962).
9. —— —— J. Irrepr. Res. *9*:43 (1961).

THE MOLECULAR THEORY OF MANAGEMENT

RUSSEL DE WAARD

It is interesting and informative to liken the growth and behavior of a company to that of a synthetized organic molecule. Take as example PVC. In unplasticized form this material is very hard, elastic, and brittle. There are many strong bonds between closely spaced charged atoms. When one adds so-called diluent plasticizers, the bonds are weakened as the inverse square law is invoked by the big putty-like molecules. The material becomes flexible, can absorb shock, and shows promise for commercial purposes; for example, shower curtains, automobile window winders, steering wheels, seat covers, and the like. These big molecules here serve a very useful purpose and furthermore they contribute in just the right way to the modern economy of "planned obsolescence." The molecules slowly lose their footing and leech out of your window winder, leaving behind a cracked handle at just about the same time as the rust eats through your right front fender.

Now, a company also starts with a small group of charged particles. A lot of energy is produced, efficiency is high, and hence business is good. This nucleus rapidly acquires more particles. Because there is no time for careful screening, a large number of the big rubber-like molecules are added to the mix. Many other types of particles are admitted in random fashion. Their quality is inversely proportional to the management stature of the interviewer and their salary directly proportional. Unfortunately, many of the big molecules are completely inelastic diluents whose function appears to be to absorb the energy generated by the charged particles.

It is interesting to contrast these rubber-like additions to the neutrino of atomic physics, whereas the latter has no charge and no mass, the former has no charge and is all mass. If a growing company can avoid gathering too many of these particles it can survive. If the converse holds, all of the energy generated by the charged particles is absorbed by the diluents and no energy or products can escape. Although the evidence pointing this way is sometimes strong, it is hard to believe that a company would consciously plan its own obsolescence.

The Innovation Myth

Actually, management is very uncomfortable with creative personnel and, with rare exceptions, has never provided an environment that motivates them to produce. Creative talent always seems to be frustrated, irascible, unpredictable, and unproductive in the corporate world.

Great numbers of corporate executives consciously are not aware of their hostility to new ideas. On a personal basis they believe to a man that new products are essential to the future of the company. But when given an opportunity to implement this conviction within the corporate environment they inevitably demonstrate negative attitudes. And in so doing, they totally reflect the basic negative corporate attitude on this point.

What prudent man is going to put his career on the line for so hazardous an undertaking as a new product venture when he personally has everything to lose and nothing to gain?

In 5 or 10 years, when the product finally begins generating profits, considering the present mobility of top executive talent, it is more than likely that he will no longer be with the company.

The Dept. of Commerce reports that of the 11 major inventions in the steel industry, four were products of European firms, seven came from independent inventors, and *none* came from American steel firms.

And in the petroleum industry, that giant among giants, of the seven major inventions in the refinig and cracking of petroleum *all* were made by small independent inventors!

Abstracts from *The Innovation Myth* by Louis Soltanoff, President, Louis Soltanoff & Associates. From *Industrial Research*, August 1971.

A Study of Basic Personality Behavior Patterns Which Characterize the Heirachry of Social Dominance or Rank in Large Corporations.

JAMES A. CUNNINGHAM
Personnel Department
Alabama Instruments, Inc.
Huntsburg, Alabama

ABSTRACT

A quantitative definition of corporate rank is established. Results are presented which show correlations between various types of salutations the audibility of salutations and behavior patterns in meetings.

INTRODUCTION

In any group of higher animals a heirachry of social dominance or rank is quickly established. A classic example is the basic pattern of social organization within a flock of poultry in which each bird pecks another lower in scale without fear of retaliation and submits to pecking by one of higher rank (1). Primates also exhibit similar behavior (2). For example, R. Nasini and A. Scala (3) describe an experiment where five East Indian gibbons were placed in a cage with a small door such that only one could exit at a time. Three males, one castrated, and two females were included. The right to exit first, i.e. the social rank, was quickly and reproducibly established with the largest male first, followed by the second largest male, a female, the castrated male, and finally, the smaller female. These studies clearly show the importance of strength and body weight in establishing social rank in animals, but they are of limited value, of course, in analyzing human behavior which in a modern society is intellectually rather than physically oriented.

Nevertheless, modern zoological and anthropological studies do show interesting correlations between lower primate behavior and man regarding social ranking and status. For example, Desmond Morris (4) lists ten basic laws which govern dominance which he claims are operative both in man and in baboons. The ten laws are:

1. You must clearly display the trappings, postures and gestures of dominance.

2. In moments of active rivalry you must threaten your subordinates aggressively.

3. In moments of physical challenge you (or your delegates) must be able forcibly to overpower your subordinates.

4. If a challenge involves brain rather than brawn you must be able to outwit your subordinates.

5. You must suppress squabbles that break out between your subordinates.

6. You must reward your immediate subordinates by permitting them to enjoy the benefits of their high ranks.

7. You must protect the weaker numbers of the group from undue persecution.

8. You must make decisions concerning the social activities of your group.

9. You must reassure your extreme subordinates from time to time.

10. You must take the initiative in repelling threats or attacks arising from outside your group.

It is not difficult to recognize that many of these behavior patterns are indeed operative in a large corporation.

Although the corporate environment represents a very dynamic system of social rank and dominance as various individuals move up and down and in and out, it is, nevertheless, a well defined system which is relatively easy to describe in quantitative terms. It is the purpose of this paper to present the results of various tests carried out which attempt to relate behavior patterns and characteristics to a precisely defined corporate rank.

RESULTS

I. Definition of Corporate Rank

The corporate rank or CR is defined as

$$CR_i = \frac{S_i}{S_p} + \frac{G_i}{G_p} + \frac{N_i}{N_T} + \frac{R_i}{R_N} + \frac{D_i}{3} + \frac{A_i}{A_T} + \frac{E_i}{E_p} \qquad (1).$$

CR_i = corporate rank of ith individual
S_p = President's salary
S_i = individual salary
G_i = individuals job grade as set by personnel department
G_p = President's job grade
N_i = number of people reporting to individual
N_T = total number of people in company
R_i = number of organizational levels from president
R_N = number of organizational levels in company
D_i = number of college degrees up to 3 maximum
A_i = number of unique office accouterments
A_T = number of unique office accouterments in president's office
E_i = number of years of related experience
E_p = number of years of related experience for the company president

Values range from a low of about 0.13, which might represent the CR of a newly employed dock worker, to a value of 7.0 held by the company president. A typical distribution of CR values in a corporation of 50,000 people would look approximately like Figure 1.

FIGURE 1

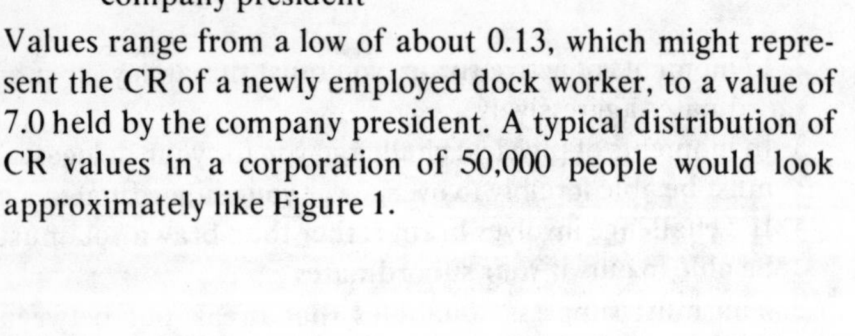

It is believed that the validity of Equation 1 is essentially axiomatic and, therefore, warrants no further discussion.

II. Basic Relationships

First, it may be mentioned that certain intracompany patterns such as (1) placing ones feet on the table, (2) the wearing of only black suits, (3) wearing bow ties, (4) wearing only blue shirts, (5) wearing only white sox, (6) smoking a pipe and others appeared to be related more to conformism and mimicry of a very highly ranked and individualistic company official than to intercompany behavior characteristics of a more general nature. Also, as far as males are concerned, no strong correlations were found between the CR and body weight or height, hair or eye color, or other such physical characteristics except for a rather mild correlation at the very highest levels with the presence of severe hemorrhoids.

Clear and unequivacal correlations were found with sex. No women with CR's above a value of about 3 appear to exist in American industry.

III. Meetings

It became clear in the very early phases of this research that a fruitful area of study would be an examination of the behavior of individuals while attending company meetings where people of various CR's are present. Accordingly, personality traits and patterns were observed and recorded by a team of three trained observers during the course of attending approximately 1600 meetings in four corporations over a period of two years.

The following personality characteristics were found to be typical of the highest ranking member of a given meeting or conference.

1. Asks questions rather than answers questions.
2. Asks questions about timing and schedules rather than about how and why.
3. Sits at the head of the table.
4. Gives commands and advice.
5. Stays on the offensive rather than on the defensive.
6. Usually comes late to a meeting.
7. Exits a meeting by having a secretary deliver a seemingly important note.
8. Rarely gives a presentation — usually is the recipient of a presentation.
9. Shows greater interest in financial matters than in technical matters.
10. Rarely appears to be snowed.
11. Never becomes emotional.
12. Responds quickly and with an authoritative tone.
13. Never lets another member of the group get the upper hand.

14. Rarely reprimands a subordinate of greatly lower CR. Does reprimand subordinates of close CR.
15. Assumes the characteristics of an extrovert rather than an introvert.
16. Looks everyone straight in the eye.
17. Never mumbles, twitches or fidgets.
18. Assigns responsibilities to others rather than to himself.
19. Is in a hurry and tries to speed up the meeting.

Universal use of all these tactics in almost all situations is, of course, reserved for the highest ranking corporate officials that is CR = 6-7 company presidents or chairmen of the board. Much lower ranking individuals, i.e. CR = 0-2, would be expected to behave, in general, according to the antithesis of the above list.

It was observed that such petty tactics as: the use of rough language, asking highly technical memorized questions or obvious attempts to embarrass a competitor were not typical of very high ranked individuals.

Let's take a look at how some of these behavior patterns operate by listening in on a meeting being held by an engineering manager, several of his engineers, three or four corporate staff people and the company president.

Dr. John Galaway, Ph.D. physics, is at the board. He is speaking and directing his remarks in the direction of Markus Hutson, President of Impact Ecotronics, Inc. Mr. Hutson is seated at the head of the table with his corporate staff members positioned immediately to his left and right. John is near the end of his presentation and is saying, "The pyridinium imino complex (related, of course, to ZFQ* activation) will probably react or enable the zeta phase of PFP via the bolonium state. This could lead us to new ortho megatypes. We feel a computer analysis of the quantized spin-orbital Gaŭdsmit integrals of the L_{II} L_{III} intermediate may lead us to the answer. (The entire analysis will have to be carried out in vector phase space, of course.) Our main delay, at this time, Mr. Hutson, is corporate funding."

Gerald Hutson, company president, unhesitatingly replies in a forceful and authoritative manner, "John, this is clearly one of our must do's for 1975. When do you think you can have the analysis finished and a full report on my desk?"

Even though the company president had no idea what the engineer was talking about, he still asserted and protected his CR by responding in the classical aggressive style. That is (1) he asked when, not how or why, (2) he answered the implied question by asking another question, (3) he passed the responsibility back to the subordinate, (4) he made it appear that he thoroughly understood the topic under discussion, (5) he postponed any decisions he might eventually have to make without the slightest hint of insipidity and finally, (6) he issued a command. A statement similar to Mr. Hutson's could

be made by anyone with the highest CR in a given meeting. Occasionally the 2nd ranked man may resort to similar tactics but at the risk of being put down by the number one man. Such statements and tactics delivered by a 3rd or 4th ranking person would be a faux pas of the first magnitude.

IV. Salutations

A brief study was made of the manner in which two people who know each other greet or acknowledge one another upon passing in the company corridors. Approximately 2500 greetings were recorded in three large corporations. The following table contains the findings.

Type of Greeting	Frequency of Use, Per Cent
1. Say Hi or Hello	33
2. Say hello, followed by name of person greeted	22
3. Raise eyebrows	10
4. Nod head	10
5. No response	10
6. Point index finger and "shoot"	5
7. Raise hand like Indian "How" sign	4
8. Military salute	4
9. Stop at shake hands followed by back slapping and considerable conversation	2

An attempt was made to correlate the various types of greeting response with the CR*. Personnel records were pulled for 10% of the greeter sample and CR's were calculated. The following correlations were found between types of greetings and the approximate difference in CR values (ΔCR).

Category	ΔCR
I. Shooters, brow raisers, howers, no responders, nodders, saluters	0-1
II. Hi'ers, name callers	1-3
III. Name callers, back slappers	3-6

From these results, it is clear that certain greeting techniques, such as shooting or howing, are avoided between greeters of high ΔCR's such as between the Executive Vice President and the Custodian. On the other hand, a response such as howing or shooting could be employed by two assembly line workers of equal CR or even the Controller and the Assistant Vice President without any fear of social recrimination.

We were also able to correlate the audible intensity of greetings as a function of the difference in CR (ΔCR) of the

---

* Male-female encounters were found to be anomolous and thus are not included in this data.

two individuals who happen to meet. Data was taken by planting a miniature transmitting device on the backs of the picture badges of a representative sample of employees. These persons were then followed with a receiving device and the response noted. The data represents the average intensity of both speakers' responses although it was noted the person of lower CR was usually more audible. Figure 2 is a plot of the response in dB vs ΔCR.

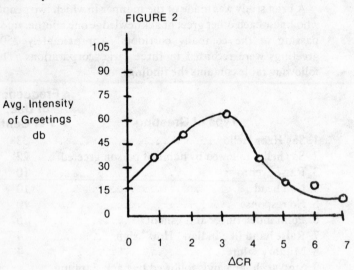

FIGURE 2

In general, the results indicate that the importance and/or intensity of salutations is proportional to the degree of competition that exists between the greeting parties. Competition is low both at low and at high values of ΔCR and peaks in the range of CR = 1-3.

CONCLUSION

These results clearly establish that strong correlatio exist between an individual's corporate rank and his beha ior. It is hoped that these findings can be used to further co porate harmony. The use of certain high CR behavior pa terns by an individual of low CR would, of course, be high unethical.

ACKNOWLEDGEMENTS

This research was made possible by a grant from t Mexican Institute de la Gringos (MIDLG-68946-AF12 The assistance of Horst Mackintose and Ellen Grantges wh conducted the greeting experiments is gratefully ackno ledged. Special thanks are extended to Max Thorbes f participating in the castration experiment (this experime was, unfortunately, unsuccessful and the results are n reported here); it is hoped his new career in The Americ Union of Women Libs is rewarding. Finally, the assistance Henry Tomlinson* who fabricated and planted several of t listening devices is acknowledged.

 * Present address, Alabama State Prison, Katoola, Alaba

BIBLIOGRAPHY

1. Maximilian Grütlich, Deut. Einsetzen für Umheimli Vogel, *39*, 864 (1939).
2. R. Nasini and A. Scala, Anal. Psychologie de Pucelag *14*, 6 (1948).
3. See for example, S. Z. Himalya, "Primate Behavior p. 86, Venuzian Book Co., Spatoona, Louisanna, 1964.
4. Desmond Morris, "The Human Zoo," pp. 42-53, McGra Hill Book Co., New York, 1969.

Department of the Army
Headquarters, 322D Civil Affairs Group
Fort DeRussy, Hawaii
18 December 1972

RCIX-K

SUBJECT: Season's Greetings

TO ALL MEMBERS OF THIS UNIT

Whatever his individual attributes may be, man is that he might have joy everlasting. The lesson of the ages suggests that the achievement of such is assured or limited neither by racial heritage nor by cultural tradition. Upon rummaging through the profoundness of ancestral insight, one is struck by the singleness of thought relative to the achievement of that universally prized goal, whatever the shades of definition. To wit: by shattering the socially, materially and biologically dictated confines of the moment, by transcending niggardly self-serving, by making all men's good each man's rule. Thereby one stands to gain poise in the face of adversity, peace in the midst of turmoil, and a perspective that spans the eternities. Can true joy be less?!

May the reflections and opportunities of the season bring you and yours such joy divine!

Nephi Georgi
Col, CA, USAR, Commanding

SOME SOCIOLOGICAL OBSERVATIONS OF REPATRIATE TECHNICIANS

R. W. PAYNE
Quiriquire, Venezuela

(With apologies to Sir Joseph Porter, K.C.B. and the famous operatic pair Goldberg and Solomon).

When I was a lad I was no fool.
I went to a technological school
I learned a little, but not a lot
And a lowly BS was all I got.

That isn't very much, the doctors say,
But I run a little project of my own today.

- - -

That small project was no accident.
I won't tell how the maneuvering went
But will quote the advice that was given to me
"A chief seldom labors in his own country."

That advice was sound and it paved my way
To the fascinating project that I run today.

- - -

As the Dutch "voortrekked" to the old Transvaal
And the Wehrmacht to Cape Canaveral,
So a scientific Gringo will waste his time
If he doen't seek his fortune in a foreign clime.

In a jungly climate, I earn my pay
On the stimulating project that I run today.

- - -

When a man has trouble with the local tongue
And butchers the grammar, like the very young,
The people smile, but still defer
To the "educated, scientific foreigner."

That "foreign complex" can take effect
For the thinking man who wants his own project.

- - -

Now Bachelors all: no matter what they say
You can have a project of your own someday.
Be careful to be guided by this golden rule:
Get a passport on the day you graduate from school.

And prolong your project with the ultimate retort,
"With a little more data, we could publish a report;"

QUOTES

J. B. Appel
THE RAT: AN IMPORTANT SUBJECT.
J. Exp. Analysis Behavior, 1964, *7*, 355

"In addition to living in a relative short time rats tend to become ill and sometimes interrupt experiments by dying."

* * *

B. Zondek and I. Tamari
EFFECT OF AUDITORY STIMULATION ON REPRODUCTION. IV. EXPERIMENTS ON DEAF RATS.
Proc. Soc. Exp. Biol. & Med., 1964, *116*, 636

". . . The experiments show that auditory stimuli during the copulation period do not cause a decrease in fertility in deafened rats in contrast to normal animals."

* * *

A. D. Cavilli and J. R. Henderson[1, 2]
ESTIMATION OF VENTILLATORY FUNCTION BY BLOWING OUT A MATCH
Amer. Rev. Respir. Dis., 1964, *89*, 680

"[2]This paper represents the personal viewpoints of the authors and should not be construed as a statement of official Air Force policy.
Acknowledgement: Staff Sergeant Sallustro and A/IC M. Penland rendered excellent technical assistance."

(lighting the matches? — Ed.)

* * *

G. Reading, W. C. Rubright, H. Rechtschaffen, and Daniels, R. S.
SLEEP PATTERN OF TOOTH GRINDING: ITS RELATIONSHIP TO DREAMING
Science, 1964, *145*, 725

* * *

Discontinuities in Social Research

SAMUEL E. WALLACE, Ph.D.

This is the only report of a study of a cross-cultural research project studying adolescents who show superior effectiveness and creativity in the academic, extra-curricular, and inter-personal spheres and especially to point up contrasts with the features observed in the adaptive behavior of students inside and outside the continental United States. (The real point, however, will be made clear in a moment).

A sample of 20 high school seniors in Spanish-speaking Puerto Rico, half boys and half girls, was selected for participation in this study. The students were interviewed various times during their senior year in order to determine the factors influencing their superior performance.

All twenty students attended an upper-middle class high school, known for its favoritism in admission practices. Although the high school accepted only those students with intelligence quotients above a certain level, the absence of a certified school psychologist permitted the parents to "shop around" the various psychological testing clinics until their child received the correct score. Therefore, students admitted tended to be those who parents had the necessary funds for "I.Q. score shopping." But the high school, interesting though it may be, is not the principal subject of this paper.

In the Fall of 1960, the author was contacted by the Institute which was carrying out (literally) the research described above. The Executive Director, Owner, President and Board of Directors of this Institute explained that a research staff was being organized, and invited me to participate. In additional conversations, the author learned that the staff was to include a psychologist, a social worker, a sociologist, and an anthropologist.[1] A federal agency was to provide the necessary funds, and work was to begin immediately, or rather, as soon as the funds became available.

After observing the Institute and talking with several members of the staff, the idea struck me that here was an excellent opportunity to study a much neglected field of research—"Discontinuities in Social Research."

During World War II, several eminent scholars had come up with the idea of studying "Continuities in Social Research".[2] They had made a lot of yardage with this idea, producing a series of books and several score of articles.

Every time I run across a reference to these "Continuities," I ask myself, what about *Discontinuities*? There are certainly projects where the investigator has a hopeless design for his research problem. There are certainly projects which adopt the worst methodology for their study area. There are certainly projects where staff changes become so frequent that not one inch[3] of continuity is possible. There are certainly projects whose publications[4] are completely unrelated to the data collected. Why is it that no one writes about these projects?

As I observed the Institute and its Executive Director, I had a hunch[5] that Fate had, at last, given me an opportunity to begin my work on "Discontinuities in Social Research." In the course of two of the most memorable years of my life, I watched a nearly complete changeover in janitorial, service, clerical, administrative, medical, clinical, etc., staffs[6]. The procession was simply fantastic. People would report for work in the morning and clean out their desks in the afternoon. The former senior accountant, bookkeeper, and treasurer, for example, seemed as well-entrenched as the Executive Director. He had worked for the Director for nearly two decades, worked hard, seemed to fulfill all the expectations of any employer, and was a personal friend. You can imagine my joy when I was told one morning that he had been summarily dismissed in the regular course of events one day, and given the remaining portion of the day to clean out his desk and go.

The (former) chief of the social workers enjoyed an excellent reputation in the social work community, devoted all her time and energy to her profession, and discovered

---

[1] An anthropologist was interviewed, but neither he nor the social worker who was supposed to be on the staff was ever seen.

[2] See: R. K. Merton and P. F. Lazarsfeld, *Continuities in Social Research:* Studies in the Scope and Method of the American Soldier, Glencoe, The Free Press, 1950.

[3] I suppose that is at least one way of measuring continuity.

[4] Usually few and quite accidentally produced in "shipsaving" operations. Their most distinguishing characteristic is their almost total lack of any relationship to the data collected. This is not to say, however, that they are always worthless. Rather one would ask, why waste money collecting data?

[5] Unkind colleagues have let it be known that perhaps it would not take a genius to have this hunch at this particular Institute.

[6] Unfortunately the record was not perfect. There were one or two notable exceptions. But the reader must keep in mind the short time period of this study.

her desk occupied by another upon returning from vacation one year.

Those who had been around twenty years seemed to go proportionally as fast as those who had just arrived. Those who worked hard departed at about the same rate as those who did nothing. Those who claimed special connections with the "inside office" cleaned out their desk about as fast as those without connections.

In September of 1960 I talked with the Executive Director, and in April of 1961 the funds finally became available and I officially began work. One week later the Research Director, the Director of the project for which the Institute had just received funds, was fired. I confess I was simply ecstatic.

My joy turned to rapture when I filed away a second Discontinuity the second week of my employment. According to the project design[7], field work for this (necessarily unnamed) study was to and did begin in the Spring of 1959. After the sample had been selected, the research staff (two psychologists) and an odd assortment of M.D.s who were studying psychiatry interviewed the students in the Fall (and maybe even the Spring) of the 1959–60 academic year. Interviewing was then suspended until funds became available, that is, until April of 1961. The students were now completing their freshman year in college. With a rather admirable dash of temerity, this federal agency was sponsoring a study of the transition from high school to college of a sample of twenty students who were completing their first year of college at the same moment the funds were approved. Talk about Discontinuities!

Naturally, I began to more closely observe the man who had helped make all this possible—the Executive Director. Here was what Max Weber would have called a Perfect Ideal Type for the study of Discontinuities[8]. The Executive Director never; (1) wrote or read a research publication, (2) interviewed an interviewer or a research subject, (3) had the least idea what data was, how it was collected, what had been collected, or what was to be collected, (4) involved himself in administration, and (5) maintained a professional relationship.

During the summer a Social Psychologist put in an appearance. He had a Ph.D. from Harvard, had published several articles, and came highly recommended. This new Research Director, Project Director, and Co-principal investigator not only knew research and was determined to get at it, but was given *carte blanche* to do anything he wanted.

The new Research Director was first told to write up the data on another major project, which had already had its own Discontinuities. The other psychologist was asked to "secure some funds" to do major study. One research assistant and a part-time sociologist were left to carry on the study of the transition from high school to college.

The next nine months were fairly dull, that is, within the research staff. However, in the late spring the Research Director announced his resignation. Actually, he had resigned himself to the situation several months earlier. It was announced that the other psychologist was to be co-principal investigator and principal writer along with the announcement that he was leaving Puerto Rico! In February the fourth Discontinuity materialized when the nonresident psychologist's salary was stopped without notice.

The two secretaries in the Research Department and the only research assistant had departed sometime earlier, providing interesting, though minor Discontinuities. The research assistant was the only staff member (ever) who spoke fluent Spanish. Consequently, when others translated certain material, Spanish words like *molestar* (to bother, annoy, make or take trouble) were translated as *to molest*. This led a later investigator to wonder about the teacher who was said to molest his female students.

In the summer of 1962, the sociologist was told the project had "shifted away" from his specialization. When this did not produce the expected resignation, his salary was simply stopped. I now had a perfect case of Complete and Continuous Discontinuity. There was now no one who knew anything about the original design. No one who knew what changes in methodology had been made. No one who knew the blind alleys that had been explored. No one who knew how the subjects had been selected. No one who knew how the subjects had been interviewed. No one who knew who interviewed the students. No one who could separate fact, fiction, and interpretation. No one who would even recognize one of the research subjects. Every possible type of Discontinuity had taken place!

Rarely does an investigator have such good fortune as I have had. With this record there is really no point in continuing. I must also confess research on Discontinuities is a bit fatiguing. Now I've taken up stunt flying, sky-diving, and shark hunting; they're so wonderfully relaxing, by comparison, you know.[9]

---

[7] A curious document which I finally discovered behind a file cabinet in a deserted office. For some strange reason it had a habit of returning to such places and was located when strongly requested only with the greatest difficulty.

[8] Max Weber, From Max Weber: *Essays in Sociology*, trans. by H. Gerth and C. W. Mills, New York: Oxford University Press, 1946.

[9] The author must add that all references to persons and places have purposely been removed and an attempt made to conceal the identity of the true location of study. I must also add that any resemblance to persons living or dead is purely coincidental, and, of course, not intended.

VETERANS ADMINISTRATION HOSPITAL

Sam Jackson Park
Portland, Oregon

EMPLOYEE RECOGNITION COMMITTEE

Minutes for the March 12, 1969, meeting which convened at 2:00 p.m.

Present: Assistant Hospital Director; Chief, Dietetic Service; Chief, Medical Administration Division; Chief, Social Work Service; Nursing Supervisor; Chief, Buildings and Grounds; Budget Analyst; Section Chief, Processing and Records; Acting Chief, Personnel Division and Personnel Specialist

COMMENDATION MEMORANDA

Dietetic Service: Albert R. Kenney, Sr. commended for reporting to Hospital due to fire alarm on 11-11-68 at 3:30 a.m.

Bldg. Mgmt. Div.: Ronald W. Agee commended for work performance as related to additional work assignments and frequent changes of tours.

Mrs. Lee L. De Berry commended for work performance on ward subjected to constant construction and completion of additional duties.

SUGGESTIONS PROCESSED UNDER DELEGATED AUTHORITY:

S-775: Installation of hinged grills in main surgery area; disapproved.
S-876: Specimen identification stickers; disapproved.
S-892: Installation of acoustical tile in dishwashing area; disapproved.
S-905: Drainage ditch near pedestrian walkway: approved with modification; certificate.
S-936: Ward designation stickers on arm bands; disapproved.
S-952: Extra special foot care; disapproved.
S-955: Automatic rinser tank; approved with $25 award.
S-959: Installation of sign giving instructions to visitors for use of phone for information; approved with certificate.
S-962: Improved lighting to metered parking lot; disapproved.
S-972: Safety hazard—automatic doors; approved with certificate.
S-976: Combining prostate study patients with tumor registry; disapproval.
S-980: Elimination of parentheses; disapproval by C.O.
S-981: Pilot program for use of radiology technologists; disapproved by C.O.
S-982: Standard evaluation sheet; approval with $15 award ($7.50 each)
S-985: Improved lighting in halls, Bldg. 25; disapproved.
S-996: Eliminating hazardous conditions in crosswalks; approved with $15.
S-998: Increase availability to dressing room #335, Bldg. 25; disapproved.
S-1004: Microphone for checker; disapproved.
S-1005: Modification of suggestion to re-use patient's toilet tissue; approved with $15 award and certificate.
S-1009: Form "Request for Volunteer Service"; approved with certificate
S-1011: Drains for cart holding green trays used on tray line; disapproved.

Publishers: We are moving heaven and earth to find out how S-1005 was implemented.

Project Management

B. SPARKS

From time to time, every professional journal publishes articles to aid their members in a particular field. Much has been written on Project Management; however, certain aspects are often overlooked. These are the practical, everyday, down-to-earth aids that make a project move. In an attempt to fill this void, the following three aids are offered to assist in obtaining irreproducible results.

I. PROJECT VOCABULARY. Knowing the terminology is the first key step in project management.

A PROJECT — an assignment that can't be completed by either walking across the hall or by making one telephone call.

TO ACTIVATE A PROJECT — to make additional copies and adding to the distribution list.

TO IMPLEMENT A PROJECT — acquiring all the physical space available and assigning responsibilities to anyone in sight.

CONSULTANT (or Expert) — anyone more than 50 miles from home.

COORDINATOR — the guy who really doesn't know what's going on.

CHANNELS — the people you wouldn't see or write if your life depended on it.

EXPEDITE — to contribute to the present chaos.

CONFERENCE (or Meeting) — that activity that brings all work and progress to a standstill.

NEGOTIATE — shouting demands interspersed with gnashing of teeth.

RE-ORIENTATION — starting to work again.

MAKING A SURVEY — most of the personnel are on a boon-doggle.

UNDER CONSIDERATION — never heard of it.

UNDER ACTIVE CONSIDERATION — the memo is lost and is being looked for.

WILL BE LOOKED INTO — maybe the whole thing will be forgotten by the next meeting.

RELIABLE SOURCE — the guy you just met.

INFORMED SOURCE — the guy who introduced you.

UNIMPEACHABLE SOURCE — the guy who started the rumor.

READ AND INITIAL — to spread the responsibility in case everything goes wrong.

THE OTHER VIEWPOINT — let them get it off their chest so they'll shut up.

CLARIFICATION — muddy the water so they can't see bottom.

SEE ME LATER ON THIS — I am as confused as you are.

WILL ADVISE YOU IN DUE COURSE — when we figure it out, we'll tell you.

IN PROCESS — trying to get through the paper mill.

MODIFICATION — a complete redesign.

ORIENTATION — confusing a new member of the project.

REORGANIZATION — assigning someone new to save the project.

II. TEN COMMANDMENTS FOR THE PROJECT MANAGER. These are the rules by which the Project Manager must run his project.

1. Strive to look tremendously important.
2. Attempt to be seen with important people.
3. Speak with authority, however, only expound on the obvious and proven facts.
4. Don't engage in arguments, but if cornered, ask an irrelevant question and lean back with satisfied grin while your opponent tries to figure out what's going on — then quickly change the subject.
5. Listen intently while others are arguing the problem. Pounce on a trite statement and bury them with it.
6. If a subordinate asks you a pertinent question look at him as if he had lost his senses. When he looks down, paraphrase the question back at him.
7. Obtain a brilliant assistant, but keep him out of sight and out of the limelight.

*Consulting Engineer

8. Walk at a fast pace when out of the office — this keeps questions from subordinates and superiors at a minimum.

9. Always keep the office door closed — this puts visitors on the defensive and also makes it look as if you are always in an important conference.

10. Give all orders verbally. Never write anything down that might go into a "Pearl Harbor File".

III. PROJECT PROGRESS REPORT. Below is a standard report that can be used by just about any project that has no progress to report.

The report period which ended .... has seen considerable progress in directing a large portion of the effort in meeting the initial objectives established.[1] Additional background information and relative data have been acquired to assist in problem resolution.[2] As a result, some realignment has been made to enhance the position of the project.[3]

One deterent that has caused considerable difficulty in this reporting period was the selection of optimum methods and techniques; however, this problem is being vigorously attacked and we expect the development phase will proceed at a satisfactory rate.[4] In order to prevent unnecessary duplication of previous efforts in the same field, it was deemed necessary to establish a special team to conduct a survey of facilities engaged in similar activities.[5]

The Project Control Group held its regular meeting and considered the broad functional aspects of all levels of coordination and cross fertilization of relevant ideas associated with the general specifications of the evolving system.[6] At the present rate of progress, it is believed that most project milestones will be met.[7] During the next quarter a major breakthrough is anticipated and will be fully covered in progress report No. ....[8]

---

[1] The project has long ago forgotten what the objective was.
[2] The one page of data from the last quarter was found in the incinerator.
[3] We now have a new lead-man for the data group.
[4] We finally found some information that is relevant to the project.
[5] We had a great time in Los Angeles, Denver, and New York.
[6] Fertilizer.
[7] Would you be happy with one or two?
[8] We think we have stumbled onto someone who knows what's going on.

Notice in an Office* about Absenteeism

Surgery: We wish to discourage any thoughts that you may need an operation as we believe that as long as you are an employee here, you will need all of whatever you have and you should not consider having anything removed. We hired you as you are and to have anything less would certainly make you less than we bargained for.

Death: (Your own) This will be accepted as an excuse, but we would like to have two weeks notice.

*ELM City Foundation, 175 St. John Street, Fredericton, N.B.

Sent by:
N.V.B. Manyam, M.D.

Irreproducible

data

impel

one

to

PUBLISH
OR PERISH

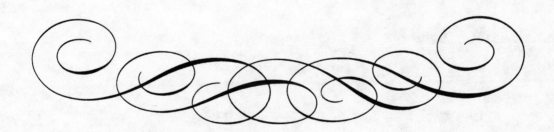

A BRIEF HISTORY OF SCHOLARLY PUBLISHING

DONALD D. JACKSON
University of Illinois Press

50,000 B.C. Stone Age publisher demands that all manuscripts be double-spaced, and hacked on one side of stone only.

1455 Johannes Gutenberg applies to Ford Foundation for money to buy umlauts. First subsidized publishing venture.

1483 Invention of *ibid*.

1507 First use of circumlocution.

1859 "Without whom" is used for the first time in list of acknowledgments.

1888 Martydom of Ralph Thwaites, an author who deletes 503 commas from his galleys and is stoned by a copy editor.

1897 Famous old university press in England announces that its Urdu dictionary has been in print 400 years. Entire edition, accidentally misplaced by a shipping clerk in 1497, is found during quadri-centennial inventory.

1901 First free desk copy distributed (Known as Black Thursday).

1916 First successful divorce case based on failure of author to thank his wife, in the foreword of his book, for typing the manuscript.

1927 Minor official in publishing house, who suggests that his firm issue books in gay paper covers and market them through drug houses, is passed over for promotion.

1928 Early use of ambiguous rejection letter, beginning, "While we have many good things to say about your manuscript, we feel that we are not now in position . . ."

1934 Bookstore sends for two copies of Gleep's *Origin of Leases* from University Press and instead receives three copies of Darwin's *Storage of Fleeces* plus half of stale peanut butter sandwich from stockroom clerk's lunch. Beginning of a famous Brentano Rebellion, resulting in temporary inprovement in shipping practices.

1952 Scholarly writing begins to pay. Professor Harley Biddle's publishing' contract for royalty on his book after 1,000 copies have been sold to defray printing costs. Total sales: 1,009 copies.

1961 Important case of *Dulany vs McDaniel,* in which judge Kelley rules to call a doctoral dissertation a nonbook is libelous per se.

1962 Copy editors' anthem "Revise or Delete" is first sung at national convention. Quarrel over hyphen in second stanza delays official acceptance.

The Dynastatic Review
Dept. of Applied Macromicrology
College of Dynastatics
Metropolitan U., Metropolis,
Metrostate

Nov. 2, 1961

Dr. Albert Bush
Dept. of Basic Micromacrology
Land Grant U., College Center
Provincia

Dear Al:

There is no need to tell you how pleased I was to have the chance to sit down with you for a few minutes during the convention last month. I am terrifically impressed by your developing research program. As I said then, I'd be most interested in an article for the *Review*.

I'm sure you realize that the *Review's* current policy is to emphasize the practical implications of pure research. Keep it solid but avoid technical terms. We prefer brief factual incidents in support of generalizations rather than details on methodology. One table of technical illustration is acceptable. Your bibliography should be brief rather than comprehensive. Please avoid footnotes.

May I plan on having something from you by the first of the year?

With warmest personal regards to you and Susan,

Herbert U. Wheel
Editor

THE DYNASTATIC REVIEW

College of Dynastatics
Metropolitan U.
Metropolis, Metrostate 999999

June 10, 1962

Your manuscript

Current Research Developments in ·Provincial Macrostatics

has been received and will be reviewed by the Editorial Board. You will be notified as soon as a decision has been reached.

THE EDITOR

The Dynastatic Review
Dept. of Applied Macromicrology
College of Dynastatics
Metropolitan U., Metropolis,
Metrostate

July 5, 1965

Albert L. Bush
Professor of Basic Micromacrology
Land Grant U., College Center
Provincia

Dear Al:

I'm ashamed to say that I've been so busy setting up our new institute that my correspondence has gotten a bit behind. It was great to have your note of April 12 and I do appreciate your patience. The manuscript reads very well and we would like very much to publish it in a forthcoming issue. However, we prefer to hold off until we have sufficient other material to include in a full issue of the *Review* devoted to a thorough and balanced treatment of minimacrostatics across the country. You may, quite understandably, prefer to submit the manuscript elsewhere for earlier publication but I do hope you decide to bear with us a little longer.

I was terribly disappointed not to see you at the convention. You missed a terrific party with the old gang but I can well imagine that the installation of your new microsplitter has kept you close to the laboratory.

Affectionately,

Herbert U. Wheel
Editor

The Dynastatic Review
Dept. of Applied Macromicrology
College of Dynastatics
Metropolitan U., Metropolis,
Metrostate 999999

Sept. 7, 1970

Dr. Albert Bush
Assistant Professor of
  Basic Micromacrology
Land Grant U., College Center
Provincia

Dear Dr. Bush:

I have very much enjoyed reading your essay, "Current Research Developments in Provincial Macrostatics," and I am genuinely appreciative of your thinking of the *Review*. Unfortunately, this piece does not quite meet our present publication needs so am returning your MS together with my thanks and best wishes. Do keep us in mind for the future, won't you?

Sincerely,

Herber U. Wheel
Editor

The Dynastatic Review
Dept of Rhythmics
College of Dynastatics
Metropolitan U., Metropolis,
Metrostate

Sept. 13, 1970

Albert L. Bush
Professor of Basic Micromacrology
Land Grant U., College Center
Provincia

Dear Professor Bush:

I am presently taking over the editorship of the *Review* from Professor Wheel who is about to go to the University of Politania. In the inevitable confusion resulting from the changeover, an error was made in the letter accompanying the manuscript just returned to you.

Through an oversight, you received the *pro forma* note ordinarily sent along with the unsolicited manuscripts that have to be rejected. We have since realized that yours was a solicited paper and that its return demands rather more explanation than you received.

As you can understand, we have decided to begin *de novo,* with the responsibility for the coming year's solicitation given to me. In the fairly sketchy plan I have at the moment, I do not find a place for your fine essay. I am, however, keeping your name and special interest on file; and I hope that, if I write with a new request, you will not hold this wielding of new brooms against me.

Sincerely,

Grace Classica
Editor

How to be a Published Mathematician Without Trying Harder than Necessary

DAVID LOUIS SCHWARTZ

Abstract

After a crisp, cogent analysis of the problem, the author brilliantly cuts to the heart of the question with incisive simplifications. These soon reduce the original complex edifice to a mouldering pile of dusty rubble.

****

The problem is that mathematicians <u>know</u> all kinds of weird things, but they publish comparatively little. It's not the <u>numbers</u> that bother them; it's the <u>words</u>. If the fill-in words necessary for a mathematical paper were provided, any mathematician could fill in the spaces with numbers, and he'd be safely through the publish-or-perish barrier. It is with this humanitarian view that I have undertaken to provide a form sheet, sort of a work-book approach. The arrangement given is based on already published material, so the plan has the advantage of having been shown to be workable at least once before.

There are numerous subtitles. One must realize that editors of mathematics magazines tend to understand either (1.) too much, or (2.) too little about the things they read. Misunderstandings arise. One way around this obstacle is don't submit things to mathematics publications. Try Ladies Home Journal, or Vogue, or Hot Rod; this is important. The possibility of "toning up" an issue with something serious can frequently appeal to a non-mathematical editor, whereas the same possibility probably never occurs to a math magazine editor. For that reason, we insert not merely connective words and phrases, but <u>whole paragraphs.</u>

Since everything basically contains part of everything else, it is always possible to relate a random paragraph to anything occurring before and after. Once this fact is taken to heart, a career as a published mathematician becomes not only possible, but inevitable.

The blanks are to be filled in with mathematical symbols. The more variety, the better. Throw in everything. Be neat. Editors love neatness.

****

From the statement
and
we obtain
in which
with
together with
we also have
and therefore, effectively,
the desired formula emerges as

Accordingly, a non-Hermitian canonical variable transformation function can serve as a generator for the transformation function referring to unperturbed oscillator energy states.

There follows
Alternatively, if we choose
there appears
Thus
and
where the latter version is obtained from

****

The next installment will discuss advanced presentation procedures, how (and why) to write an abstract, and the role of mathematics in our Judeo-Christian heritage.

EATING BY WRITING

OR

Pot-Boilers in Science*

ROBERT SOMMER

The pot-boiler has a long and respected history among writers, composers, and playwrights. Most men of letters have consciously written second-rate stories for second-rate magazines simply to stay alive. Often the alternative was book reviews, translations, or ghost writing. Sometimes this was done under a *nom de plume* or the influence of alcohol. Most reviewers will not begrudge a young writer the opportunity to earn a few dollars for consciously doing work of an inferior quality.

However some people cannot imagine any place for the pot-boiler in science. The stereotype exists that science is above the lure of pecuniary motivation. The belief persists that the scientist is so well-paid and secure that he has no need for the dubious rewards gained by producing second-rate articles. Both of these assumptions are tenuous.

Has the scientist any need to write pot-boilers? The answer is an emphatic "YES." In many universities, as is well known, promotions depend on the number of papers written. Since the people who pass on promotions are the academic deans or university presidents who are usually trained outside the scientist's field, they cannot assay the quality of an article. They must leave assays of quality to the editors of professional journals. Furthermore the deans are unable even to judge the quality of the various journals. Sometimes their judgments are based on criteria that invariably assign the greater weight to the poorer journal. Because of local pride or regionalism, the dean may be more influenced by an article in a second or third-rate local periodical than in a first-rate international journal. He may resent the professor at Isthisa State University who never bothers sending an article to Is-

thisa Journal of Chemistry or presents a paper at the anual Isthisa convention. Since academic deans are unable to judge the merit and potential contribution of most papers, they are compelled to use systems based on a combination of counting and weighing[1]. It may be decided that a heavy book is worth ten light articles, or that three published experiments are better than one review article. However a dean will usually conclude that eight articles are better than two articles, and three reviews are better than one. People are impressed by anyone who has done anything *several times*. One success may be an accident, but several "successes" indicate a genuine talent, a person who can be relied upon.

The rewards system in science may be less direct than in writing, but there is still a very real connection between the number of articles published and the size of one's paycheck. The scientist who waits several years for supporting data before publishing his results is rapidly becoming a relic of the past. As in exploring, fame and fortune come to those who are the first to land. Later arrivals may become known as homesteaders or substantial citizens, but they will never have statues erected in their honor. The pressure to be the first to publish is endemic through the scientific community; it is not limited to missile laboratories. The disinterested, relaxed and scholarly scientist is fast becoming extinct. To protect his job and guarantee his next promotion, he is compelled

---

* Reprinted with permission of the editor and author from THE MALPIGHII (Montreal).
[1] Young F. N. and Crowell, S. The application of gamesmanship to science, J. Irrepr. Res. 1957, 4, 12.

to read and heed the circulars on research grants sent out by the NSF, NRC and other foundations. Needless to say, officials who pass on research grants and awards are not unaware of the number of publications a man has to his credit. "Him that has, gits" is a good rule of thumb for understanding the logic of grants and awards.

But doesn't the ethical code of the scientist militate against the writing of second-rate articles? Certainly not, for as any scientist knows, there are second-rate scientific journals, and as long as these exist there will be a ready market for second-rate articles. As far as I know, all scientific fields have journals of varying degrees of merit. In some cases, the national journal is considered the best, while the regional and local journals contain papers that could not reach the standard of the national journal. This is also true of local and regional meetings of professional societies. Usually the papers are presented by graduate students or recent graduates, and are of dubious merit. The usual attendance at the scientific sessions of such meetings is far below the number of people registered for the meeting. Woe betide anyone scheduled to present the first paper of the morning, or the last before dinner.

Another occasion when the scientist consciously produces a second-rate study is when he is instructed to do a piece of research by his superior and he lacks interest in the topic or sufficient facilities. For example, if a biochemist is instructed to do a study of a thiamine derivative and he lacks the necessary equipment, he may know beforehand that he cannot hope to turn out anything resembling a first-rate study.

Although science has a ready market for second-rate work, it lacks the demand. No editors are clamoring for mediocre articles. Perhaps the chief reason for this is that articles pour in regardless. Authors have such a need to turn out articles that editors have no difficulty in securing material*. In some fields, not only are the authors unpaid, they must even pay to have articles published. There are several journals in psychology that exist solely on articles that are paid for by their authors. (Many articles in these "pay as you go" journals are supported by federal and foundation grants. In such cases the researcher is able to use part of his grant to finance the publication of an article which was not of sufficient quality to be accepted by a better, non-paying journal.)

I have often seen the look of amazement on the faces of friends and relatives when they learn that I am not paid for articles. They consider my motives are compounded of either egoism or altruism. I dread to think of their reaction if they learned that I write some articles to advance my job or facilitate transfer to another position.

In one laboratory I was in the middle of a personal feud between two superiors. One of them continually urged me to "produce articles" in order to embarrass the other person, who had been employed for three years and had written nothing.

Needless to say, my second superior looked upon each of my papers as a personal threat, and was not my most enthusiastic fan. I soon learned that research was a powerful weapon in inter-departmental warfare. If one department was able to publish a score of articles and reviews and receive mention in a national magazine or alumni publication, it was soon able to dominate the entire organization. They would soon receive preference in allocation of office space, secretaries, and graduate students.

In this highly specialized culture, it is extremely difficult for a lay administrator or specialist in another discipline to judge the merits of a scientific paper, especially if it is neatly packaged in technical jargon. The chances of a scientific pot-boiler being mistaken for an article of merit are correspondingly greater than would be the case with a poem, symphony, or novel. The fine arts have a cadre of reviewers and judges who are hired to assess the merits of a symphony or painting. Most often the public becomes acquainted with a play or book only through reviews. No such group of middlemen exists in science. Public acclaim very often comes to the scientist with a flare for publicity or whose work borders on a controversial area.

So then, let us drink a toast to the pot-boilers. Writers need them, scientists need them. But does anyone read them?

****
****

---

* This is also true for the *J. Irrepr. Results* (Editors).

A LETTER

DALHOUSIE UNIVERSITY
Halifax, N. S.

Faculty of Medicine
Department of Paediatrics

February 26, 1970

Dr. Lyle A. David
Department of Veterinary & Parasitology &
Public Health
Oklahoma State University
Stillwater, Oklahoma 74074
U.S.A.

Dear Lyle:

Thank you for your letter of February 18, and I apologize for the long delay in getting you some information on our manuscript, however there were a few minor problems which I wanted to get cleared up before I wrote again.

Initially I had a little bit of a problem getting the manuscript from the Post Office and Customs Officials when it arrived. However, as they explained, it was all a mistake which could have happened to anyone. Do you remember that little problem you had about possibly being held up at the Border when you left B.C. a few years ago? Well apparently the usual circulars were forwarded to Post Office and Custom and Immigration Departments and when the whole problem was cleared up naturally they did not bother to cancel any of the usual information that authorities circulate to Post Offices. At least if they did they have not found out about it in the Halifax Post Office. It seems that Customs Officials routinely check all communications from individuals on their Border crossing check list. When your manuscript (which did not seem to make any sense to them) arrived they were sure it was some sort of coded message that you were trying to get across the border. It seems that their decoding process involves cutting the manuscript into single worded bits and in some case even splitting compound words. They eventually called me in and I was able to explain the whole thing and regain possession of the manuscript. Unfortunately it arrived in the form of a couple of large envelopes full of typed words in single pieces. However, I must admit they were most careful and did not misplace one single word.

Of course this meant a bit of time for the secretary and I to piece together the words but I think we managed to get most of them into the proper order.

Since this meant a bit of time I thought maybe I could have the people in photography take a look at our photographs. They have a real hot-shot in photography working in the medical illustration department down here and he is doing a marvelous job at constructing his own computerized photograph printing processes. He felt that if he had all possible information in (i.e. photographs, negatives, color prints etc. in other words all the photographic evidence we have in this particular bit of work) he was quite sure that he could improve the quality of our prints. He really is an absolute genius when it comes to both photography and computers and had a system just about perfect. However, there was a small problem concerning a power supply source for one of the connections between the computer and the printer-enlarger equipment, and he had very neatly overcome this problem by using a battery. Unfortunately the battery was one of the little imperfections in his system and some of the acid leaked out overnight and destroyed most all the material on the bench including all of our data (i.e. prints and negatives).

He was most apologitic about the whole thing and really was sorry that he had destroyed all of our material, however he assures me that this little accident enabled him to pin-point all the problems and go on and perfect his system.

These things will happen and although it was a bit of a problem and, although the manuscript seemed a bit incomplete without photographic evidence I managed to make the necessary changes deleting references to figures and got the manuscript back together again.

I then sent it on to Dr. Miller who was really quite pleased with the manuscript as a whole. However, he felt our method of gluing the words on pages was a little bit unprofessional and decided to have the whole thing typed up properly before he sent it on to the editors. Things were a bit slow at that end because he was having secretarial problems at the time and was sharing a secretary with Dr. Vince. It appears that the poor girl was terrible overworked and in trying to do too many things at one time some of the manuscript pages got mixed up with some of Dr. Vince's reports.

283

As Dr. Miller knew from experience Dr. Vince never gets around to looking over his reports for at least a month and he probably quite rightly felt that any further delay would be just too much. Since the missing pages primarily involved descriptions of the photographs which has already been left out, he felt that he could put the manuscript together without these details and finally got what he felt was a very good, although somewhat reduced in length, manuscript off to the editor.

Now that I have brought you up to date I am pleased to advise you that none of the above, of course, happened but I wanted you to get the whole thing in its proper prospective before I told you the following.

Twenty-four hours after receiving your letter of inquiry I received the manuscript back from the editors informing me that they are not interested in publishing the manuscript.

I will be writing again in a day or two—mostly because I didn't want to clutter this letter with details. Chow ! ! !

Yours sincerely,
Margaret J. Corey, Ph.D.
Assistant Professor

MJC/mb

VIDE·INFRA

DR. TIM HEALEY, F.F.R., M.I.Nuc.E.
Yorkshire

As a keen[1] student[2] of footnotes,[4] I have long[14]

[1] Enthusiastic, not necessarily sharp.[13]

[2] When the late Dr. John Wilkie[18] stood up and said "As a mere student in these matters . . ." the listeners knew that they were about to hear some words of wisdom from a very experienced expert.[16,24] Modesty[17a] forbids me to draw a parallel.

[3] Blaise[17b] Pascal used the same trick with his phrase "It is easy to show that . . .". Experienced mathematicians soon recognised that these words warned them that the next step would take them three days of complex calculations to understand.

[4] I have been fascinated by footnotes ever since I obtained several editions of a book[5] which has some of the best footnotes[6] I have ever encountered.[7]

[5] Samson Wright's "Applied Physiology".[8]

[6] E.g. text. "Never occurs." Footnote: "What never? Well, hardly ever".

[7] A book called "Useless Facts in History" has a good pair[9] also.

[8] The footnotes disappeared after the ninth edition, when Samson Wright died. His major work has been continued,[10] but the footnotes that gave it individuality are no longer given: a grave mistake.

[9] There are only two in the book.[11]

[10] Tenth edition by C. A. Keele and E. Neil. O.U.P. London 1961.

[11] The first says "Do you like footnotes?" The second says "Aha![12] Caught you again"

[12] Note the similar style to Lucy.[15]

[13] Though I do not deny it.

[14] There is no room for the rest of this article, as my allotted space is entirely taken up with footnotes. However, I was merely going to state that it has been my ambition to write an article wholly composed of footnotes.[20] My resolution weakened and I included a first line.

[15] In the Peanuts strip cartoon by Schultz[24] in the Daily Sketch.[19]

[16] He was never wrong.[6]

[17] This juxtaposition no doubt reflects my admiration for the work of Mr. Peter O'Donnell.

[18] Of Sheffield.

[19] Now defunct. The Sketch and the strip have gone to the Mail.

[20] Footnotes should not be confused with references. Thus, 10 is a footnote, not a reference. References have a special charm of their own. I cherish a reprint of an article, describing one case, with seven alledged co-authors and 73 references. Famous physics papers include those by Bhang and Gunn; Alfa, Bethe and Gamow; Sowiski and Soda, etc. In my capacity of Science Editor for an international journal, I get not a few "crank" papers for assessment. I have learned to recognise these at a glance by the facts that a) the references always come first, and b) the list includes (always at number 5 or 6, for some unknown reason) "5: "Some inane observations on some perfectly well worked out phenomena" by N.A.D.[21] Six copies, privately circulated, six years ago."[22]

[21] The author of the paper being considered. They always use only initials here.

[22] You will observe that not all footnotes are brief. A recent article[23] I wrote was originally subtitled "A Footnote to History". It occupied two sides of news-sheet with 3000 words. The subeditorial pencil removed the subtitle, but a comment on the article in the People restored my faith in the subeditorial class. This genius[24] dreamed up the heading "Queen of Drag".

[23] "Was the Virgin Queen a Man?" Pulse. September 1971

[24] Credit where credit is due.

A Psychological Study
of Journal Editors

S. A. RUDIN
F.S.B.I.R.

The clinical psychologist Anne Roe studied the manner in which a scientist is seduced by his field of study, and she reported her findings in her book, *The Making of a Scientist* (Roe, 1955). She obtained interviews and test results from the 20 most eminent physical scientists, the 20 most eminent biological scientists, and the 20 most eminent social scientists in the USA. She concluded that the biological scientists tended to be preoccupied with death, that the physical scientists had difficulty locating themselves in the physical world, and that the social scientists disliked and could not get along with people.

This study extends her methods to the study of editors of scientific journals. The editors chosen for study were in charge of all major scientific journals in the USA, making a total of 318,991 subjects. Each subject was studied exhaustively by a combination of depth interview, case history, and numerous psychological tests of intelligence, aptitude, interests and personality.

RESULTS

First impression and general appearance. Subjects ranged from tall* to short, fat to thin, and warped to degenerate in general appearance. Despite this heterogeneity, each was marked by certain tell-tale characteristics: the eyes were narrowed; the mouth was pursed into a snarl; and the writing hand was cramped and taut from stamping REJECTED thousands of times. Upon first perceiving the experimenter, each subject exclaimed, "NO!" before noticing that no manuscript was being tendered.

Childhood background. That childhood experiences strongly influence the developing personality is well known. Again, great diversity of backgrounds was noted: they came from every conceivable environment, from palatial mansions in Hollywood to wretched hovels on some university campuses, but all had in common a peculiar set of family relationships. In every case, the father turned out to have been an alcoholic, drug addict, professional . . .**, or the editor of a scientific journal. The mother was found to spend but little time with her children, devoting herself to such pursuits as managing a house . . .**, selling drugs to adolescents, smuggling diamonds past customs officials, or editing a scientific journal. But of greatest interest for the purposes of this study was the discovery that in every case, the child had been beaten often and severely *with a book*. Naturally, such traumatic stimulation eventually led to a deep-seated hatred of anything associated with reading, writing, learning, knowledge, and scholarship. Some showed this tendency as early as the second year by tearing pages out of the Encyclopaedia Britannica, setting them afire in the middle of the living room floor, and executing an exultant war dance around them in the fashion of certain American Indian tribes.

Intelligence and aptitudes. These were measured by a variety of instruments including the Wechsler Adult Intelligence Scale (WAIS), the Draw-A-Person Test and various special aptitude tests. Considerable difficulty was encountered since none of the subjects could read. The use of oral and non-verbal tests, however, finally yielded usable data. It was found that the subjects were uniformly below IQ 71. This highest IQ was attained by the editor of a widely-read psychology journal who was himself the author of one of the intelligence tests used. The pattern of abilities measured by the specialized aptitude tests showed the subjects to be well below the standardization group (which was made up of college sophomores, white rats, and some persons from mental hospitals) on verbal reasoning, numerical reasoning, perceptual speed, spatial reasoning, verbal recall, clerical ability, map-reading ability, needle-threading ability, and the capacity to pronounce words of more than three syllables. Indeed, the only tests on which the subjects performed well were one requiring the use of a spade to pick up and transfer material from one pile to another and the ability to ignore noxious odors.

Interest tests. On the Strong Vocational Interest Blank and the Kuder Preference Record-Vocational, subjects tended to score lower than average on activities

285

and occupations associated with originality, critical thinking, creativity, scientific research, and literary production and appreciation. They scored relatively high, however, on scales measuring interest in mild manual labor and evading work altogether.

Personality tests. All subjects were found to register insane on Rohrschach Ink-Blot Test, Thematic Apperception Test, Minnesota Multi-Phasic Personality Inventory and the House-Three-Person Test. Exceptions were two subjects, both neurotic, ulcer-ridden, and compulsive shoe-lace cleptomaniacs. All subjects perceived themselves as God, except for one who claimed that he had created God. Another signed his name omitting all vowels.*** Yet another claimed that the ink-blots were actually reprints of old copies of his Journal, and sued the experimenter for plagiarism.

CONCLUSIONS

The reasons for the success of these subjects in editing journals is clear. First, by preventing new ideas from appearing in print, they make it easier to keep up with the literature. Second, by requiring the experimenter to repeat his study dozens of times and re-write his paper hundreds of times, they enforce the consumption of materials and labor, thus stimulating the national economy. Third, if *they* can understand a paper, *anyone* can.

*e.g. J. Bacteriol. (the rest of description does not apply).
**censored
***He was from Israel.

QUOTES

Brit. Med. J., March 16, p. 743 (1963).

"On March 5, 1963 pickets appeared in front of the White House and called on Mrs. Jackie Kennedy to clothe her horse. They belonged to the Society for Indecency to Naked Animals (SINA). The first preposition should have been "against," but I gather they can't change it because of legal registration of the original society. According to the Guardian, SINA has designed bikinis for stallions, petticoats for cows, and knickers for bulldogs. Just think of the dogs in Hyde Park tearing the pants off each other."

* * *

V. Spužić, I. Spužić, S. Djordjević, L. Ivković, Jasmina Ljalević and Milica Živković.
LE RÔLE DU PAPRIKA DANS L'APPARITION DES MANIFESTATIONS ALLERGIQUES
Acta Allergologica, *17*:516 (1962)

* * *

Jerusalem Post, March 21, 1963 (Quotation from Lord Shackelton's Speech in the House of Lords).

"Cannibals in Polynesia no longer allow their tribes to eat Americans because their fat is contaminated with chlorinated hydrocarbon. Recent figures published show that we [English] have two parts per million DDT in our bodies, whereas the figure for Americans is about 11 p.p.m."

* * *

THE CROWDED CROSSROADS

J. BRUCE MARTIN, Ph.D

REFERENCES

Asch, A. B. "Engineering Education at the Crossroads," *Jour. Eng. Ed., 57* No. 8, (April 1967), 576–578.

Bose, Subhas O. *Crossroads: Collected Works,* Asia (1938–40).

Brode, Douglas. *Crossroads to the Cinema.* Holbrook (1975).

Collins, James. *Crossroads in Philosophy: Existentialism, Naturalism, Theistic Realism.* Regnery (1969).

Cox, Lionel A. "Why Is Industrial R&D at the Crossroads?" *Pulp Pap. Mag. Can. 73* No. 7 (July 1972), 93–96.

Ewing, David W. "Corporate Planning at a Crossroads," HBR *45* No, 4 (July–Aug. 1967), 77–86.

Fehrenbach, T. R. *Crossroads in Korea.* Macmillan (1968).

Forcey, Charles. *Crossroads of Liberalism: Croly, Weyl, Lippmann, & the Progressive Era, 1900–1925.* Oxford U. Pr. (1967).

Goland, Martin. "Professionalism in Engineering: At the Crossroads," *Mech. Eng.,* (March 1974), 18–22.

Hale, Arlene. *Crossroads for Nurse Cathy.* Ace Bks. (1974).

Kakonis, Tom E. & Wilcox, James C., Ed. *Crossroads: Quality of Life Through Rhetorical Modes.* Heath (1972).

MacDonald, John D. *Crossroads.* Fawcett World (1974).

Maritain, Jacques. *Education at the Crossroads.* Yale U. Pr. (1943).

Miers, Earl S. *Crossroads of Freedom: The American Revolution & the Rise of a New Nation.* Rutgers U. Pr. (1971).

Morgenthau, Hans J., Ed. *Crossroad Papers.* Norton (1965).

Namier, Lewis B. *Crossroads of Power.* Bks for Libs. (1962).

Norton, Andre. *Crossroads of Time.* Ace Bks. (1974).

Olsen, James & Swinburne, Laurence, Ed. *Crossroads Series.* Noble (1969).

Pappas, Lou S. *Crossroads in Cooking.* Ritchie (1973).

"Publication at the Crossroads," *Anal. Chem. 37,* (April 1965), Sup. 27A–30A.

Sherif, M. & Wilson, M. O., Ed. *Group Relations at the Crossroads.* Harper Bros. (1953).

Sykes, Christopher. *Crossroads to Israel 1917–1948.* Ind. U. Pr. (1973).

Taylor, Erwin K. "Management Development at the Crossroads," *Personnel, 36* No. 2 (Mar.–Apr. 1959), 8–23.

Thompson, Daniel C. *Private Black Colleges at the Crossroads.* Greenwood (1973).

Tomlinson, Monette W. *Crossroads Cameos.* Naylor (1964).

Verissimo, Erico. (Tr. by Kaplan, L. C.). *Crossroads.* Greenwood (1943).

Vitz, Evelyn B. *Crossroad of Intentions: A Study of Symbolic Expression in the Poetry of Francois Villon.* Humanities (1974).

Webster, David. *Crossroad Puzzlers.* Natural Hist. (1967).

Witton, Dorothy. *Crossroads for Chela.* Archway

Women's Bureau. *American Women at the Crossroads: Directions for the Future.* Proc. 50th Conf. (June 11–13, 1970)

Wyatt, Arthur R. "Accounting Profession at the Crossroads," *Mich. Bus. Rev.* XVIV, No. 5, (Nov. 1972), 20–26.